WITHDRAWN

Law Dictionary for Nonlawyers

Third Edition

Law Dictionary for Nonlawyers

Third Edition

Daniel Oran, J.D.

Mark Tosti, J.D.
Contributing Author

West Publishing Company
St. Paul   New York   Los Angeles   San Francisco

Cover Image   *Detail of hand silkscreen printed textile design entitled "Castle in Spain," copyright © 1990 Dawn Zero Erickson. Photograph by Daniel A. Erickson*

Copy Editor   *Judy Lary, Naples Editing Services*

Composition   *Carlisle Communications*

Library of Congress Cataloging-in-Publication Data

Oran, Daniel.
  Law dictionary for nonlawyers / Daniel Oran; Mark Tosti, contributing author. — 3rd ed.
      p. cm.
    ISBN 0-314-87535-2 (soft)
      1. Law—United States—Dictionaries.   I. Tosti, Mark.   II. Title.
KF156.07 1991
349.73'03 —dc20
[347.3003]
                                              91-2759
                                    ∞   CIP
                                          AC

 # About the Authors

Daniel Oran is a graduate of Hamilton College and Yale Law School. He has practiced law in Connecticut and the District of Columbia. In addition, he has been Assistant Director of the National Paralegal Institute, Professor of Law at Antioch Law School, staff counsel to a member of Congress and the House Appropriations Committee, and president of Foresight, Incorporated. He has written an internationally reprinted novel and business text as well as professional and popular articles on paralegal education, psychiatry and law, poverty law, and individual rights.

Mark Tosti, contributing author, is a graduate of Princeton University, Columbia College, and the Washington College of Law of The American University. He practices general business, entertainment, and intellectual property law, and is Professorial Lecturer of Law at The American University. In addition, he has been the producer, director, and editor of several feature films.

ontents

I ntroduction

This is a guidebook to a foreign language. The language of Law uses mostly English words, but they rarely mean what they seem. Many look like everyday English, but have technical definitions totally different from their ordinary uses. Some mean several different things, depending on the area of law or business they come from. The language of Law also contains more "leftovers" than most languages. Hundreds of Latin, Old French, Old English, and obsolete words are still used in their original forms.

This dictionary has two main purposes. Like any specialized dictionary, it helps you to understand and use a technical vocabulary. It also helps you to recognize and discard the many vague words that sound precise and that lawyers use as if they were precise. I have tried to write a complete, clear, and easy-to-use guidebook. Using it, you should be able to understand contracts, laws, court decisions, and even lawyers.

Acknowledgments

This third edition is both a revision of the original *Law Dictionary for Nonlawyers* and a portable condensation of *Oran's Dictionary of the Law,* Second Edition. I have omitted the many friends and colleagues acknowledged in these other books, but their extensive help is, as lawyers say, "incorporated by reference." I would also like to thank the many readers who, though strangers, took the time to suggest additions and corrections to prior editions. This book would not have been the same without their help.

My special thanks go to Mark Tosti, who is responsible for many of the improvements in this edition; to my wife, Elaine; to the Boris family, who suffered along with yet another book; and to my parents, Max and Minerva, who always knew it could be done. Many thanks also to Kenneth Zeigler, Theresa J. Lippert, and Mary Garvey Verrill, the West Publishing team who produced this edition.

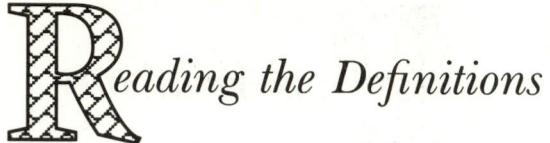eading the Definitions

Finding the Word
Skim the area near where the word should be. The word you want may be printed in the definition of a nearby word. Also, look up both parts of a compound word.

Boldface
If a word in a definition is in **boldface,** it is defined elsewhere in the dictionary. Look it up if you do not know it.

Italics
Italics are used to emphasize a word or to illustrate its use.

Ordinary English
Everyday English definitions of legal words are omitted unless needed to avoid confusion.

"Person"
"Person" is used in this dictionary to mean "person," "man or woman," "human being," and "corporation." Also, many old feminine forms of words, such as executrix, are omitted.

Pronunciation

Most Words

Most words in this dictionary are easy to pronounce. No pronunciations are given for these words. The same is true for most Latin words, which may be pronounced almost any way they are read because they have at least three acceptable pronunciations: "classical," "church," and "English" Latin.

Accent Marks

Some words need accent marks for the strong syllable. This is done by underlining the emphasized part: "Testimony."

Problem Words

Legal words that are hard to pronounce have the pronunciations in square brackets after the definitions. For example, after the definition for "indictment," you will find "[pronounce: in-dite-ment]." This dictionary uses English sounds, not technical pronunciation marks.

$\mathcal{T}$he Basic 50

These fifty words are used frequently in definitions. They are among the most basic words in the law. If you are using this dictionary as a learning tool, rather than as an occasional reference, look up those words you do not know and those for which you know only an ordinary English meaning:

Action	Duty	Opinion
Agency	Estate	Party
Appeal	Evidence	Plaintiff
Bill	Executive	Pleading
Case	Federal	Property
Civil	Grounds	Regulate
Complaint	Judgment	Right
Constitutional	Judicial	Security
Contract	Jury	Sentence
Conviction	Law	Statute
Corporation	Legislate	Testimony
Court	Liability	Title
Creditor	Mortgage	Tort
Criminal	Motion	Trust
Debtor	Negligence	Verdict
Deed	Negotiable	Will
Defendant	instrument	Witness

A *1*. (Latin) From, for, with, in, of, or by. For "*a*" as the first word of several Latin phrases, see the entries following abbreviations. *2*. Atlantic Reporter (see **National Reporter System**).

AA **Affirmative action.**

AAA *1*. American **Accounting** Association. *2*. American **Arbitration** Association.

AALS Association of American Law Schools.

ABA **American Bar Association.**

ACLU American Civil Liberties Union.

AG **Attorney general.**

AKA Also known as.

ALI American Law Institute.

ALJ **Administrative law judge.**

ALR **American Law Reports.**

APA **Administrative procedure act.**

APR **Annual percentage rate.**

AR (Latin) Anno Regni. "In the year of the reign of." Used in England to date cases and laws by the year of a particular king or queen's reign.

ARM Adjustable rate **mortgage.**

ATLA American Trial Lawyers Association.

A (Latin) *1. A coelo usque ad centrum.* "From the heavens to the center of the earth." A landowner's property right to the air space above and the earth below the surface of land, sometimes limited by stronger rights such as **mineral rights** or **air rights.** *2. A contrario sensu.* On the other hand; in a contrary sense. *3. A fortiori.* "With stronger reason; by force of logic." If a twenty-one-year-old is an adult, *a fortiori,* a thirty-year-old is also. [pronounce: ah for-she-<u>o</u>-ri] *4. A gratia.* By **grace.** *5. A latere.* **Collateral.** *6. A mensa et thoro.* "From bed and board." A type of legal **separation** or limited **divorce.** *7. A posteriori.* "From the effect to the cause." A method of reasoning that starts with experiments or observations and attempts to discover general principles from them. *8. A priori.* "From the cause to the effect." A method of reasoning that starts with general principles and attempts to discover what specific facts or real-life observations will follow from them. [pronounce: ah pri-<u>o</u>-ri] *9. A quo.* "From which." A *court a quo* is a court from which a case has been removed, and a *court ad quem* is the court to which a case is transferred. *10. A vinculo matrimonii.* "From the marriage bonds." Either an **annulment** or a **divorce.**

Ab *1.* (Latin) Same as **A** (first word in dictionary) but used in front of words starting with a vowel. *2. Ab ante.* Before. *3. Ab antiquo.* Since ancient times. *4. Ab inconvenienti.* "From inconvenience." A weak argument offered only because you must make an argument. *5. Ab initio.* From the very beginning. [pronounce: ab in-<u>ish</u>-i-o]

Aba̲ction Forcibly carrying something away.

Abandonment The complete and final giving up of property or rights with no intention of reclaiming them and to no particular person. For example, throwing a book away is abandonment, but selling or giving it away is not; a lawsuit may be thrown out of court as abandoned if no action is taken on it for too long a time; children are abandoned if they are no longer cared for; and a husband or wife is abandoned if the other leaves without consent, without just cause, and with the intent of staying away permanently.

Abatement *1*. Complete elimination. For example, an *abatable nuisance* is a **nuisance** that is easily stopped or made harmless. *2*. A reduction or decrease. *3*. A proportional reduction; for example, reduction of each person's share if a pot of money is not large enough to pay all of them. *4*. The order of reduction or elimination; for example, the order in which persons take all the money owed to them from a pot that is not large enough to pay them all. *5*. See **dismissal.**

Abbroachment Buying up goods at wholesale to control supplies and sell at much higher prices.

Abdication The act of a king or other monarch giving up the throne, or the act of an official giving up a public office by ceasing to perform its functions.

Abduction The criminal offense (or the **tort**) of taking away a person in the care of another; for example, **kidnapping.**

Abet Encourage, request, order, or help another person to commit a crime. This is done by an *abettor.*

Abeyance In suspension, waiting, or temporarily held off.

Abide Obey, accept the consequences of, or wait for something.

Abjuration Taking an oath to give up property, rights, or personal convictions. For example, to become a citizen of the United States as an immigrant, you must *abjure* (promise to give up) allegiance to all foreign governments.

Abnegation   Denial or renunciation.

Abode   Home or dwelling place.

Aboriginal   Belonging to the first natives or residents since ancient times.

About   Near in time, distance, quality, or quantity; approximately.

Above   *1.* A higher or **appellate** court. *2.* Before or earlier in a document.

Abridge   *1.* Shorten or condense. *2.* Infringe upon; to "abridge a right" is to make it less useful or complete.

Abrogation   The ending or **annulling** of a former law.

Abscond   Hide or sneak away to avoid arrest, a lawsuit, or creditors.

Absentee   A person who is not there. For example, an *absentee landlord* does not live on the premises and often cannot be easily contacted by the tenants, and *absentee voting* is voting by mail or another approved method if you are unable to vote in person on election day.

Absolute   Complete, final, and without restrictions. For example, an absolute **deed** is a transfer of land without a **mortgage** or **lien**; absolute **liability** is responsibility for harm to another whether or not you are at fault; and an *absolute nuisance* is a **nuisance** that is not caused by **negligent** conduct.

Absorption   The continued life of a thing (a right, a company, etc.) by its becoming a part of another thing.

Absque   (Latin) Without; but for. [pronounce: ab-skway]

Abstain   Refrain, hold off, keep hands off. The *abstention doctrine* is the principle that a federal court should refuse to decide certain cases if they can be better handled by a state court.

Abstract *1*. A summary. For example, an *abstract of title* is a condensed history of the ownership of a piece of land that includes other rights such as **liens.** *2. Abstraction* is taking something with the intent to commit **fraud.**

Abuse *1*. Sexually molest or regularly injure a child. *2*. Insult forcefully. *3*. Misuse. For example, *abuse of discretion* is the failure to use sound, reasonable judgment when a person (such as a judge) is under a legal duty to do so; and *abuse of process* is using the legal system unfairly, in a way it was not meant to be used.

Abut Border on or physically touch (with nothing in between). For *abutter's rights,* see **ancient lights.**

Accede *1*. Come into a job or public office. *2*. Agree, consent, or give in.

Acceleration Shortening of the time before a future event will happen. For example, an *acceleration clause* in a **note** or contract makes an entire debt come due immediately if certain specified things happen.

Acceptance *1*. Agreeing to an **offer** and thereby forming a **contract.** *2*. Taking something offered by another person with the intention of keeping it. For example, one way a buyer can accept goods from a seller is to tell the seller that the goods received are right. *3*. Technical rules govern the *acceptance* of **negotiable instruments.** For example, a person may accept a check by signing and depositing it. *4*. A *banker's (or trade) acceptance* is a form of *acceptance credit,* a trade device in which a bank (or company) promises to pay a certain amount at a future date (a negotiable time **draft** or a guaranteed **bill of exchange**).

Access Either the opportunity or the right to approach and use something.

Accession The right to own something because it becomes a part of something one already owns. See also **accede.**

Accessory Something connected to something more important; for example, a person who helps commit a crime without being present. An *accessory before the fact* is a person who, without being present, encourages, orders, or helps another to commit a crime; and an *accessory after the fact* is a person who finds out that a crime has been committed and helps to conceal the crime or the criminal.

Accident An unexpected event, especially one with harmful effects. The event may be predictable or unpredictable, somebody's fault or nobody's fault.

Accommodation A favor done for another person, usually involving a **cosigner** who helps another person get a loan. A **bill** or **note** signed in this way, promising to pay if the person getting the loan fails to pay, is called **accommodation paper.**

Accomplice A person who knowingly and voluntarily helps another person to commit or conceal a crime. This includes persons who **aid**, **abet**, or act as an **accessory.**

Accord An agreement, especially one to pay (on one side) and to accept (on the other side) less than all a debt or obligation is worth as full payment for that obligation. An *accord and satisfaction* is an accord that has been completed by payment and a full **release.**

Account A list of money paid and owed by one person or business to another. An *account payable* is a debt not yet paid, an *account receivable* is a debt not yet collected, and an *account stated* is an exact, agreed-upon amount of money owed.

Accountant A person who specializes in preparing and analyzing financial records. Duties include **auditing, bookkeeping,** and preparing financial **statements.** Accountants who satisfy state professional requirements are called *certified public accountants.*

Accounting *1.* A system of setting up financial record books, especially for tax purposes. See **accrual basis** and **cash basis.** *2.* Giving a full financial explanation of, or making good on, a transaction or an entire business.

Accredit Give official status or recognition.

Accretion A gradual accumulation, such as the growth of a riverbank due to silt deposited by the river.

Accrual basis An **accounting** method that shows expenses **incurred** and income earned in a given time period, whether or not cash payments have actually changed hands during that period. *Accruals* are regular, short-term business obligations.

Accrue Become due and payable.

Accusatory instruments Papers (such as an **indictment**, an **information**, or a **presentment**) that charge a person with a crime.

Accused A criminal **defendant**; charged with a crime.

Acknowledgment An admission or declaration that something is genuine or has happened.

Acquiescence Silent agreement or, by silence, appearing to be satisfied.

Acquittal *1.* A formal legal determination that a person who has been charged with a crime is innocent. *2.* A **release** from an obligation.

Acquittance A written discharge (such as a **receipt**) of an obligation to pay money.

Act *1.* A law passed by one or both **houses** of a **legislature.** *2.* Something done voluntarily that triggers legal consequences. *3.* An *act of God* is an event caused entirely by nature. *4.* The *act of state doctrine* is the principle that a court should not question the legality of acts done in a foreign country by that country's government.

Acting   Holding a temporary rank or position.

Actio   (Latin) A **right** and the legal proceedings taken to enforce that right. See also **action.**

Action   *1.* A civil lawsuit or criminal prosecution. Actions are categorized in many ways. See, for example, **civil action** and **common law action.** *2.* An act or related series of acts; conduct or behavior. See **actus.**

Actionable   Providing a legal basis for a lawsuit; for example, *actionable words* are statements by one person that are serious enough to support a lawsuit (or **action**) for **libel** or **slander** by another person.

Actual   Real, substantial, and presently existing as opposed to possible or theoretical. For example, in the law of **agency,** *actual authority* is the right and power to act that a **principal** (often an employer) intentionally gives to an **agent** (often an employee) or at least allows the agent to believe has been given. This includes both **express** and **implied** authority. For *actual cash value,* see **market value.**

Actuarial method   A system of accounting for finances in a record book. For example, the *actuarial method* mentioned in the Uniform Consumer Credit Code is the application of payments first to **interest** and finance charges, then to paying off **principal.**

Actuary   A person who specializes in the mathematics of **insurance.**

Actus   (Latin) An **act.** An *actus reus* is a "wrongful deed" (such as killing a person), which, if done with

mens rea, a "guilty mind" (such as **malice afore-thought**), is a crime (such as *first-degree* **murder**).

Ad *1.* (Latin) To, for, by, because, until, or near. *2. Ad damnum.* "To the **damages**." That part of a **plaintiff's** original court papers that specifies the amount of money sought. *3. Ad hoc.* "For this." For this special purpose or one time. *4. Ad interim.* Meanwhile; for now. *5. Ad litem.* "For this lawsuit." For example, a *guardian ad litem* is a person appointed to represent a child (or other person lacking legal **capacity**) in a lawsuit. *6. Ad quem.* "To which." See **a quo** for its use. *7. Ad sectam.* "At the suit of." "Ad sectam Jones" means that Jones is the **plaintiff**. *8. Ad valorem.* "According to value." An *ad valorem* tax is based on a percentage of a thing's cost or value.

Addict A person who regularly uses something (especially a drug) to the extent that he or she no longer has control over its use.

Additur Either the power of a trial court to increase the amount of money awarded by a **jury** to a **plaintiff**, or the power of an **appeals** court to deny a new trial to the plaintiff if the defendant agrees to pay the plaintiff a certain amount of extra money.

Add-on clause A provision in an **installment** contract that combines payment obligations for previously and newly bought things so that nothing is owned "free and clear" until everything has been paid for.

Adduce Present **evidence** in a **trial**.

Ademption *1.* The pre-death disposal of something left in a **will** with the effect that the person to whom it was left does not get it. *2.* The gift, before death, of something left in a will to the person to whom it was left. Compare **advancement**.

Adequate Enough. *Adequate* has no precise legal meaning.

Adhesion   A *contract of adhesion* is a deal in which all the bargaining power (and the contract terms) favors one side, usually when buyers have no choice among sellers of a particular item and when sellers use preprinted contracts to unfair advantage.

Adjacent   Near or close by, but not necessarily touching.

Adjective law   Procedural law. Compare **substantive law.**

Adjournment   Putting off business or a session to another time or place. The decision of a court, legislature, or other meeting to stop meeting either temporarily or permanently. See **recess.**

Adjudicate   To judge. An *adjudication* is the formal giving, pronouncing, or recording of a **judgment** for one side in a lawsuit. An *adjudicated form* is a **form** that a court has called legally binding or has interpreted in a way that makes it useful for later users.

Adjudicative facts   The "who, what, where, when, and how" facts about persons having a dispute before an **administrative agency.** See **legislative facts.**

Adjust   Settle or arrange; bring persons to agreement, especially as to an amount of money owed. The process is *adjustment.* An *insurance adjuster* acts for an insurance company to determine and settle claims.

Adjusted gross estate   A dead person's **estate** minus deductions for the cost of handling the estate, funeral expenses, and so on.

Adjusted gross income   A person's **income** minus certain investment and business deductions, certain employee expenses, alimony paid, and so on.

Adjustment securities   Stocks and other **securities** issued during a *corporate* **reorganization.**

Administration _1._ Managing a business, organization, or part of a government. _2._ Supervising the **estate** of a dead person. This usually includes collecting the property, paying debts and taxes, and giving out what remains to the **heirs.**

Administrative _1._ An _administrative agency_ is a subbranch of government (such as a local police department or the federal Department of Defense) set up to carry out the laws. _2. Administrative board_ is a broad term for _administrative agency_ or for a courtlike body set up by an agency to hold **hearings.** _3. Administrative discretion_ is a public official's right to do things that are not precisely "covered" by a law or rule and that require the use of professional judgment. _4. Administrative law_ is either laws about the duties and proper running of an _administrative agency_ that are imposed on agencies by **legislatures** and courts, or it is **rules** and **regulations** written _by_ administrative agencies. An _administrative law judge_ is an official who conducts hearings for an administrative agency. _5._ An _administrative procedure act_ is a law that describes how U.S. (and some state) agencies must do business and how disputes go from these agencies into court. _6._ An _administrative remedy_ is a means of enforcing a right by going to an administrative agency either for help or for a decision. If you must "exhaust administrative remedies," you must submit your problem to the proper agency for decision before taking it to court.

Administrator A person appointed by a court to carry out the **administration** of a dead person's **estate.** If named in a **will,** the administrator is called an **executor.** See also **cum testamento annexo** and **de bonis non.**

Ad<u>mi</u>ralty Maritime (seagoing) law, such as that dealing with shipping claims or collisions between ships, or the court (usually a federal **district court**) that handles these matters.

Ad<u>mi</u>ssible Proper to be used in reaching a decision; **evidence** that should be "let in" or introduced in court; evidence that a **jury** may use.

Ad<u>mi</u>ssions Confessions, concessions, or voluntary acknowledgments that a fact is true. Statements made by a **party** to a lawsuit (or by the party's representative) that a fact exists that helps the other side or that a point the other side is making is correct.

Ad<u>mo</u>nition *1*. Oral advice by a judge to a jury. *2*. A reprimand given by a judge.

Ad<u>mo</u>nitory tort An intentional **tort** of the type for which punishing the wrongdoer is more important than compensating the person hurt.

Adopt *1*. Accept, choose, or take as your own; for example, legally accept a child of another (or, in some states, an adult) as your own, with all the rights and duties there would have been if the child had been your own. *2*. Pass a law and put it into effect.

Adult A person over the legal age a state has set for full rights and responsibilities to begin.

Adulteration Mixing inferior, cheaper, or harmful things in with better ones (to increase volume, lower costs, etc.).

Adultery Voluntary heterosexual intercourse between a married person and a person who is not the husband or wife.

Advance *1*. Pay money before it is due; loan money; supply something before it is paid for; increase a price; or hold a trial sooner. *2*. *Advance sheets* are "hot off the press" unbound copies of case **decisions** that will later be printed with others in bound form.

Advancement Money or property given to an **heir** (usually a child) that is intended to be deducted from the heir's eventual share upon the giver's death. See also **ademption.**

Adventure A (risky) commercial venture, often a shipment of goods by sea.

Adversary system The system of law in the United States in which a judge acts as a decision maker between opposite sides. Compare **inquisitorial system.**

Adverse Opposed; having opposing interests; against. For example, *adverse possession* is a method of gaining legal **title** to land by openly occupying the land continuously for a number of years (as set by state law) while claiming ownership of the land.

Advice The **counsel** given to a client by a lawyer.

Advisement Consideration; under review.

Advisory Giving an opinion when not responsible for a decision.

Advocate *1.* A person, such as a lawyer, who speaks for another. *2.* To speak, write, etc., in favor of something.

Affiant A person who "swears to" an **affidavit.** [pronounce: a-fi-ant]

Affidavit A written statement, usually about the truth of a set of facts, sworn to before a person who is officially permitted by law to administer an **oath.**

Affiliate *1.* A person or company with an inside business connection to another company. *2.* An *affiliation proceeding* is a **paternity suit.**

Affinity Related through marriage.

Affirm Make firm; repeat agreement; confirm; or state positively. For example, when a higher court declares that a lower court's decision was correct, it "affirms" the decision; and when someone reaccepts and makes solid a **contract** that was breakable, he or she "affirms" it.

Affirmation   A solemn, formal declaration in place of an **oath** for persons whose religion forbids oath taking.

Affirmative   *1*. Taking special steps; going forward. *2*. *Affirmative action* is an administrative action to right a wrong rather than to punish anyone for causing it. The most common form is the requirement that an organization take steps to remedy past **discrimination** in hiring or promotion. *3*. An *affirmative defense* is that part of a defendant's **answer** to a **complaint** that goes beyond denying the facts and arguments of the complaint and sets out new facts and arguments that might win for the defendant even if everything in the complaint is true. **Contributory negligence** is a possible affirmative defense to negligence in a **civil** case, and **insanity** is a possible affirmative defense to murder in a **criminal** case. *4*. *Affirmative relief* is money (**damages**) or other benefit (such as *specific* **performance**) awarded to a **defendant** in a lawsuit.

Aforesaid   A vague word meaning "previously identified" or "already mentioned."

Aforethought   Planned in advance; done with **premeditation.**

After-acquired property clause   A provision in a **mortgage** that anything added to the mortgaged property is subject to the mortgage just as if it were mortgaged directly.

After-acquired title rule   The legal principle that if a person transfers ownership to land without possessing good **title** to it, then gets good title, the title automatically goes to the person to whom the property was transferred.

After-born child rule The legal principle that if a child is born after a **will** is made, and if the will does not exclude later children, that child should inherit a child's share.

Age *Age of consent* is the age at which you may marry without parent's approval or legally consent to sexual intercourse. *Age of majority* is the age at which you may make **contracts,** vote, etc. *Age of reason* is the age at which you may **testify,** commit a crime, etc. These ages vary from state to state and from situation to situation.

Agency *1.* See **agent.** *2.* Short for **administrative agency.**

Agent A person requested or permitted by another person to act for him or her; a person entrusted with another's business.

Aggravated assault A criminal **assault** that is more serious or dangerous than a simple assault. In some states it means "assault with a deadly weapon."

Aggressive collection Debt collection by **attachment, garnishment, execution,** etc.

Aggrieved party A person whose rights are violated by another or whose interests are harmed by a court's **judgment.**

Agreement *1.* A **contract.** *2.* Complete understanding between persons, often called a "meeting of minds." *3.* An intention of two or more persons to enter into a **contract** with one another, combined with an attempt to form a valid contract.

Aid and abet Intentionally help or encourage another person to commit a crime.

Aid and comfort the enemy Commit **treason.**

Aider The legal conclusion that once a jury gives a **verdict,** those facts that the jury logically needed to reach the verdict are assumed to be properly **alleged** and proved.

Air rights *1.* A landowner's ownership rights to the air space above the land. *2.* The right to use part of the air space above another's land.

Aleatory Having effects and results that depend on an uncertain event; for example, an insurance contract is aleatory. [pronounce: <u>a</u>-le-a-<u>to</u>-ri]

Alia (Latin) Other things or other persons.

Alias *1.* (Latin) Short for *alias dictus* or "otherwise called," a fictitious name used in place of a person's real name. *2.* An *alias* **writ** or **summons** is a second (or third, etc.,) one put out through the court if the first one did not work.

<u>Ali</u>bi (Latin) "Elsewhere." The claim that at the time a crime was committed, a person was somewhere else.

Alien Any person who is not a U.S. **citizen**, whether or not that person is living in the United States permanently; more generally, any foreigner.

Alienation The transfer or other disposal of property or rights to another person. For example, an *alienation clause* in an **insurance** policy **voids** (ends) the policy if the insured property is sold or otherwise disposed of; and *alienation of affection* is taking away the love, companionship, or help of another person's husband or wife. When something *can* be transferred or taken away, it is called *alienable*.

<u>Ali</u>mony Payments by a divorced husband or wife to the ex-spouse for ongoing personal support.

Aliquot (Latin) A part; a fractional or proportional part. [pronounce: <u>al</u>-i-quo]

Aliunde (Latin) From another place; from outside this document; from a separate, independent source; etc. See **extrinsic evidence.** [pronounce: al-ee-<u>und</u>]

All fours Two cases or decisions are "on all fours" if they are generally similar and are exactly alike in all legally important ways.

Allegation A statement in a **pleading** that sets out a fact that the side filing the pleading expects to prove.

Allege State, assert, charge, or make an **allegation.** "Alleged" often means "*merely* stated" or "*only* charged."

Allocation *1.* Putting something in one place rather than in another; for example, crediting all of a payment to one **account** when there are several possible accounts to credit. *2.* Proportional distribution (of money, of blame, etc.).

Allocution The procedure in which a judge asks a prisoner whether he or she has any way to show that **judgment** should not be **pronounced** or has any last words to say before a sentence is given out.

Allodial An old word for land owned freely and completely.

Allograph A document written or signed by one person for another.

Allonge A piece of paper attached to a **negotiable instrument** to provide space for **indorsements** (signatures).

Allowance Either a **deduction** or a regular payment.

Alteration *1.* A change or modification that does not destroy a thing's identity. *2.* Writing or erasing on a document that changes its meaning.

Alternative pleading (**or relief**) Asserting facts (or asking for help) in a **pleading** in ways that may contradict each other.

Alternative writ **Show cause order.**

Am. Jur. **American Jurisprudence,** a multivolume legal encyclopedia.

Ambit Boundary line, limit, or border.

Ambulance chaser   A lawyer or person working for a lawyer who improperly solicits business, originally by following up on street accidents.

Ambulatory   Movable; capable of being changed or revoked.

Amend   Improve, correct, change, or review.

Amendment   *1.* A change made to a **bill** during its passage through a **legislature** or to a law already passed. *2.* One of the provisions of the U.S. **Constitution** enacted since the original Constitution became law. *3.* A change made to a **pleading** that is already before the court.

American   *1.* The *American Bar Association* is the largest voluntary organization of lawyers in the country. *2.* The *American Digest System* is a giant collection of summaries of every **reported** case (written **opinion**) in America since the sixteen hundreds. The Century Digest contains the years before 1897; each ten-year period after that is in a Decennial Digest; and the latest few years are in a General Digest. Each digest has many volumes, each organized by the **key number** system. *3.* *American Jurisprudence* is a multivolume legal encyclopedia that is cross-referenced with *American Law Reports,* a large series of books that selects important cases, prints them in full, and gives an **annotation** (a commentary) that often discusses a whole area of the law.

Amicable action   A lawsuit (involving a real, not a made-up, problem) that is started by agreement of the two sides.

Amicus curiae   (Latin) "Friend of the court." A person who is allowed to appear in a lawsuit (often only to file a **brief**) even though the person is not a **party** to the lawsuit. [pronounce: a-me-kus cure-e-eye]

Amnesty   A wiping out, by the government, of guilt for persons guilty of a crime; a general governmental forgiving.

Amortization   _1_. Paying off a debt in regular and equal payments. To _amortize_ an ordinary loan, calculate the total interest for the whole time, add that to the loan amount, and divide the sum by the number of payments. _2_. Any dividing up of benefits or costs by time periods.

Analogy   Reasoning or argument by similarities. For example, when no previous case exactly decides an issue (a **precedent**), lawyers will argue from cases that are factually similar or are decided by the same general principles.

Anarchy   The absence of government or law. _Anarchism_ is the belief that no government is the best government.

Ancient   A word meaning "old," but without a precise legal definition. For example, _ancient lights_ are windows that have had outside light for more than a certain length of time (often twenty years) and that for this reason cannot be blocked off by adjoining landowners in some states; and _ancient writings_ are documents that are presumed to be genuine because they have been kept in continuously proper **custody** for a certain number of years.

Ancillary   Supplementary or "on the side." For example, _ancillary administration_ is a legal proceeding in a state where a dead person had property but which differs from the state where the main **estate** is **administered;** and _ancillary jurisdiction_ is a court's power to handle matters that are a "side" part of a case even if it could not handle them separately.

Animo (or animus)   (Latin) "With intention." For example, _animo furandi_ (with intention to steal), _testandi_ (to make a will), *revertendi* (to return), *donandi* (to make a gift), or *revocandi* (to revoke).

Annex Attach (usually something small or less important to something large or more important).

Annotation *1.* A note or commentary intended to explain the meaning of a passage in a book or document. A *legal annotation* is usually an explanation of a **case** and a comparison to similar cases. *2. Annotated statutes* are a set of books containing the laws of, for example, a state, plus commentary such as history, explanations, or cases discussing each law.

Annual percentage rate The true cost of borrowing money, expressed in a standardized, yearly way to make it easier to understand **credit** terms and to "shop" for credit.

Annuity A fixed sum of money, usually paid to a person at fixed times, for a fixed time period or for life.

Annulment The act of making something **void** or wiping it out completely. For example, the *annulment* of a marriage "wipes the marriage off the books" because it was **invalid** in some way, as opposed to a **divorce,** which only ends the marriage.

Answer The first **pleading** by a **defendant** in a lawsuit. This pleading responds to the charges and demands of the *plaintiff's* **complaint.** The defendant may deny the plaintiff's charges, may present new facts to defeat them, or may show why the plaintiff's facts are legally invalid.

Ante (Latin) Before.

Antenuptial agreement A **contract** between persons about to marry that usually concerns the way property will be handled during the marriage or divided in case of divorce.

Anticipation The act of doing something before its proper time or simply doing it "before" something else; for example, paying off a **mortgage** before it comes due.

Anticipatory breach Breaking a **contract** by refusing to go through with it once it is entered into but before it is time to fully perform (do one's share).

Antitrust acts Federal and state laws to protect trade from **monopoly** control and from price fixing and other **restraints of trade.** The main federal antitrust laws are the **Sherman, Clayton,** Federal Trade Commission, and **Robinson-Patman Acts.**

Apparent authority The **authority** an **agent** seems to have, judged by the words or actions of the person who gave the authority or by the agent's own words or actions.

Appeal *1.* Ask a higher court to review the actions of a lower court in order to correct mistakes or injustice. The process is called "an appeal." An appeal may also be taken from a lower level of an **administrative agency** to a higher level or from an agency to a court. *2.* An *appeal bond* is money put up, by someone appealing a court's decision, to pay the other side's costs in case the person appealing fails to go forward with an honest appeal.

Appearance The formal coming into court as a party (**plaintiff** or **defendant**) or a lawyer in a lawsuit.

Appellant The person who **appeals** a case to a higher court.

Appellate An *appellate court* is a higher court that can hear **appeals** from a lower court. *Appellate jurisdiction* is the power of this higher court to take these cases and make decisions about them without holding a trial. The process is called *appellate review.*

Appellee The person against whom an **appeal** is taken. This person is usually, but not always, the person who won in the trial court.

Apportionment Dividing up by shares; dividing fairly and proportionately; dividing up land to create voting districts.

Appose Examine the keeper of written records about the records.

Appraisal (or appraisement) *1.* Estimation of the value of property, especially if done by an impartial expert. This is *not* **assessment.** *2.* The fixing of the fair value of **stock** by a court when stockholders in a **corporation** quarrel and some must be bought out.

Appreciate *1.* Increase in value. (*Appreciation* is sometimes the increase in a property's value excluding improvements.) *2.* Estimate the value of something. *3.* Understand or realize.

Apprehension *1.* The capture or arrest of a person on a criminal charge. *2.* Fear. *3.* Understanding; knowledge of something.

Appropriation *1.* A **legislature's** setting aside for a specific purpose of a portion of the money raised by the government; for example, a highway appropriation. *2.* A governmental taking of land or property for public use. *3.* Taking something wrongfully; for example, using a person's picture and name in an advertisement without permission.

Approval A sale "on approval" means that the buyer may return the goods if they are unsatisfactory even if they are all the seller claims they are.

Appurtenance Something that belongs to or is attached to something else; for example, a barn on a farm.

Arbiter A person who is chosen to decide a disagreement.

Arbitrage The simultaneous buying and selling of **stocks** or other **securities** to profit from the price difference.

Arbitrary *1.* Done according to a person's desires, without supervision, general principles, or rules by which to decide. *2.* Done capriciously, in bad faith, or without good reason.

Arbitration Resolution of a dispute by a person (other than a judge) whose decision is binding. This person is usually called an *arbitrator*, and the submission of the dispute for decision is often the result of an agreement in a contract.

Areawide agreement One **union** making the same **labor contract** with many companies in the same geographical area. The process is *area bargaining*.

Arguendo (Latin) Assume something is true (whether true or false) for the sake of argument.

Argument Persuasion by laying out facts, law, and the reasoning that connects them, usually done orally and in court.

Argumentative *1.* Stating not only facts but also conclusions. *2.* Disputatious and controversial.

Arise Originate or come into being.

Arm's length Not on close terms; not an "inside deal."

Arraign Bring a **defendant** before a judge to hear the charges and to enter a **plea** (guilty, not guilty, etc.) The procedure is called *arraignment*. [pronounce: ah-rain]

Arrangement with creditors See **Chapter Thirteen.**

Array The entire group of persons from which a **jury** is chosen. A *challenge to the array* is an objection to the procedures by which the *group* was chosen.

Arrears (or arrearages) Money owed that is overdue and unpaid.

Arrest *1.* The official taking of a person to answer criminal charges. This involves at least temporarily depriving the person of liberty and may involve the use of force. *2. Arrest of judgment* is a judge's temporary stopping of the enforcement of a **judgment** because of some apparent defect in the proceedings.

Arrogation *1.* Claiming or taking something without having any right to it. *2.* To **adopt** an adult.

Arson The **malicious** and unlawful burning of a building.

Articled clerk A lawyer's apprentice in England.

Articles The separate parts of a document, book, set of rules, agreement, law, and so on, or the document itself that contains these parts. For example, *Articles of Confederation* was the document that held together the thirteen original colonies before the adoption of the **Constitution,** and *articles of incorporation* is the document that sets up a **corporation.**

Artificial person An entity or "thing" that the law gives some of the legal rights and duties of a person; for example, a **corporation.**

As is Sold in a possibly defective condition and bought with no promises except that the thing is as seen and described.

Ascendants Parents, grandparents, etc.

Asportation Taking things and carrying them away illegally.

Assault An intentional threat, show of force, or movement that could reasonably make a person feel in danger of harmful physical contact. It can be a crime or a **tort.**

Assembly *1.* A large meeting. *2.* The lower **house** of many state **legislatures**.

Assess *1.* Set the value of something; for example, set the value of property for the purpose of taxing it. *Assessed valuation* is often less than **market value.** *2.* Charge part of the cost of a public improvement, such as a sidewalk, to each property directly benefiting from it.

Assessable Liable to make payments, pay extra, or be taxed.

Assessment *1*. See **assess.** *2*. Deciding the amount to be paid by each of several persons into a common fund. *3*. A periodic payment. *4*. An extra payment.

Assets Money, property, and money-related rights (such as money owed to you) that you own. In a business, *capital assets* or *fixed assets* are those assets (such as buildings) that cannot be turned into cash easily; *current assets* or *liquid assets* are those things (such as cash or goods for sale) that can be turned into cash easily; and *frozen assets* are tied up legally, often by a lawsuit.

Assign *1*. To formally transfer property, rights, or money to another person; for example, see **wage** *assignment*. *2*. To point out, set forth, or specify; for example, to "assign errors" is to specify them on a legal document. *3*. An *assigned account* is a debt owed to a company that the company uses as **security** for its own debt to a bank. *4*. *Assigned counsel* is a court-appointed, often free, lawyer. *5*. *Assigned risk* is a type of **insurance,** such as automobile insurance for a person who has had many accidents, that insurance companies handle only because they are required to do so by law. *6*. An *assignee* is a person to whom something is given or transferred. *7*. An *assignor* is a person who gives or transfers something. *8*. *Assigns* means persons to whom property is or will be transferred.

Assise (or assize) An old word for various English courts, laws, **writs,** etc.

Associate justice The title of each judge (other than the chief justice) on an **appeals** court.

Association Any group of persons joined together for a particular purpose.

Assumpsit (Latin) "He promised." An old word meaning a promise to do or pay something. Certain types of lawsuits, including several that involved no actual promise, had this name.

Assumption *1.* The assumption of a **mortgage** is the taking over of a seller's mortgage debt when buying a property. *2. Assumption of risk* is the legal rule in some states that if someone exposes self or property to certain kinds of known dangers, he or she cannot collect **damages** if harmed.

Assurance *1.* **Insurance.** *2.* A **pledge** or **guaranty.**

Asylum One country's protection of a fugitive from criminal **prosecution** by another country. This protection is limited by **extradition** treaties.

At bar Currently being handled by this court.

At issue A legal point is *at issue* when one side in a lawsuit clearly asserts it and the other side clearly denies it. The lawsuit itself is *at issue* when all major legal points are clearly asserted and denied.

At large *1.* Unlimited; fully; in detail; everywhere. For example, an *at-large election* is one in which a voter may choose from among all the candidates rather than from among those in one geographical subarea. *2.* Free; unrestrained; uncontrolled.

Attachment *1.* Formally seizing property (or a person) to bring it under the control of a court. For example, a **defendant's** bank account may sometimes be *attached* to make sure that money will be available to pay a **judgment** if the defendant loses the lawsuit. *2.* A **security** interest, such as a **mortgage,** *attaches* if it is valid and can be enforced.

Attainder The wiping out of **civil rights** (and often the governmental taking of property) that occurs when a person is convicted of a **felony** or is sentenced to death. A *bill of attainder* was a **legislative** act pronouncing a person guilty, usually of **treason,** without a trial and sentencing the person to death and attainder. This is now prohibited by the U.S. Constitution.

Attempt *1.* An act that goes beyond preparation but is not completed. *2.* An effort to commit a crime that goes beyond preparation and that proceeds far enough to make the person who did it guilty of an "attempt crime" such as attempted murder.

Attest Swear to; act as a witness to; certify formally. *Attestation* usually refers to the act of witnessing the signing of a document and signing that one has witnessed it.

Attorney *1.* Lawyer (*attorney at law*). *2.* A person who acts formally for another person (*attorney in fact*). *3.* An *attorney general* is the chief law officer of a state and of the United States. *4.* An *attorney of record* is the lawyer listed in court papers as representing a person and who is responsible to the person for all work on the case. *5.* An *attorney's lien* is the right of lawyers, in some circumstances, to hold a client's money, property, or court papers to pay attorney's fees.

Attornment Agreeing to pay rent to, and be a tenant of, a new landlord who buys the land you rent.

Attractive nuisance A legal principle, used in some states, saying that if a person keeps dangerous property in a way that children might be attracted to it and be able to get at it, that person is responsible even if the children are trespassing or at fault when they get hurt.

Audit An official examination of an **account** or of a person's or an organization's financial situation.

Authentication *1.* A formal act certifying that a public document is official and correct so that it may be admitted as **evidence.** *2.* Any evidence that proves a document is what it seems to be.

Authority *1.* The permission, power, or legal right to do something. For **apparent, express,** and **implied** authority, see those words. *2. Authorities* are **citations** to references taken from laws, decisions, texts, and so on to support a legal position.

Autopsy Examination of a dead body to find out the cause of death.

Autre (or auter) (French) "Another." For example, *autre vie* means "during another person's lifetime." [pronounce: oh-tr vee]

Auxiliary Aiding, **subsidiary, ancillary.**

Avails Profits or **proceeds.**

Aver Declare, assert, **allege,** set out clearly and formally. An *averment* is a statement of facts.

Avoidance *1.* Escaping or evading. Compare **evasion.** *2.* **Annulling** or **cancelling.** *3.* In **pleading**, admitting facts in the other side's pleading while showing why these facts should not have the legal effect intended by the other side.

Avowal An offer of **proof** (made out of the **jury's** hearing) to have the proof available in case an **appeals** court says that the witness should have been allowed to **testify** before the jury.

Award Give or grant by formal process. For example, a jury *awards* **damages,** a company *awards* a **contract** to a bidder, and an **arbitrator** *awards* a decision to one side in a dispute.

BF **Bona fide.** A *BFP* is a *bona fide purchaser.*

BIA Bureau of Indian Affairs.

BJ Bar Journal.

BNA Bureau of National Affairs. A publisher of **loose-leaf services.**

Backbond A **bond** given by a person to the **surety** who backs the person's debt.

Bad faith Dishonesty in dealing with another person, whether or not **fraud** is involved.

Badge of fraud A strong suspicion of **fraud.**

Bail *1.* A person who puts up money or property to allow the release of another person from jail. *2.* The money or property put up by the person in #1. This money, often in the form of a bail **bond,** may be forfeited if the person released does not appear in court.

Bailee A person to whom property is loaned or entrusted. See **bailment.**

Bailiff A local official, usually a **sheriff**'s deputy or an official who keeps the peace in court.

Bailment A temporary delivery of property by the owner into another person's custody (keeping); for example, by loan, for storage, or for repair. A *bailment for term* is delivery into custody for a set time period.

Bailor A person who entrusts property to another.

Bait and switch The practice of advertising one item to get people to come into a store, then persuading them to buy a different item. This may be illegal if the original item is not available as advertised.

Balance   An amount left over. For example, the difference between a debt and payments already made is called a *balance due*. In **bookkeeping,** a balance is the difference between the **debit** and **credit** columns. If no difference exists, the account is "balanced." A *balance sheet* is a summary of the financial worth of a company broken down by **assets** and **liabilities.**

Balloon loan   A loan in which the last payment (the "balloon payment") is much larger than any of the other regular payments. This may give the false impression that low payments will pay off the debt, but the payments are often only **interest,** not **principal.** Federal truth-in-lending laws require clear disclosure of balloon loans, and many states prohibit them.

Banc (or bank)   (French) "Bench"; place where the judges hear cases. A court "sitting in banc" (or "en banc") is a session of all the judges together.

Banker's lien   A bank's right to take for its own the money or property left in its care by a customer if the customer owes an overdue debt to the bank and if the money, to the bank's knowledge, belongs fully to the customer.

Bankruptcy   The procedure, under the Federal Bankruptcy Act, by which a person is relieved of most debts once the person has placed all property and money under the court's supervision, or by which an organization in financial trouble is either restructured by the court or ended and turned into cash to pay **creditors** and owners. *Bankruptcy* is triggered by **insolvency** but does not mean the same thing. See **Chapter Seven, Chapter Eleven,** and **Chapter Thirteen** for the different types of bankruptcy.

Bar _1_. The entire group of lawyers permitted to practice law before a particular court. _2_. The part of some courtrooms where prisoners stand. _3_. The court itself or the judge at work in court. _4_. A barrier or prohibition. _5_. A _bar act_ is a state law that says what a lawyer may and may not do. _6_. A _bar association_ is a voluntary group of lawyers, as opposed to a group of lawyers who are required to be members of a court's **integrated bar.** _7_. A _bar examination_ is the written test a lawyer must pass to practice law. Some states use the "multistate" exam, some use their own tests, and some use a combination of the two.

Bare With very limited legal rights, duties, or effects.

Bargain A mutual understanding, **contract,** or agreement.

Bargaining agent A **union** that has the exclusive right to represent all the employees of a certain type (a _bargaining unit_) at a company.

Barratry The offense of stirring up quarrels or lawsuits (usually applied to a lawyer stirring up a lawsuit from which the lawyer can profit).

Barrister _1_. A British lawyer who argues in actual court trials. Compare **solicitor.** _2_. A lawyer.

Barter An exchange of things (or services) for other things, as opposed to an exchange of things for money.

Basis In tax law, the adjusted "cost" of property used in calculating gain or loss on the sale, exchange, or other transfer of property. This is usually purchase price plus the cost of **improvements** minus the amount of **depreciation** deductions.

Bastardy action **Paternity suit.**

Battery An intentional, unconsented-to, physical contact by one person (or an object controlled by that person) with another person.

Bearer A person in possession of a **negotiable instrument** (for example, a check) that is made out "payable to bearer," that is indorsed in **blank** (signed, but with no name filled in on the "payable to" line), or that is made out to "cash" or other indication that no one specific person is meant to cash it. This type of document is often called *bearer paper* or a *bearer instrument*.

Belief A sense of firmness about the truth of an idea that lies somewhere between "suspicion" and "knowledge."

Below A lower court.

Bench *1.* Judges collectively are "the bench." *2.* The place where judges sit in court. A *bench conference* is a private meeting at the judge's bench of lawyers for both sides in a lawsuit. A *bench warrant* is a paper issued directly by a judge to the police or other peace officers ordering an arrest.

Beneficial Giving a profit or an advantage. A *beneficial interest* (or *use*) is the right to profits resulting from a **contract, estate,** or **property,** rather than the legal ownership of these things.

Beneficiary *1.* A person (or organization, etc.,) for whose benefit a **trust** is created. *2.* A person to whom an **insurance** policy is payable. *3.* A person who inherits under a **will.**

Benefit Any advantage, profit, or privilege; especially money paid by an insurance company, by a retirement plan, by an employer (other than wages), etc.

Benefit of clergy *1.* The right that clergymen had in old England to avoid trial by all nonchurch courts. *2.* Married.

Bequeath *1.* Give **personal** property or money (as opposed to real estate) by **will.** *2.* Give anything by will. Compare **devise.**

Bequest *1.* A gift by **will** of **personal** property. *2.* Any gift by will.

Best efforts More than **good faith** efforts, but less than a promise to do a thing.

Best evidence A rule of **evidence** that requires that the most reliable available proof of a fact must be produced. For example, if a painting is available as evidence, a photograph of the painting will not do.

Best use Land use that would bring in the most money.

Bestow Give or **grant** something.

Betterment An **improvement** rather than a **repair.**

Beyond a reasonable doubt The level of proof required to **convict** a person of a crime. For a **jury** to be convinced "beyond a reasonable doubt," it must be fully satisfied that the person is guilty. This is the highest level of proof required at any trial. It does not mean "convinced 100 percent," but it comes close to that meaning.

Bias *1.* A preconceived opinion that makes it difficult to be impartial. *2.* A preconceived opinion by the judge about a person involved in the lawsuit, as opposed to an opinion about the subject matter.

Bicameral Having two chambers. A legislature with two "houses," such as the U.S. Congress (composed of the Senate and House of Representatives), is bicameral.

Bid An offer to pay a specific price, supply goods, or perform work at a given price, etc.

Bifurcated trial Separate hearings for different issues in the same case, such as for guilt and punishment.

Bigamy The crime of being married to two or more husbands or wives at the same time.

Bilateral contract A deal that involves promises, **rights,** and **duties** on both sides. For example, a contract to sell a car is *bilateral* because one person promises to transfer ownership of the car, and the other person promises to pay for it. Compare *unilateral* **contract.**

Bill *1.* A formal written statement sent to a higher court either to inform it of certain facts or to request certain actions; for example, a *bill of exceptions* (a list of objections to the rulings and actions of the trial judge by one side). *2.* A draft of a law proposed to a **legislature** or working its way through the legislature. *3.* A law passed by a legislature acting as a court; for example, a *bill of impeachment.* *4.* An unusually important declaration, such as the **Bill of Rights.** *5.* A list of debts, contract terms, or items; for example, a **bill of lading** (list of goods shipped). *6.* A type of **negotiable instrument** promising the payment of money; for example, a *bill of exchange* (a written **order** from A to B, telling B to pay C a certain sum of money). *7.* A statement of details in court; for example, a *bill of indictment* (the formal accusation of a crime presented to a grand jury).

Bill of attainder See **attainder.**

Bill of lading A document given by a railroad or other **carrier** that lists the goods accepted for transport and sometimes lists the terms of the shipping agreement.

Bill of particulars A detailed statement of charges or claims by a **plaintiff** or the **prosecutor** (given upon the **defendant's** request).

Bill of Rights The first ten amendments (changes or additions) to the U.S. Constitution that provide for the following: *1.* **Freedom of speech,** religion, press, assembly, and to petition the government. *2.* The right to keep weapons. *3.* Freedom from being forced to give room and board to soldiers. *4.* Freedom from unreasonable searches and seizures and the requirement that **warrants** be supported by **probable cause.** *5.* The requirement that crimes be **indicted,** the prohibition against **double jeopardy,** the freedom from being a witness against oneself in a criminal trial, and the requirement that no rights or property be taken away without **due process of law** and just compensation. *6.* The right to a speedy criminal trial, an impartial jury, knowledge of the charges, **confrontation** of adverse witnesses, **compulsory process** of witnesses, and the help of a lawyer. *7.* The right to a jury trial in most civil cases. *8.* The prohibition against excessive **bail,** excessive fines, and cruel and unusual punishment. *9.* The fact that some rights are spelled out in the Constitution does not mean that these are all the rights the people have. *10.* Any power not kept solely for the United States belongs to the states and the people.

Bind *1.* Hold by legal obligation. *2.* See **binding over.**

Binder A temporary, preliminary contract and payment, such as for insurance or a home purchase.

Binding authority Sources of law that *must* be taken into account by a judge in deciding a case; for example, **statutes** from the same state or decisions by a higher court in the same state.

Binding over *1.* A court requiring a **bond** or **bail** money. *2.* Transferring a criminal **defendant** to another court in the same system. *3.* Sending a defendant to jail pending a trial's outcome.

Black Acre A fictional piece of real estate used for hypothetical examples in teaching law; often used together with "White Acre."

Black letter law Important legal principles that are accepted by most judges in most states.

Blackmail Illegal pressure or **extortion** of money by threatening to expose a person's illegal or embarrassing act. In some states, the threat must be in writing to be blackmail.

Blank *1.* A space left in a document. *2.* A printed document (a "form") with spaces to be filled in.

Blank indorsement Signing a **negotiable instrument,** such as a check, without specifying to whom it is being signed over (leaving a blank in the space), not limiting who can cash it.

Blanket Covering most (or many) things.

Blotter The police record form for **booking** a **defendant** and for keeping a cumulative record of arrests.

Blue Book Any of several different books of lists, prices, or specifications, such as the book that shows the proper form of case **citations.**

Blue law A state or local law that forbids selling or other activities on Sunday.

Blue ribbon jury A jury specially chosen for important or complex cases. This is rarely permitted.

Blue sky law Any state law **regulating** sales of **stock** and other investment activities to protect the public from fly-by-night or **fraudulent** stock deals or to give investors enough information to make informed decisions.

Board A publicly appointed or elected group chosen to oversee a public function (such as the *board of supervisors* that runs some county governments) or a private governing body (such as a *board of directors* that runs a **corporation**).

Body *1.* A person or an organization, such as a "body corporate" (a **corporation,** a city, etc.,) or "body politic" (the government, citizens as a group, etc.). *2.* The main or most important part of a document. *3.* A collection of laws. *4. Body execution* is the legal authority to deprive a person of freedom. *5.* For *body of the crime,* see **corpus delicti.**

Boilerplate Standardized, recurring language found in many legal documents, such as those sold in stationery stores.

Bona fide (Latin) Honest; real; in **good faith** (see that word.)

Bond _1._ A document that shows a debt owed by a company or a government to a bond purchaser. The purchaser is promised specific interest for a set time period with repayment on a set date. _2._ A document that promises to pay money if a particular future event happens, or a sum of money that is put up and will be lost if that event happens; for example, a **bail bond.**

Book value _1._ **Net worth;** clearly proven **assets** minus **liabilities.** _2._ The worth of something as recorded on a company's **financial statement.**

Booking The writing down, by the police, of facts about a person's arrest and charges along with identification and background information. Booking sometimes includes questioning the person and setting **bail** before a judge.

Bookkeeping Writing down the financial transactions of a business in a systematic way.

Boot Something extra thrown into a bargain.

Bottomry A loan to repair or equip a ship.

Boycott The refusal to do business with and the attempt to stop others from doing business with a company. In labor law, a _primary boycott_ involves a union and an employer, whereas a _secondary boycott_ involves companies that do business with (usually by buying from) the union's employer.

Breach Break a law or fail to perform a duty. For example, _breach of contract_ is failure, without legal excuse, to live up to a significant promise made in a

contract; and *breach of peace* is a vague term for any illegal public disturbance.

Breaking   Using force, or some kind of tampering or destruction, to get into property.

Bribery   The offering, giving, receiving, or soliciting of anything of value to influence the actions of a public official.

Brief   A written summary or condensed statement of a series of ideas or of a document. It may be a written statement prepared by one side in a lawsuit to explain its case to the judge (containing a fact summary, law summary, and argument about how the law applies to the facts), a document prepared by one side to use at a trial (containing lists of **witnesses, evidence, citations,** and **arguments),** or a summary of a published **opinion** in a case (prepared to help study the case and to review it later.)

Bright line   Simple or straightforward; avoids or ignores ambiguity.

Bring suit (or an action)   Start a lawsuit, usually by filing the first papers.

Broker   An **agent** who is employed by many different persons to buy, sell, make bargains, or enter into **contracts.**

Brother   An old expression for "fellow lawyer."

Budget   *1.* Money allowed for a particular purpose. *2.* An estimate of money that will be taken in and spent during a time period.

Buggery   Sodomy.

Building line   A certain distance inside the border of a lot, outside of which no new building may extend.

Bulk transfer   According to the **Uniform Commercial Code,** a *bulk transfer* is "not in the ordinary course of business" and of "a major part of materials, supplies, or other inventories." Rules against *bulk sales, bulk mortgages,* etc., are to protect a merchant's **creditors** from being cheated.

Burden of going forward (or burden of proceeding) The requirement that one side in a lawsuit produce evidence on a particular issue or risk losing on that issue.

Burden of proof The requirement that to win a point or have an issue decided in your favor in a lawsuit, you must show that the weight of evidence is on your side. Compare **standard** of proof.

Bureaucracy An organization, such as an **administrative agency** or the army, with the following traits: a chain of command with fewer people at the top than at the bottom; well-defined positions and responsibilities; fairly inflexible rules and procedures; "red tape" (many forms to be filled out and different procedures to go through); and **delegation** of authority downward from level to level.

Burglary **Breaking** and entering the house of another person at night with the intention of committing a **felony** (usually theft). Some states do not require a breaking, or that the building be a house, or that it be at night for it to be *burglary.*

Business expense Any normal expense necessary for producing income, not merely those expenses that are part of a "business."

Business entry rule **Business records exception.**

Business judgment rule The principle that if persons running a **corporation** make honest, careful decisions within their corporate powers, no court will interfere with these decisions, even if the results are bad.

Business records exception A principle that allows original, routine records (sometimes even if not part of a "business") to be used in a trial even though they would otherwise be excluded as **hearsay.**

Business trust   A company set up in the form of a **trust** that is similar to a **corporation** in most ways.

"But for" rule   Negligence alone will not make a person responsible for damage unless "but for" that negligence the damage would not have happened. For example, a failure to signal a turn may be negligent, but if the other driver was looking the other way, the failure to give the signal did not cause the accident.

Bylaws   Rules or **regulations** adopted by an organization.

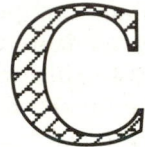

C   © is the symbol for **copyright.**

CA   Court of appeals.

CC   Any of several types of *courts, cases, codes,* etc., such as *circuit, city, civil, criminal,* and so on.

CCA   Circuit court of appeals.

CCH   Commerce Clearing House, a publisher of **loose-leaf services.**

CFR   Code of Federal Regulations.

CFTC   Commodity Futures Trading Commission.

CJ   *1.* Chief judge or justice; circuit judge. *2.* **Corpus** *Juris.*

CJS   Corpus *Juris Secundum.*

CL   Civil law.

CLA   A certified legal assistant who has passed the **NALA** exams.

COGSA   Carriage of Goods by Sea Act.

CP   Common pleas.

CPA   Certified public **accountant.**

CPSC   Consumer Products Safety Commission.

CSC   Civil Service Commission.

CTA   Cum testamento annexo.

Cabinet   The official advisory board of a head of government. Cabinet members are usually the heads of government departments.

Calendar   A court's day-by-day trial schedule or a court's **docket.**

Call   *1.* Public announcement, usually of a list. *2.* A formal demand for payment according to the terms of a contract. *3.* For *calling the prisoner,* see **allocution.**

Calumny   **Defamation** and false accusation.

Camera   Room; chamber. See **in camera.**

Cancel   *1.* Wipe out, cross out, or destroy the effect of a document by defacing it (by drawing lines across it, stamping it "canceled," etc.). *2.* Destroy, **annul,** set aside, or end. The process is called *cancellation.* *3.* Under the **Uniform Commercial Code,** *cancellation* means ending a **contract** because the other side has **breached** (broken) the agreement.

Canon   *1.* A law, rule, or principle. *Canon law* is Christian religious law. *2. Canons of construction* are principles to guide the **interpretation or construction** of written documents to decide their legal effect. *3. Canons of Ethics* and *Canons of Judicial Ethics* are the older forms of the lawyers' **Code of Professional Responsibility** and judges' **Code of Judicial Conduct.**

Capacity The ability to do something, the legal right to do something, or the two in combination.

Capias (Latin) "That you take." A **writ** from a judge to the **sheriff** or to the police, commanding them to take a **defendant** into **custody.** *Capias ad respondendum* is to bring the defendant to answer a claim or defend a charge, and *capias ad satisfaciendum* is to bring a defendant to pay a **judgment.**

Capital *1.* Head, chief, or major. For example, *capital crimes* are punishable by death. *2.* **Assets** or worth. *3.* Relating to wealth, especially to assets held for a long time. For example, *capital assets* are almost all property owned other than things held for sale. Personal capital assets include personally owned stocks, land, trademarks, jewelry, and so on. Business capital assets are described under **assets.** A *capital gains tax* is a tax on the profit made when a capital asset is sold.

Capitalize *1.* Treat the cost of something (a purchase, an improvement, etc.,) as a **capital** *asset* by breaking the cost into annual parts and taking an annual tax **deduction** for each part. *2.* Issue **stocks** or **bonds** to cover an investment. *3.* Figure out the **net worth** or **principal** on which an investment is based.

Capitation tax A tax on a person at a fixed rate, regardless of income, assets, etc.; a "head tax."

Capricious Not based on fact, law, or reason.

Caption The heading or introductory section of a legal paper that has, for example, the names of the **parties,** the court, the case number, etc.

Care *1.* Safekeeping or **custody.** *2.* Attention, heed, or caution.

Carnal knowledge Sexual intercourse.

Carrier A person or organization that transports persons, property, or information. A _common carrier_ does this for the general public.

Carry back (over) rule A tax rule that sometimes allows a person or company to use current-year losses to reduce taxes in the years before (after) the loss.

Carrying charges _1_. The costs of owning property, such as land taxes, mortgage payments, etc. _2_. **Interest.**

Cartel A close (often formal) association of companies carrying on the same or similar businesses. The companies limit competition among themselves and drive out competition by others.

Case _1_. A dispute that goes to court (a lawsuit), the **evidence** and arguments presented by each side, or the judge's **opinion** deciding that dispute. _2_. A _case-in-point_ is a prior decision of the same court or a higher court that decides a similar legal question. _3_. The _case method (or system)_ teaches law by studying cases in each legal subject historically and by drawing general legal principles from them. _4_. A _casebook_ is an edited collection of written court opinions, usually by **appeals** judges, used for teaching a single law school subject. _5_. A _case-in-chief_ is the main **evidence** offered by one side in a lawsuit. It does not include evidence to oppose the other side's case. _6_. _Caselaw_ is all reported judicial decisions; the law drawn from reading judges' opinions. _7_. _Cases and controversies_ are real (not hypothetical or faked) disputes that turn into lawsuits; the U.S. **Constitution** allows the courts to decide only these real disputes. _8_. _Case_ is also short for _trespass on the case,_ an old form of lawsuit seeking recovery for indirect injury.

Cash basis A method of accounting that reflects income and expenses only when actually received or paid. Compare **accrual basis.**

Cash value *1.* The same as **market value;** the price something would bring if sold for cash on the open market. *2. Cash surrender value* is the amount of money an insurance policy will bring if cashed in with the company.

Casual Accidental, by chance, unexpected, unintentional.

Casual ejector See **ejectment.**

Casualty *1.* Any accident; an unexpected accident; an inevitable accident. *2.* An injured or killed person.

Categorical assistance Financial help programs with requirements in addition to financial need; for example, Aid to the Blind.

Causa (Latin) *1.* Cause, reason, or motive. *2.* For *causa causans* or *causa proxima,* see **proximate cause.** *3. Causa mortis* means "because of impending death." A *gift causa mortis* is a gift made by a person who thinks he or she is dying; if the person recovers, the gift is **void.** [pronounce: <u>cow</u>-sa]

Cause *1.* That which produces an effect. *2.* Motive or reason. *3.* Lawsuit or legal action. *4.* Short for *just cause* in the removal of a person from office or dismissal from a job.

Cause of action *1.* Facts sufficient to support a valid lawsuit. For example, a *cause of action* for **battery** must include facts to prove an intentional, unconsented-to physical contact. *2.* The legal theory upon which a lawsuit is based.

Caveat (Latin) "Beware"; warning. *Caveat emptor* means "let the buyer beware." Although this is still an important warning, recent laws and court decisions provide many safeguards to the buyer. [pronounce: <u>kav</u>-ee-aht]

Cease and desist order An **administrative agency's** command that a person or organization stop doing something. It is similar to a court's **injunction.**

Cede **Assign, grant,** give up, or **transfer.**

Censorship *1.* Denial of **freedom of speech** or of the press. *2.* Review of books, movies, etc., to prohibit publication and distribution, usually for moral or state security reasons.

Censure Formal reprimand.

Century Digest (Cent. Dig.) See **American Digest System.**

Certificate A written acknowledgment that something has been done or some formal requirement has been met. For example, a *certificate of occupancy* permits a building to be used because it meets building, health, or **zoning** requirements.

Certification *1.* The process by which a federal court sometimes refers a question about state law to a state court and delays deciding the case until the question is answered. *2.* A *certification mark* is placed on goods by an organization other than the manufacturer or seller to show that they meet quality standards, were made by a union, come from a certain region, etc. *3.* A *certification proceeding* is an **NLRB** procedure to find out if a company's employees want a particular union to represent them.

Certified check A check that a bank has marked as "guaranteed cashable" for its customer.

Certiorari (Latin) "To make sure." A request for *certiorari* (or "cert." for short) is like an **appeal,** but one which the higher court is not required to take for decision. It is literally a **writ** asking the lower court for the case **record.** [pronounce: sir-sho-<u>rare</u>-ee or <u>sir</u>-sheo-<u>rare</u>-ee]

Cession   A giving up of something. See **cede.**

Cestui que trust   (French) **Beneficiary** of a **trust.** [pronounce: <u>set</u>-i-kuh or ce-<u>twee</u>-kuh]

Chain of title   A list of the consecutive passing of the legal ownership of a piece of land.

Chain referral   **Pyramid sales scheme.**

Challenge   An objection; for example, to the qualifications of a prospective **juror.**

Chambers   A judge's private office.

Champerty   "Buying into" another person's lawsuit. This is restricted by law in most states.

Chancery   An old court that handled **equitable** actions. These lawsuits are now handled by regular courts in most places. [pronounce: <u>chance</u>-ery]

Chapter Eleven   A reorganization of an **insolvent** (broke) **corporation** under federal **bankruptcy** law in which ownership is transferred to a new corporation made up of old owners and **creditors.**

Chapter Seven   A regular **bankruptcy** for individuals.

Chapter Thirteen   A procedure under federal **bankruptcy** law for an individual or small business in financial trouble to pay off only a proportion of its debts (called a *composition*), get extra time to pay them (called an *extension*), or both. This process is also called *rehabilitation.*

Character evidence   **Testimony** about a person's personal traits and habits drawn from close associates' opinions, community reputation, and past actions.

Charge   *1.* A **claim, obligation,** burden, or **liability.** *2.* A judge's final summary of a case and instructions to the jury. *3.* A formal accusation of a crime.

Charitable trust   A **trust** set up for a public purpose such as to support a school, church, charity, etc.

Charter An organization's basic starting document, such as a corporation's **articles of incorporation.**

<u>Chattel</u> Personal property; any property other than **land.** A *chattel mortgage* is a **mortgage** on personal property, and *chattel paper* is a document that shows both a debt and the fact that the debt is **secured** by specific goods.

Check *1.* A type of **negotiable instrument** on which the "maker" instructs a bank to pay a certain amount of money to another person. *2.* A restraint; for example, each branch of the federal government *checks and balances* the others, so no one branch dominates.

Choate Complete; valid against all later claims. [pronounce: ko-ate]

Chose (French) "A thing"; a piece of personal property. A *chose in action* is a right to recover a debt or to get **damages** that can be enforced in court; also, the thing itself, such as the contract being sued on. [pronounce: shows]

Circuit The geographical area served by a single *circuit court* (different types and levels of courts in different states). For *circuit court of appeals,* see **United States Court of Appeals.**

Circumstantial evidence Fact that *indirectly* tend to prove a main fact in question. For example, **testimony** that a person was seen walking in the rain is **direct evidence** that the person walked in the rain, but testimony that the person's clothing was wet is *circumstantial evidence* that the person walked in the rain.

Citation *1.* A notice to appear in court; also, a notice of a violation of law, such as a *health board citation. 2.* A reference to a legal authority and where it is found. For example, "17 UDlLR 247" is a citation to an article that begins on page 247 of volume 17 of the University of Dull Law Review.

Citator A set of books (or a data base) that uses tables of **citations** to tell what happened to a **case** or **statute** after it came out. It will tell, for example, if a case has been **overruled** or **distinguished.**

Cite *1.* Summon a person to court. *2.* Refer to specific legal references or **authorities.** *3.* Short for **citation.**

Citizen *1.* A person born in or naturalized in the United States. *2.* A person is a citizen of the state where he or she has permanent residence, and a corporation is a citizen of the state where it was legally created.

Civil Either "having to do with the government" or "other than **criminal.**" A *civil action* is every lawsuit other than a criminal proceeding. It is brought to enforce a right or **redress** a wrong. A *civil commitment* is confinement by a noncriminal process to a mental hospital, drug treatment facility, and so on. *Civil death* is the loss of all rights, such as the right to sue, that occurs in some states to persons convicted of serious crimes (usually those sentenced to life imprisonment). *Civil disability* is the loss of some rights, such as the right to vote, that occurs in some states when a person has been convicted of a crime. *Civil disobedience* is breaking a law to demonstrate its unfairness or to focus attention on a problem. *Civil law* may refer to law handed down from the Romans, to law based on one elaborate document or **code** rather than on a combination of many laws and judicial **opinions,** to government by civilians rather than by the military, or to the law used in a *civil action. Civil procedure* is the laws and rules that govern how *civil actions* are handled by individuals and by the courts. *Civil rights* are the rights of all citizens that are guaranteed by the U.S. **Constitution** and other laws; for example, **freedom of speech.** The *civil rights acts* are federal laws that prohibit discrimination based on race, color, age, sex, religion, or national origin. The *civil rights amendments* are the Thirteenth, Fourteenth, and Fifteenth **Amendments** to the U.S. **Constitution** that deal with slavery, **discrimination,** and the right to vote. The *civil service* is all nonmilitary government employees chosen by a standardized method rather than by political appointment or election. A *civil suit* is a *civil action*.

Claim *1*. Demand as your own; assert. *2*. A *claim for relief* is the core of a modern **complaint** (first **pleading** in a lawsuit). It may be a short, clear statement of the claim being made that shows that if the facts **alleged** can be proved, the **plaintiff** should get help from the court in enforcing the claim against the **defendant.** *3*. A *claimant* is either a **plaintiff** or a person who claims property or a right.

Class action A lawsuit brought for yourself and other persons in the same situation.

Class gift A gift, usually in a **will,** to a group such as "my grandchildren," whose shares will depend on the number of such persons at the time the persons actually receive the gift.

Classified *1*. Secret. *2*. Put in a special category or "class."

Clause A single paragraph, sentence, or phrase.

Clayton Act A 1914 federal law that extended the **Sherman Act's** prohibition against **monopolies** and price discrimination.

Clean bill Either a legislative **bill** that has been substantially rewritten by a committee or a commercial **bill** that is clear and in final, unqualified, unmarked form.

Clean hands Acting fairly and honestly in all matters concerned with a lawsuit that you are bringing, especially if the lawsuit involves a request for **equitable** *relief*.

Clear *1*. Final payment on a check by the bank on which it was drawn *clears* the check. *2. Clear title* means legal ownership that may pass freely to another person. *3*. Free of taxes, **liens,** or other **encumbrances** or claims.

Clear and convincing evidence Stronger **evidence** than a **preponderance of the evidence** (evidence that something is more likely to be true than false) but not as strong as **beyond a reasonable doubt** (evidence that something is almost certainly true.)

Clear and present danger A test of whether speech may be restricted or punished. According to this test, speech may be restricted or punished if it will probably lead to immediate and direct violence or if it threatens a serious, immediate weakening of national security.

Clemency Either lenient sentencing of a criminal or reduction of the criminal's punishment.

Clerical error A mistake in writing or copying, as opposed to a mistake in judgment or in decision making.

Clerk *1*. A court official who keeps records and official files. *2*. A law student or lawyer temporarily employed by a judge.

Client *1*. A person who employs a lawyer; sometimes, a person who merely discusses with a lawyer hiring that lawyer. *2*. A person whose aversion to the other side in a lawsuit exceeds his or her aversion to lawyers.

Clifford trust A **trust** that you set up that gives the trust's income to someone else but that eventually returns the **principal** (original money put in) to you.

Close *1.* Old word for an enclosed or well-marked piece of land. *2.* A *close (or closed) corporation* is a **corporation** with total ownership in a few hands. *3.* A *closed shop* is a company for which only members of a particular **union** may work in certain jobs. *4. Closely held* stock (or a closely held company) is owned by a family or by another company.

Closing The final meeting for the sale of land at which all payments are made, the property is formally transferred, and the **mortgage** is fully set up by filling out all necessary papers for the mortgage lender. *Closing costs* are all charges for finishing the deal, such as transfer taxes, mortgage fees, credit reports, etc. These costs are all set down on a *closing statement,* also called a "settlement sheet."

Cloture A formal process of ending debate in a meeting.

Cloud on title A **claim** or **encumbrance** against property that, if valid, would lower the property's value or weaken its legal ownership.

Co A prefix meaning with, together, or unitedly; for example, a *codefendant* is a person who is a defendant along with another person in a trial.

Coaching A lawyer telling a **witness** how to **testify.** This is sometimes improper or even illegal.

Cobuyer A person with an ownership right in a thing being purchased; a person who merely put up some of the money; or a **cosigner.**

Coconspirators rule The principle that statements by a member of a **conspiracy** are valid **evidence** against the other conspirators.

Code *1.* Either a collection of laws or a complete, interrelated and exclusive set of laws. *2. Code Civil* is the law of France as established in 1804 and used with revisions since. *3. Code of Federal Regulations* is the compilation of all the **rules** and **regulations** put out by federal **agencies.** *4. Code of Hammurabi,* written four thousand years ago in Babylon, was the first full-scale set of laws. *5. Code of Judicial Conduct* is the set of rules for judges' conduct adopted by the **American Bar Association** and used by many states. *6. Code of Military Justice* is the set of laws and rules governing all **military law,** courts, punishment, etc. *7. Code of Professional Responsibility* is the set of rules that governs lawyers' conduct. It contains both general ethical guidelines and specific rules prohibiting things that may be punished. It was written by the **American Bar Association** and adopted (with modifications) by the states. *8. Code pleading* is the system of **pleading** that replaced **common-law** and **equity** pleading with a standardized system.

Codicil   A supplement or addition to a **will** that adds to it or changes it. [pronounce: cod-i-sill]

Codification   The process of collecting and arranging by subject matter the laws of an area into one complete system, approved in one piece by a **legislature.**

Coercion   Compulsion or force; making a person act against free will.

Cognizance   **Judicial** power to decide a matter; a judge's decision to "take notice" of a matter and accept it for decision.

Cognovit note   A written statement that a **debtor** owes money and "confesses judgment," or allows the **creditor** to get a **judgment** in court for the money whenever the creditor wants to or when a certain event, such as a failure to make a loan payment, happens.

Cohabitation   Living together; living together as if the persons were husband and wife; living together and having sexual intercourse; having sexual intercourse.

Co̲i̲nsurance A sharing of an insurance **risk** between an insurance company and its customer. This is often a percentage payment on a partial loss when the property is not insured at full value. For example, if a $100 watch is insured for $50 and suffers $50 in damage, coinsurance might pay $25.

Coll̲a̲teral *1.* Money or property put up to back a person's word when taking out a loan. *2.* "On the side." Often, the opposite of **direct.** For example, *collateral ancestors* include uncles, cousins, and persons similarly related but not direct ancestors such as grandparents. *3. Collateral attack* is an attempt to avoid the effect of a court's action or decision by taking action in a different court proceeding. *4. Collateral estoppel* is being stopped from making a claim in one court proceeding that has already been disproved by the facts raised in a prior, different proceeding. *5.* A *collateral warranty* is a **warranty** of **title** to land made by someone other than the person selling it.

Collective bargaining Negotiation between a union and an employer of union members, usually concerning wages, hours, and working conditions. Federal law often requires an employer to collectively bargain with a union. A *collective bargaining agreement* is the **contract** that results from these negotiations. A *collective bargaining unit* is all employees of one type or all the employees of one department in a company.

Coll̲o̲quy A discussion, often private, among lawyers and the judge during a trial.

Coll̲u̲sion Secret action taken by two or more persons together to cheat another or to commit **fraud.** For example, it is *collusion* if two persons agree that one should sue the other because the second person is **covered** by insurance; and it is *collusion* if a husband

and wife agree that one of them will commit an act that will allow the other to get a divorce.

Color Appearance or semblance; looking real or true on the surface, but actually false. Sometimes this involves deliberate falseness. For example, acting "under *color of law,* authority, or office" is taking an action that looks official or appears to be backed by law, but which is not. Sometimes, however, "color" does not involve an attempt to deceive. For example, *color of title* is apparent, but not actual, ownership, based on a **deed,** a court **decree,** etc.

Colorable *1.* False; having the appearance but not the reality. *2.* **Prima facie.**

Comaker A second (or third, etc.,) person who signs a **negotiable instrument** such as a check and who, by doing so, promises to pay on it in full.

Combination *1.* A group of persons working together, especially for an unlawful purpose. *2.* A putting together of inventions, each of which may be already **patented,** but which working together produce a new, useful result that may itself be patented.

Comity Courtesy and respect. A willingness to do something official, not as a matter of right but from good will and tradition. For example, nations often give effect to the laws of other nations out of *comity,* and state and federal courts depend on *comity* to help keep their decisions consistent with each other.

Commerce clause Article I, Section 8 of the U.S. **Constitution.** It gives Congress the power to control trade with foreign countries, trade from state to state, and things that "affect" this trade.

Commercial code See **Uniform Commercial Code.**

Commercial paper A **negotiable instrument** related to business, such as a **bill** *of exchange.*

Commingling Mixing together, such as putting two persons' money into one bank account in a way that makes separate accounting difficult.

Commission *1*. A written grant of authority to do a particular thing, given by the government to one of its branches or to an individual or organization. *2*. An organization like one mentioned in #1. *3*. Payment (to a salesperson or other **agent**) based on amount of sales, percentage of profit, etc. *4*. Doing a criminal act.

Commissioner *1*. The name for the heads of various government **boards** and **agencies.** *2*. A person appointed by a court to handle special matters, such as to conduct a court-ordered sale or to take **testimony** in complicated, specialized cases.

Commitment The formal process of putting a person into the official care of another person, such as the warden of a prison or head of a psychiatric hospital. See **civil commitment.**

Committee *1*. A subgroup that a larger group appoints to do specialized work. *2*. A **trustee** appointed by a court to take care of a mentally **incompetent** person's property. *3*. *Committee of the whole* is a procedure in which a **legislature** acts as if it is a committee to get business done quickly and informally.

Commodity Anything produced, bought, or sold; a raw or partially processed material; a farm product.

Common *1*. A piece of land used by many persons. *2*. Usual, ordinary, regular; applying to many persons or things. *3*. For *common carrier,* see **carrier.** *4*. A *common council* is a town or city **legislature.** *5*. For *common count,* see **count.** *6*. A *common disaster* occurs when two or more persons die in the same accident with no way to tell who died first. *7*. *Common law* may refer to judge-made (rather than legislature-made) law or to law that had its origins in England and grew from ever-changing custom and tradition (rather than king-made law). *8.* A *common-law action* may refer to a lawsuit based on the *common law* rather than on a **statute,** or it may refer to a **civil** (as opposed to **criminal**) lawsuit that is between private individuals and that contains a request for **damages.** *9.* A *common-law marriage* is a legally binding marriage that occurs without license or ceremony under the laws of many states when a heterosexual couple holds itself out as married (or lives together as if married) for a specified time period. *10.* A *common-law trust* is a **business trust.** *11. Common pleas* is the name for several different types of **civil** trial courts. *12.* A *common scheme, plan, or design* may refer to two or more different crimes planned together, two or more persons planning the same crime, or dividing a piece of land into lots with identical restrictions on land use. *13. Common situs picketing* is a union's **picketing** an entire construction site because of a dispute with only one **contractor.** This is generally illegal. *14. Common stock* is **shares** in a **corporation** that depend for their value on the value of the company. These shares usually have voting rights but usually earn **dividends** only after other types of company obligations are paid.

Community *1.* A vague term that can include very large or very small areas, groups with common interests, etc. *2. Community property* is property owned *in common* (both persons owning it all) by a husband and wife. In *community property states,* most property acquired during a marriage belongs to both partners, no matter whose name it is in.

Commutation Changing a criminal punishment to one less severe. Compare **pardon** and **reprieve.**

Compact An agreement or contract, usually between governments. The *compact clause* of the U.S. **Constitution** prohibits states from making agreements with other states or with foreign countries without congressional approval.

Company Any organization set up to do business.

Comparative negligence rule A legal rule, used in many states, by which the amount of "fault" on each side of an accident is measured, and the side with less fault is given **damages** (money) according to the difference between the magnitude of each side's fault. Compare **contributory negligence,** in which any fault usually precludes damages.

Comparative rectitude rule A legal rule, used in some states, by which a divorce is given to the person in a marriage who the judge decides has behaved better. Also called a "least fault divorce."

Compelling state interest A strong-enough reason for a state law to make the law **constitutional** even though the law classifies persons on the basis of race, sex, and so on or uses the state's police powers to limit a person's **constitutional rights.**

Compensatory damages **Damages** awarded for the actual loss suffered by a **plaintiff.** Compare **punitive damages.**

Competent *1.* Properly qualified; adequate; having the right natural or legal qualifications. For example, a person may be *competent* to make a **will** if he or she understands what making a will is, knows that he or she is making a will, and knows generally how making the will affects relatives and those named in the will. *2.* A *competency proceeding* is either a hearing to determine whether a person should undergo **civil commitment** or a hearing to determine whether a person is mentally capable of standing trial in a **criminal** case. *Competency* may be different from *sanity* (see **insanity**). *3. Competent evidence* is **evidence** that is both relevant to the point in question and the proper type of evidence to prove the point; evidence that cannot be kept out by any **exclusionary rule.**

Complainant A person who makes an official complaint or who starts a lawsuit (see **plaintiff**).

Complaint *1.* The first main paper filed in a **civil** lawsuit. It includes, among other things, a statement of the wrong or harm done to the **plaintiff** by the **defendant** and a request for specific help from the court. *2.* A *criminal complaint* is a formal document that charges a person with a crime.

Compliance Acting in a way that does not violate a law or an agreement.

Composition A formal agreement, involving a **debtor** and several **creditors,** that each creditor will take less than the whole amount owed as full payment. For *composition in bankruptcy,* see **Chapter Thirteen.**

Compound interest Interest on interest. Adding interest to the **principal** (main debt) at regular intervals and then computing the interest on the newly increased principal plus interest.

Compounding a felony A person's accepting money or other gain in exchange for not prosecuting, or not testifying about, a major crime.

Comptroller The top financial officer of a company or the government. [pronounce: con-troll-er]

Compulsion *1.* **Duress.** *2.* An overpowering impulse.

Compulsory process Official action to force a person to appear in court or before a **legislature** as a witness.

Compurgator See **wager of law.**

Conciliation The process of bringing two sides together to agree to a voluntary compromise.

Conclusion of law An argument or answer arrived at not only by drawing a conclusion from facts but also by applying law to the facts. For example, saying that a person hit another person with a car is only a conclusion of fact, but saying that the accident was the driver's fault is a *conclusion of law.*

Conclusive Beyond dispute; ending inquiry or debate; clear. For example, a *conclusive presumption* is a legal conclusion that cannot be changed by any facts.

Concur Agree. A *concurring opinion* is one in which a judge agrees with the result reached in an **opinion** by another judge in the same case, but not necessarily with the reasoning that the other judge used to reach the conclusion.

Concurrent Together; having the same authority; at the same time. For example, courts have *concurrent jurisdiction* when each court has the power to deal with the same case; and *concurrent sentences* are prison terms that run at the same time.

Condemn (and condemnation) *1.* Find guilty of a criminal charge. *2.* A governmental taking of private property, usually with payment but not necessarily with consent. *3.* An official ruling that a building is unfit for use.

Condition *1.* A future, uncertain event that creates or destroys rights and obligations. For example, a **contract** may have a *condition* in it that if one person should die, the contract is ended. Conditions may be **express** or **implied.** Also, they may be **precedent** (if a certain future event happens, a right or obligation is created) or *subsequent* (if a certain future event happens, a right or obligation ends). *2.* A requirement.

Conditional Depending on a **condition;** unsure; depending on a future event. For example, a *conditional sale* is a sale in which the buyer gets **title** (full legal ownership) only after full payment. For *conditional use,* see **special** *use permit.*

Condominium Several persons owning individual pieces of a building and managing it together. Compare **cooperative.**

Condonation Willing forgiveness by a wife or husband of the other's actions that is enough to stop those actions from being **grounds** for a **divorce.** Actions that imply forgiveness, such as resuming sexual relations after knowledge of adultery, can also be condonation.

Confession *1.* A voluntary statement by a person that he or she is guilty of a crime. *2.* Any admission of wrongdoing. *3.* For *confession and avoidance,* see **avoidance.** *4. Confession of judgment* is a process in which a person who borrows money or buys on credit signs in advance an agreement to allow the lawyer for the lender to get a court judgment without even telling the borrower. See **judgment** and **cognovit note.**

Confidential relation Any relationship in which one person has a right to expect a higher-than-usual level of care and faithfulness from another person; for example, client from attorney or child from parent. If a very strong duty exists, it is a **fiduciary** relationship.

Confidentiality *1.* The requirement that a lawyer, or anyone working for a lawyer, not disclose information received from a client. One exception is if the lawyer is told that the client is planning to commit a crime. *2.* The requirement that certain other persons (such as clergy, physicians, husbands and wives, etc.,) not disclose information that is considered to be *privileged communication.*

Confirmation   Formal approval, especially formal written approval of a prior act.

Confiscation   Governmental taking of private property without payment.

Conflict of interest   Being in a position, intentionally or unintentionally, in which your own needs and desires might lead you to violate your duty to another who has a right to depend on you (for example, if you are a judge holding XYZ stock trying a case involving the XYZ company) or in which you must serve competing masters (if you are a lawyer with competing clients).

Conflict of laws   The situation that exists when the laws of more than one state or country may apply to a **case** and a judge must choose among them. *Conflict of laws* is also the name for the legal subject concerned with the rules used to make such choices.

Conformity hearing   After a judge decides in favor of one side in a lawsuit, the judge may tell the winner's lawyer to write a **judgment** or **decree** to carry out the decision. A *conformity hearing* may then be held to decide whether the judgment or decree is correct.

Confrontation   The **constitutional** right of a criminal **defendant** to see and cross-examine all **witnesses** against him or her.

Confusion   Mixing or blending together. *Confusion of goods* is a mixing together of the property of two or more persons, with the effect that telling which belongs to whom is not possible.

Congress   *1.* A meeting of officials. *2.* The **legislature** of the United States (composed of the Senate and House of Representatives).

Congressional Record   A daily printed record of proceedings in the U.S. **Congress.** It tells how each **bill**

was voted upon, which bills were sent to and from each **committee,** what was said, etc.

Conjugal   Having to do with marriage. *Conjugal rights* are a husband and wife's legal interest in the other's companionship, love, and sexual relationship.

Connecting up   A thing may be conditionally admitted into **evidence** subject to *connecting up* (subject to a later showing that it is **admissible**).

Connivance   The consent (or help) of a husband or wife to the other's acts in order to get a **divorce** based on those acts.

Consanguinity   Blood relationship; kinship.

Consecutive sentence   A **cumulative sentence.**

Consent   Voluntary and active agreement. A *consent decree* is either a **divorce** that is granted against a person present in court (or represented in court) who does not oppose the divorce, or a settlement of a lawsuit or prosecution in which a person or company agrees to take certain actions without admitting fault or guilt for the situation causing the lawsuit.

Consequential damages   Court-ordered compensation for *indirect* losses or other indirect harm. Also, in contract law, sometimes called *special damages.*

Conservator   A guardian or preserver of another person's property appointed by a court because the other person is not legally competent to manage it.

Consideration   The reason or main cause for a person to make a **contract;** something of value received or promised to induce (convince) a person to make a deal. For example, if Ann and Sue make a deal for Ann to buy a car from Sue, Ann's promise to pay a thousand dollars is *consideration* for Sue's promise to hand over the car and vice versa. Without *consideration* a contract is not valid.

Consignment   Handing over things for transportation or sale, but keeping ownership.

Consolidation   Combining separate things, such as lawsuits on the same subject between the same persons.

Consortium   The right of a husband or wife to the other's love and services. **Damages** are sometimes given to one spouse to compensate for the *loss of consortium* that occurs when the other spouse is wrongly killed or injured. [pronounce: con-<u>sor</u>-shum]

Conspiracy   A crime that may be committed when two or more persons agree to do something unlawful (or to do something lawful by unlawful means). A person can be guilty of both conspiracy to commit a crime and the crime itself, but certain crimes that require two persons, such as bribery, are not usually also conspiracy.

Constable   A local peace officer who does court-related work.

Constitute   Make up. *Duly constituted* means properly put together and formally valid and correct.

Constitution   A document that sets out the basic principles and most general laws of a country, state, or organization. The *U.S. Constitution* is the document on which U.S. laws are based and to which all laws in the United States must yield.

Constitutional   *1.* Consistent with (not in conflict with) the **constitution.** *2.* Depending on the constitution; for example, a *constitutional court* is one established by the U.S. Constitution. *3.* A *constitutional convention* is a meeting of representatives of the people of a country to write or change a **constitution.** Article V of the U.S. Constitution allows a convention if two-thirds of the state **legislatures** call for one. *4. Constitutional law* is the study of the law that applies to the organization, structure, and functions of the government, the basic principles of government, and the validity (or *constitutionality*) of laws and actions when tested against the requirements of the **constitution.** *5.* A *constitutional right* is a right or freedom guaranteed to the people by the **constitution** (and thus safe from **legislative** or other governmental attempts to limit or end it).

Construction A decision (usually by a judge) about the meaning and legal effect of ambiguous or doubtful words that considers not only the words themselves but also surrounding circumstances, relevant laws and writings, etc. (Looking at just the words is called **interpretation.**)

Constructive *1.* True legally even if not factually; "just as if"; established by legal interpretation; inferred; implied. *2.* A *constructive contract* is a **quasi contract.** *3. Constructive desertion* is forcing a husband or wife to leave; for example, when Mary is forced to leave because John has made it unsafe for her to stay, John has "constructively deserted" Mary. *4. Constructive knowledge (or notice)* is knowledge that a person should have and that the person would have if he or she used reasonable care to keep informed; for example, knowledge of a properly recorded mortgage on a house a person plans to buy. *5.* A *constructive trust* is a situation in which a person holds legal **title** to a property, but the property should, in fairness, belong to another person. A court may say that it is held in **trust.**

Consular court A court held by the *consuls* (representatives below ambassador rank) of one country inside another country.

Consumer *1.* A person who buys (or rents, travels on, or uses) something for personal rather than for business use. *2. Consumer credit* is money, property, or services offered to a person for personal use "on time" if there is a finance charge or if there are more than four **installment** payments. *3.* The *Consumer Credit Protection Act* is a federal law that requires the clear disclosure of consumer credit terms, gives consumers the right to back out of some deals, restricts wage **garnishments,** and so on. Also called Truth in Lending Act.

Contemner   A person who commits **contempt** *of court.*

Contemplation of death   See **causa mortis.**

Contempt   *1.* An act that obstructs a court's work or lessens the dignity of a court. *2.* A willful disobeying of a judge's command or official court order. It is also possible to be in *contempt* of a **legislature** or an **administrative agency.**

Contest   Oppose or defend against a lawsuit or other action; oppose the validity of a **will,** etc.

Contingent   Possible, but not assured; depending on some future events or actions (*contingencies*) that may or may not happen. A *contingent estate* is a right to own or use property that depends on an uncertain future event for the right to take effect. A *contingent fee* is payment to a lawyer of a percentage of the possible "winnings" from a lawsuit rather than a flat amount of money or payment by hourly fee.

Continuance   The postponement of court proceedings to a later day or session of court.

Contra   Against; on the other hand; opposing.

Contraband   Things that are illegal to import, export, transport, or possess.

Contract   *1.* An agreement that affects or creates legal relationships between two or more persons. To be a *contract,* an agreement must involve: at least one promise, **consideration** (something of value promised or given), persons legally capable of making binding agreements, and a reasonable certainty about the meaning of the terms. A contract is called **bilateral** if both sides make promises (such as the promise to deliver a book for the promise to pay for it) or **unilateral** if the promises are on one side only. According to the **Uniform Commercial Code,** a contract is the "total legal obligation which results from the parties' agreement," and according to the Restatement of the Law of Contracts, it is "a promise or a set of promises for the breach of which the law in some way recognizes a duty." *2.* The *contract clause* is the provision in Article I of the U.S. **Constitution** that no state may pass a law abolishing contracts or denying them legal effect. *3.* A *contract for deed* is a **land sales contract.** *4.* A *contract under seal* was an old form of contract requiring a **seal** but no **consideration.**

Contractor   An **independent contractor.**

Contravention   Violation of law, rule, or custom.

Contribution   The sharing of payment for a debt (or **judgment**) among persons **liable** for it.

Contributory negligence   **Negligent** conduct by a person who was harmed by another person's negligence; a **plaintiff's** failure to be careful that is a part of the cause of his or her injury.

Controller   **Comptroller.**

Controversy   Any **civil** lawsuit involving real legal rights.

Controvert   Dispute, deny, or oppose.

Contumacy   **Contempt;** especially the refusal to appear in court.

Contumely   Rudeness or scornful treatment.

Conventional *1.* Usual and ordinary. *2.* Caused by an agreement between persons rather than involving the courts or government.

Conversion *1.* Any act that deprives an owner of property without that owner's permission and without just cause. *2.* The exchange of one type of property for another.

Conveyance A transfer of **title,** especially title to land.

Convict *1.* Find a person guilty of a crime. *2.* A person in prison.

Cooling off period *1.* A period of time during which no action of a particular sort may be taken by either side in a dispute. For example, after the filing of a **grievance,** a month in which a union may not strike and an employer may not **lock out** employees; or an automatic delay between filing divorce papers and the **hearing.** *2.* A period of time, often three days, during which a buyer may cancel a purchase contract.

Cooperative An organization set up to help the persons who form it and use it. An *apartment co-op* is owned by residents who **lease** the individual apartments.

Coordinate **Concurrent.**

Copartnership **Partnership.**

Copyright The right to control the copying, distributing, performing, displaying, and adapting of *works* (paintings, music, books, movies, etc.). The right belongs to the creator, or to persons employing the creator, or to persons who buy the right from the creator. The symbol for copyright is ©.

Coram (Latin) "Before"; in the presence of. For example, *coram nobis* (before us) is a request that a court change its **judgment** because the **defendant** has an excuse for failing to raise facts that would have won the case.

Co-respondent See **correspondent.**

Coroner An official who conducts inquiries into the cause of violent or suspicious deaths. Serious cases may require a *coroner's inquest* or hearing. See **medical examiner.**

Corporal punishment Physical punishment such as beating.

Corporate Belonging to a **corporation.** The *corporate veil* is the legal assumption that actions taken by a corporation are not the actions of its owners, and that these owners cannot usually be held responsible for corporate actions.

Corporation An organization that is formed under state or federal law and exists, for legal purposes, as a separate being or **artificial person.** It may be public (set up by the government) or private (set up by individuals), and it may be set up to carry on a business or to perform almost any function. A *corporation counsel* is a lawyer who represents a town or city in **civil** matters.

Corporeal Having body or substance; visible and tangible. [pronounce: cor-<u>por</u>-e-al]

Corpus (Latin) *1.* "Body"; main body of a thing as opposed to attachments. For example, a **trust** *corpus* is the money or property put into the trust, as opposed to interest or profits. *2. Corpus delicti* means "the body of the crime." It is either the material substance upon which a crime has been committed (dead body, burned house, etc.,) or the fact that proves that a crime has been committed. *3. Corpus Juris* is a legal encyclopedia cross-referenced with the **American Digest System.** *Corpus Juris Secundum* is its update. *4. Corpus juris civilis,* "the body of the civil law," is the main writings of Roman law.

Correspondent *1.* The "other" man or woman in a divorce suit based on **adultery.** *2.* A bank or other financial institution that performs regular services for another, such as collecting mortgage payments.

Corroborate Add to the likely truth or importance of a fact; give additional facts or evidence to strengthen a fact or an assertion; back up what someone else says.

Corrupt practices act Either a state law that regulates political campaigns or a federal law that regulates international **corporate** financial activities.

Corruption of blood An old punishment by which a criminal was deprived of the right to take, hold, or pass on property.

Cosigner A general term for a person who signs a document along with another person. A cosigner may have *primary* responsibility (to pay a debt if the lender comes first to the cosigner for the money) or only *secondary* responsibility (to pay only if the borrower does not).

Costs Expenses of one side in a lawsuit that the judge orders the other side to pay or reimburse.

Cotenancy Property ownership by two or more persons with each having a right to the whole property.

Council A local **legislature.**

Counsel *1.* A lawyer for a client. *2.* Advice (usually professional advice). *3.* See **of counsel.** *4.* The *right to counsel* is the Sixth Amendment **constitutional** right of a **defendant** to have a lawyer at every important stage of a criminal proceeding that might lead to imprisonment.

Counselor Lawyer.

Count *1.* Each separate part of a **civil complaint** or **criminal indictment.** Each count must stand alone as a separate **claim** or **charge.** *2.* The *common counts* were once the various **forms of action** (for example, **assumpsit**) for money owed.

Counterclaim A claim made by a **defendant** in a **civil** lawsuit that, in effect, sues the **plaintiff.** It can be based on entirely different things from the plaintiff's **complaint** and may even be for more money than the plaintiff is asking.

Counterfeit Forge, copy, or imitate without right, to pass off the copy as the original. The copy itself is also a counterfeit.

Counteroffer A rejection of an **offer** and a new offer made back, even if it looks like an **acceptance** with new terms attached. Under the **Uniform Commercial Code,** however, a *counteroffer* for the sale of goods may be an acceptance plus new proposed contract terms.

Counterpart A copy or duplicate of a document.

Countersign Sign a document in addition to the primary or original signature in order to approve the document's validity.

Course *Course of business* is what is normally done by a company. ("Custom" or "usage" is what is normally done by a *type* of company.) *Course of dealing* is the prior history of business between two companies. *Course of employment* means directly related to work, during work hours, or in the workplace.

Court The place where judges work, all the judges working for a particular **jurisdiction,** or a judge at work. (When a judge says "the court will," it means "I will.") A *court-martial* tries members of the armed forces according to the **Code of Military Justice.** The least serious type is "summary," next "special," and most serious "general." A *court of appeals* decides **appeals** from a trial court. In most states, it is a middle-level court (similar to the U.S. Court of Appeals), but in some states, it is the highest. A _court of probate_ handles **wills** and **estates** and sometimes handles the problems of **minors** and other legally **incompetent** persons.

Covenant A promise, agreement, or restriction, usually in a **deed** or **contract.** A _covenant for quiet enjoyment_ is a promise that the seller of land will protect the buyer against a defective **title** to the land and against anyone who claims the land. A _covenant running with the land_ is any agreement in a deed that is binding for or against all future buyers of the land.

Cover _1._ Make good. _2._ Protect. _Coverage_ is the amount and type of **insurance.** _3._ Protect oneself from the effects of a business deal that falls through or is not made good on.

Coverture An old word for the special rights and legal limitations that a married woman used to have.

Credibility The believability of a **witness** and of **testimony.**

Credit _1._ The right to delay payment for things bought or used. _2._ Money loaned. _3._ See **credits.** _4._ A _tax credit_ is a direct subtraction from tax owed, such as for other taxes paid. _5._ A _credit bureau_ is a place that keeps records on persons' credit use and financial reliability. _6._ For _credit line,_ see **line of credit.** _7._ A _credit rating_ is an evaluation of a person's or business's ability to pay debts, usually compiled by a credit bureau and given out to businesses in _credit reports_. _8._ A _credit union_ is a financial organization that uses money deposited by a closed group of persons and lends it out again to the same persons.

Creditor A person to whom a debt is owed. A _creditor's meeting_ is a meeting of persons to whom a **bankrupt**

person owes money or who hold a **security** interest in the bankrupt's property.

Credits Records in a person's account book of money owed to that person or of money that person has paid out. (The opposite of **debits.**)

Crime Any violation of the government's **penal** laws. An illegal act. For *crime against nature,* see **sodomy.**

Crimen falsi (Latin) "Crime of **fraud** or falsehood." Any crime, such as **perjury,** that might affect a **witness's** believability.

Criminal *1.* Having to do with the law of crimes and illegal conduct. *2.* Illegal. *3.* A person who has committed a crime. *4.* A *criminal action* is the procedure by which a person accused of a crime is brought to trial and given punishment. *5. Criminal conversation* is the **tort** (not crime) of causing a married person to commit **adultery.** Most states now prohibit lawsuits against the seducer.

Criminology The study of the cause, prevention, and punishment of crime.

Cross *1.* A *cross-action* (or *cross-bill*) is a **counterclaim,** a *cross-claim,* or a separate lawsuit against someone suing another. *2.* A *cross-claim* is a claim brought by one **defendant** against another, or by one **plaintiff** against another, that is based on the same subject matter as the plaintiff's suit. *3.* A *cross-complaint* or *cross-demand* is either a **counterclaim** or a *cross-claim.* *4. Cross-examination* is the questioning of an opposing **witness** in a trial or hearing. See **examination.** *5. Cross-picketing* is **picketing** by two or more **unions** that claim to represent the same workers. *6.* A *cross-remainder* is property that is inherited by several persons as a group. As each person dies, the others share that portion.

Crown case A **criminal** case brought by the British government.

Cruel and unusual punishment Punishment, by the government, that is prohibited by the U.S. **Constitution.** Courts have required the discontinuance of many types of punishment as *cruel and unusual* if they shock the moral sense of the community.

Cruelty In **divorce** law, harsh treatment by a husband or wife that gives the other person **grounds** for divorce. Its definition is different in each state and may vary widely from the common meaning. The formal definition has little relation to what it takes to get a divorce nominally based on the definition. Some phrases that mean the same thing as *cruelty* are "extreme cruelty," "willful cruelty," and "intolerable severity."

Culpable Blamable; at fault; having done a wrongful act.

Cum testamento annexo (Latin) "With the **will** attached." A court-appointed **administrator** who hands out a dead person's property when there is a will but no **executor.**

Cumulative evidence **Evidence** that is offered to prove what has already been proved by other evidence.

Cumulative sentence An additional prison term given to a person who is already **convicted** of a crime, with the additional term to be served after the previous one is finished.

Curator A person appointed by a court to take care of a person (and the person's property) who cannot take care of himself or herself (such as a child or someone mentally **incompetent**), or, in the case of a **spendthrift,** to take care of the property only.

Cure *1.* It is a *cure* when a seller delivers goods, the buyer rejects them because of some defect, and the seller then delivers the proper goods within the proper time. *2.* An **error** in the course of a trial is *cured* if the **judgment** or **verdict** is in favor of the side complaining of the error. Compare **aider.**

Curia (Latin) Old English word for court.

Curtesy A husband's right to part of his dead wife's property. This right is now **regulated** by state **statutes**. Compare **dower.**

Curtilage An area of household use immediately surrounding a home.

Custody Rightful possession without ownership; a general term meaning care and keeping. Parents usually have legal *custody* of their children, a warden has *custody* of prisoners, and a person has *custody* of a book borrowed from another person.

Custom Regular behavior (of persons in a geographical area or type of business) that gradually takes on legal importance so that it will strongly influence a court's decision. See **unwritten law.**

Customs Taxes or **duty** payable on goods brought into or out of a country; the government department that oversees these taxes.

Cy pres (French) "As near as possible." When a dead person's **will** can no longer be legally or practically carried out, a court may (but is not required to) order that the dead person's **estate** be used in a way that *most nearly* does what the dead person would have wanted. The doctrine of *cy pres* is now usually applied only to **charitable trusts.** [pronounce: see-pray]

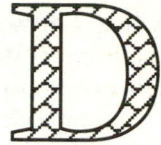

D **Defendant; dictum; digest; district;** and many other law-related words.

DBA Doing business as.

DC District court.

DJ District judge.

DUI Driving under the influence (of alcohol or drugs).

DWI *1.* Driving while intoxicated. *2.* Died without issue (child).

Damages Either the money that a court orders paid to a person who has suffered a loss (or injury) by the person whose fault caused it, or a **plaintiff's** claim in a legal **pleading** for this money. *Damages* may be **actual and compensatory** (directly related to the amount of the loss) or, in addition, *exemplary* and **punitive** (extra money given to punish the **defendant** and to help keep a particularly bad act from happening again). Also, merely **nominal** *damages* may be given (a small sum when the loss is either very small or of unproved amount). See **consequential, incidental, liquidated,** and **treble** for other types of *damages*.

Damnum absque injuria (Latin) A loss without legal injury (without any way of suing for it).

Dangerous instrumentality Things that are potentially harmful by their mere existence, such as electricity, or that are designed to be harmful, such as guns.

Day certain A specific future date.

Day in court The right to be notified of a court proceeding involving your interests, and the right to be heard when the case comes up in court.

De (Latin) *1.* Of, by, from, affecting, as or concerning. Often the first word of the name of an old English **statute** or **writ.** *2. De bene esse* means "as well done (as possible)"; provisional; temporary; subject to later challenge or change. *3. De bonis non* means "of the goods not (already taken care of)." It refers to an **administrator** appointed to hand out the property of a dead person whose **executor** has died. *4. De bonis propriis* means "from his or her own goods." When a person managing another's property has committed **waste,** personal repayment may be required. *5. De facto* means "in fact, actual; a situation that exists in fact whether or not it is lawful." For example, a *de facto corporation* is a company that has failed to follow some of the technical legal requirements to become a legal **corporation** but that carries on business as one in good faith. Often the opposite of *de jure*. *6. De jure* means either "of right, legitimate, lawful, whether or not true in actual fact" or it means "the result of government action." Often the opposite of *de facto*. [pronounce: de joo-re] *7. De minimis* means "small or unimportant." It is often short for *de minimis non curat lex* (the law does not bother with trifles). *8. De novo* means "new, completely new from the start." A *de novo trial* is a completely new trial ordered by the judge, ordered by an **appeals** court, or provided as a right by **statute**. *9. De son tort* is a mixture of law-Latin and French meaning "of his own wrong." An **executor** *de son tort* is a person who takes on the duty of distributing property under a **will** without any right to do so, and who will be held responsible for all actions taken.

Dead man's acts   Laws, now mostly abolished, that prevented a person from **testifying** in a **civil** lawsuit against a dead person's representative about things to which the dead person might have testified.

Deathbed declaration   Dying declaration.

Debar   Exclude from doing something. *Not* **disbar.**

Debenture   A **corporation**'s obligation to pay money (usually in the form of a **note** or a **bond**) that is usually not **secured** (backed up) by any specific property. [pronounce: de-<u>ben</u>-chur]

Debit card   A card that allows a person to make a purchase by direct subtraction from the person's bank account. It looks like a credit card but works like writing a check.

Debits   Records in a person's **account** book of money that the person owes or of money paid to that person. (The opposite of **credits.**)

Debt adjusters (or consolidators or poolers)   Persons (or organizations) who take a person's money and pay it out to **creditors** by getting the creditors to accept lower monthly payments, less money, etc.

Debt service   Regular payments of **principal,** interest, and possibly other costs made to pay off a loan.

Debtor   A person who owes money.

Decedent   A dead person.

Deceit   Intentionally misleading another person by making false statements that cause that person harm.

Decennial Digest   (Dec. Dig.) See **American Digest System.**

Decision   A formal resolution of a dispute, such as a judge's resolution of a lawsuit. A *decision on the merits* is a final decision that fully and properly decides the subject matter of a case, with the effect that other lawsuits may not be brought by the same person on the same subject against the same opponent.

Declaration   *1.* An unsworn statement made out of court. For example, a *declaration against interest* is a statement that, when made, is so contrary to the speaker's interests that it would not likely have been made unless it were true. *2.* A formal statement of facts. For example, a *declaration of trust* is a written statement by a person owning property that it is held for another person. *3.* A public proclamation, such as the Declaration of Independence. *4.* An old name for a **complaint.** *5.* An announcement of a set-aside of money, such as a *declaration of dividends,* a **corporation's** setting aside of part of its profits to pay stockholders.

Declaratory judgment   A judge's decision (about a real problem with legal consequences) that states the rights of the **parties** or answers a legal question without awarding any **damages** or ordering that anything be done.

Decree   *1.* A **judgment** of a court that announces the legal consequences of the facts found in a case and orders that the court's decision be carried out. Specialized types of decrees include a **consent** *decree* and a *decree* **nisi.** *2.* A proclamation or **order** put out by a person or group with **absolute** authority to give orders.

Dedication   *1.* The gift or transfer of land or rights in land to the government for a specific public use, such as a park, and its acceptance for that use by the government. *2.* Voluntarily or involuntarily giving a **copyright** (or other right) to the public.

Deductible   That which may be taken away or subtracted. For example, an **insurance policy** with a "$100 deductible **clause**" will pay $200 on a $300 loss. See also **deduction.**

Deduction *1.* A conclusion drawn from principles or facts already proved. *2.* Any subtraction of money owed. In income tax law, *itemized deductions* are those nonbusiness expenses, such as home mortgage payments and charitable contributions, that may be subtracted from **adjusted gross income.** See also **credit, exclusion,** and **exemption.**

Deed A document by which one person transfers the legal ownership of land and what is on the land to another person.

Deed of trust *1.* A document, similar to a **mortgage,** by which a person transfers the legal ownership of land to independent **trustees** to be held until a debt on the land is paid off. *2.* Compare **declaration** of trust.

Deem *1.* Treat as if. For example, if a fact is *deemed true,* it will be treated as if true unless proven otherwise. *2.* Hold to be; determine to be. For example, if a **statute** says that a certain act is *deemed a crime,* it is a crime.

Deep pockets Capacity to pay a lot of money. The one person or organization, among many possible **defendants,** best able to pay a **judgment** has the *deepest pockets* and is the one a **plaintiff** is most likely to sue.

Defalcation *1.* Failure to account for money entrusted to one's care, with the assumption that the money was misused. *2.* Setting off one claim against another; deducting a smaller debt owed to a person from a larger debt owed by that person.

Defamation Transmission to others of false statements that harm the reputation, business, or property rights of a person. Spoken defamation is **slander,** and written defamation is **libel.**

Default *1.* A failure to perform a legal duty, observe a promise, fulfill an obligation, or pay a debt that is due. *2.* A failure to take a required step, such as filing a paper on time, in a lawsuit. This can lead to a *default* **judgment** against that side.

Defeasance clause The part of a **mortgage** document that says that the mortgage is ended once all payments have been made.

Defeasible Subject to being defeated, ended, or undone by a future event or action.

Defect *1.* An error in the design (design defect) or production (manufacturing defect) of a product. *2.* The absence of some legal requirement that makes a thing legally insufficient or nonbinding. For example, a *defective title* is one that is improperly drawn up, is inaccurate, fails to comply with a law, or is obtained by unlawful means.

Defendant The person against whom a legal action is brought. This legal action may be **civil** or **criminal.**

Defense The sum of the facts, law, and arguments presented by the side against whom legal action is brought.

Deficiency judgment (or decree) A court's decision that a person must pay more money to a **creditor** than the amount brought by the sale of property used to **secure** the debt.

Deficit Something missing or lacking; a "minus" **balance.**

Definite sentence Determinate sentence.

Definitive Capable of finally and completely settling a legal question or a lawsuit.

Deforcement An old word for using force to keep a person from possessing his or her own land.

Defraud Cheat.

Degree A step, grade, or division; for example, a "step removed" between two relatives (brothers are related in the *first degree,* grandparent and grandchild in the *second*). Also, a *degree* describes a division of a crime (or group of crimes) into different levels of severity (*first-degree murder* carries a more severe maximum punishment than *second-degree murder*).

Del credere   (Italian) An **agent** who sells goods for a person and also **guarantees** to that person that the buyer will pay in full for the goods. [pronounce: del cred-er-e]

Delectus personae   (Latin) "Choice of persons." Describes a **partner**'s right to choose or reject additional partners.

Delegate   *1.* A person who is chosen to represent others. *2.* Choose a person as a representative or to do a job you would otherwise do.

Delegation   *1.* A group of **delegates** or representatives. *2.* The giving of authority to one person by another. *3. Delegation of powers* is the **constitutional** division of authority among branches of government and also the handing down of authority from the president to **administrative agencies.**

Deliberate   *1.* To consider carefully, discuss, and work toward forming an opinion or making a decision. *2.* Well advised; carefully considered; thoroughly enough planned. *3.* Planned in advance; premeditated; intentional.

Delictum   (Latin) A crime, **tort,** or wrong. Also *delict.*

Delinquency   Failure, omission, or violation of duty; misconduct. An overdue debt is called a *delinquency.*

Delinquent   *1.* Overdue and unpaid. *2.* Willfully and intentionally failing to carry out an obligation. *3.* Short for *juvenile delinquent,* a **minor** who has done an illegal act or who seriously misbehaves.

Delivery   The handing over of property other than land from one person to another; usually the transfer of sold goods. Sometimes acts other than handing over an object (such as handing over **title** to the object) have the legal effect of *delivery*.

Demand *1*. A forceful claim that presupposes that there is no doubt about its being won. *2*. The assertion of a legal right; a legal obligation asserted in the courts. *3*. *On demand* is a phrase put on some **negotiable instruments** (such as *demand notes*) indicating that a specified amount of money must be paid immediately when the **holder** requests payment.

Demeanor Physical appearance and behavior. The demeanor of a witness is not what the witness says but how the witness says it, including tone of voice, hesitations, gestures, etc.

Demise *1*. A **lease.** *2*. A transfer of property, especially land. *Not* **devise.** *3*. Death.

Demonstrative evidence All **evidence** other than **testimony.**

Demonstrative legacy (or bequest) A gift of a specific sum of money in a **will** that is to be paid out of only a particular part of a dead person's property.

Demur Make a **demurrer.**

Demurrer A legal **pleading** that says, in effect, "even if, for the sake of argument, the facts presented by the other side are correct, those facts do not give the other side a legal argument that can possibly stand up in court." The *demurrer* has been replaced in many courts by a **motion** to dismiss.

Denial *1*. Any part of a **pleading** that contradicts claims made in an opponent's previous pleading. *2*. Refusal; rejection; withholding; or deprivation.

Dependent *1*. A person supported primarily by another person. *2*. Conditional. For example, a *dependent contract* is one in which one side does not have to do something in the contract until the other side does something it is required to do. _3. Dependent relative revocation_ is the legal principle in some states that if a person **revokes** a **will** with the intention of making a new one, and that new one either is never made or is defective, there is a **rebuttable** _presumption_ (an assumption) that the person would have preferred the old will to no will at all.

Depletion Using up a finite natural resource (such as coal or oil). A _depletion allowance_ is the amount allowable, under tax rules, as a **deduction,** corresponding theoretically to the loss in value of property caused by the removal of oil, gas, or minerals.

Deponent A person who gives sworn **testimony** out of court. See **deposition.**

Depose _1._ Give sworn **testimony** out of court. See **deposition.** _2._ Ask questions of the person in #1. (The questions are usually asked by a lawyer.)

Deposit Place money or property in another's hands for safekeeping, as part payment, as **earnest money,** as **security** for a purchase, to earn interest, to pay a possible **judgment,** etc.

Deposition _1._ The process of taking a witness's sworn out-of-court **testimony**. The questioning is usually done by a lawyer, with a lawyer from the other side being given a chance to attend and participate. _2._ The written record of #1.

Depreciation _1._ A fall in value or reduction in worth that is due to deterioration. _2._ In tax law, a _depreciation deduction_ is the amount allowable as a **deduction,** theoretically corresponding to the loss in value of investment or business property (such as an office building or computer) that is due to the assumed physical deterioration of the property.

Derivative action A lawsuit by a stockholder of a corporation against another person (usually an officer of the company) to enforce claims the stockholder thinks the corporation has against that person.

Derivative evidence **Evidence** that is collected by following up on evidence gathered illegally. It may only rarely be used in a trial.

Derogation *1.* Partial **repeal** or partial abolishment of a law by a later law. *2.* A *derogation clause* in a **will** is a phrase stating that no later will lacking that phrase should be treated as valid. It is an attempt to protect against fakes; it will not be automatically enforced by a court but will be treated as **evidence.**

Descent *1.* **Inheritance** from parents or other ancestors. *2.* Getting property by inheritance of any type rather than by purchase or gift.

Descriptive word index A large set of books in dictionary form that allows you to find cases on a topic by tracking down exact words or catch phrases. For example, to find cases involving tires that blow out during a skid, you might look up "tires," "blowout," or "skid."

Desertion Abandoning a job or duty without permission and with no intention of returning; abandoning a wife, husband, or child with no intention of returning or resuming the duties of marriage or parenthood.

Design A purpose plus a plan to carry it out.

Desire Anything from a small preference to a total command.

Despoil Take something from a person illegally, usually by force or threats.

Destination contract An agreement for the sale of goods in which the risk of loss of or damage to the goods passes from seller to buyer when the goods are delivered to a specific destination.

Destroy   You can *destroy* a document's *legal effect* by less extreme methods than total physical ending; for example, you can do it by tearing the document in half or by writing over it.

Detainer   *1.* The unlawful keeping of another person's property even if keeping that property was originally lawful. *2.* **Detention.** *3.* A **warrant** or court **order** to keep a person in **custody** when that person might otherwise be released.

Detention   Holding a person against his or her will. *Detention for questioning* involves a police or similar officer holding a person without making a *formal* arrest.

Determinable   *1.* Possibly ended; subject to being ended if a certain thing happens. *2.* Can be found out or decided upon.

Determinate sentence   An exact prison term set by law, rather than one that may be shortened by "good time credit" for good behavior or by a **parole** board.

Determination   A formal decision, usually a final one.

Determine   *1.* Decide. *2.* End. When a right ends, it *determines.*

Detinue   A legal action to get back property held unlawfully by another person, plus **damages** resulting from the wrongful withholding. [pronounce: det-i-new]

Detriment   Loss; harm. For *detrimental reliance,* see **promissory estoppel.**

Devest   **Divest.**

Devise   A gift by **will,** especially of land or things on land. A *devisor* makes this gift and a *devisee* gets it. *Not* **demise.** [pronounce: de-vize]

Devolution   The transfer or transition by process of law from one person to another of a right, **liability, title,** property, or office (often by death). To *devolve* is to go by devolution.

Dicta (Latin) Views of a judge that are not a central part of the judge's decision, even if the judge argues them strongly and even if they look like conclusions. One way to decide whether a particular part of a judge's **opinion** is *dicta* is to examine whether it was needed to reach the result. If it could be removed without changing the result, it is probably dicta and thus not binding **precedent** on later court decisions. Compare **holding.**

Dictum (Latin) Singular of **dicta** and short for *obiter dictum* (a remark by the way, as in "by the way, did I tell you . . ."); a digression or discussion of side or unrelated points.

Digest A collection of parts of many books, usually giving not only summaries but also excerpts and condensations. The **American Digest System** is a set of legal digests that collects **headnotes** (summaries originally printed before each **case**) and arranges them by subject categories.

Dilatory Tending or intending to cause delay or gain time.

Diligence Carefulness, prudence, or doing your duty.

Diminution Reduction or lessening; incompleteness.

Direct *1*. Immediate or straight. In different settings, *direct* is the opposite of *indirect* (not direct), *collateral* (on the side), *cross* (opposing), *derivative* (drawn from something else), and other specialized words, such as *circumstantial*, that are not necessarily *direct's* logical opposite. *2*. A *direct attack* is an attempt to have a judge's decision overturned (**annulled, reversed, vacated, enjoined,** etc.,) by a proceeding started for that specific purpose (an **appeal,** an **injunction** hearing, etc.) *3*. For *direct cause*, see **proximate cause.** *4*. *Direct evidence* is proof of a fact without the need for other facts leading up to it. For example, *direct* evidence that dodoes are not extinct would be a live dodo. See **circumstantial evidence.** *5. Direct examination* is the first questioning in a trial of a **witness** by the side that called the witness.

Directed verdict A **verdict** in which the judge takes the decision out of the jury's hands by telling them what they must decide or by actually making the decision.

Director *1.* The head of an organization, group, or project. *2.* One of a group of persons elected by the shareholders (owners) of a **corporation** to decide basic corporate policy, such as the hiring of the **officers** (president, etc.) to run the company's day-to-day operations.

Directory *1.* Required; mandatory; for example, a *directory trust* leaves no **discretion** to the **trustee.** But see #2. *2. Not* required or mandatory; for example, *directory language* in a **statute** merely instructs a public official. But see #1.

Disability *1.* A *legal disability* is the lack of legal capacity to do an act; for example, a person is *disabled* from marrying a second time while married. *2.* A *physical or mental disability* is the absence of adequate physical or mental powers or the lowering of earning ability because of this absence.

Disaffirm Repudiate; take back consent once given; refuse to honor former promises or stick by former acts (usually in situations in which the person has the legal right to do so).

Disallow Refuse, deny, or reject.

Disbar Take away a lawyer's right to practice law. *Not* **debar.**

Disburse Pay out of a fund of money.

Discharge Release; remove; free; dismiss (or the document that shows that this release, etc., has taken place). For example, to discharge a **contract** is to end the obligation by agreement or by carrying it out; to discharge a prisoner is to release him or her; to discharge a court **order** is to cancel or revoke it; to discharge a person in **bankruptcy** is to release the person from all or most debts; and to discharge a **bill** is to force it out of a **committee** by a vote of the **legislature** to consider it.

Disciplinary rules The part of the **Code of Professional Responsibility** that lists and explains specific things that lawyers are prohibited from doing. Compare **ethical considerations.**

Disclaimer *1.* The refusal, rejection, or renunciation of a claim, a power, or property. *2.* The refusal to accept certain types of responsibility. For example, a *disclaimer clause* in a written sales contract might say, "we give you, the purchaser, promises A, B, and C, but *disclaim* all other promises."

Discontinuance Either a **nonsuit** or a **dismissal.**

Discovered peril doctrine See **last clear chance doctrine.**

Discovery The formal and informal exchange of information between sides in a lawsuit. Two types of *discovery* are **interrogatories** and **depositions.**

Discretion *1.* The capacity to act intelligently and prudently. *2.* The power to act within general guidelines, rules, or laws, but without either specific rules to follow or the need to completely explain or justify each decision or action.

Discrimination The failure to treat equal persons equally; in particular, illegally unequal treatment based on race, religion, sex, age, handicap, etc.

Disfranchise (or disenfranchise) Formally take away certain rights, such as the right to vote, from a **citizen.**

Dishonor   Refuse to accept or pay a **negotiable instrument** when it comes due.

Disinterested   Impartial; not biased or prejudiced; not affected personally or financially by the outcome. *Disinterested* does *not* mean "uninterested" or "lacking an opinion."

Dismissal   A court **order** or **judgment** that ends a lawsuit. If dismissed "with **prejudice**," no further lawsuits may be brought by the same persons on the same subject.

Disorderly conduct   A vague term for actions that disturb the peace or shock public morality. Few states define it precisely.

Disparagement   Discrediting or belittling something or someone.

Dispensation   An exemption from a law prohibiting something.

Disposable earnings   **Gross** or "total" pay minus only those payments required by law.

Disposition   *1.* Giving something up or giving it away. *2.* A final settlement or result. A court's *disposition* of a case may be to give a **judgment,** dismiss the case, **sentence** a criminal, etc.

Dispossession   *1.* **Ouster.** *2.* **Eviction.**

Dispute   A disagreement between persons about their rights or their legal obligations to one another.

Disqualify   Make ineligible. For example, a judge may *disqualify* himself or herself from a case if the judge is not **disinterested.**

Disseisin   **Ouster.** [pronounce: dis-see-zin]

Dissent   A judge's formal disagreement with the decision of the majority of the judges in a lawsuit. If the judge puts it in writing, it is called a *dissenting opinion.*

Dissolution Ending or breaking up. *Dissolution* of a
contract is a **mutual** agreement to end it. *Dissolution*
of a **corporation** is ending its existence. *Dissolution* of
a marriage is legally ending the marriage any way
but by **annulment.**

Distinguish Point out basic differences. To *distinguish*
a **case** is to show why it is irrelevant (or not very
relevant) to the case being decided.

Distrain Take and hold another person's personal
property.

Distress *1.* The process of **distraining** property.
2. Forced.

Distribution Division by shares; for example, giving
out what is left of a dead person's **estate** after taxes
and debts are paid. A *distributee* is a person who inherits. A *distributive finding* is a jury **finding** partly in
favor of each side. A *distributor* is a wholesaler.

District A subdivision of many different types of areas
for judicial, political, or administrative purposes. A
federal *district attorney* (called the "U.S. attorney") is
the top **criminal** prosecuting lawyer of each federal
district (a whole state or part of a state). A state
district attorney is the same for state districts. Federal
district courts are U.S. **trial** courts, one in each federal
district. State *district courts* may be trial or **appeals**
courts.

Disturbing the peace A vague term, defined in different ways in different places, for interrupting the
peace, quiet, or good order of a neighborhood.

Divers *1.* Many; several. *2.* Different; many different. [pronounce: <u>dive</u>-ers]

Diversion A turning aside; for example, the unauthorized use of **trust** funds. *Pretrial diversion* is a turning
aside of persons from the regular course of criminal

prosecution into special programs that avoid the stigma of a criminal conviction.

Diversity of citizenship The situation that occurs when the persons on one side of a case in federal court come from a different state than the persons on the other side. This usually lets the court take and decide the case based on *diversity* **jurisdiction.**

Divest Deprive, take away, or withdraw; for example, you can *divest* yourself of a car by selling it.

Dividend A share of profits or property; usually a payment per **share** of a **corporation**'s **stock.**

Divorce The ending of a marriage by court order. It is different from an **annulment** and from a *limited divorce*, which is also called a "legal **separation**" or "divorce **a mensa et thoro**".

Docket A list of cases, usually with file numbers, set down for trial in a court, or a list of specific actions taken by a court.

Doctrine A legal principle or rule.

Document Something with a message on it, even a map carved on a tree. A *document of title* is a piece of paper that is normally accepted in business as proof of a right to hold goods; for example, a **bill of lading.** For *documentary originals rule*, see **best evidence rule.**

Doing business A flexible term meaning carrying on enough business within a state so that another person can sue the company in that state, the state can tax the company, or the state can otherwise claim **jurisdiction** over it.

Domain Ownership and control (usually by the public). National forests are in the *public domain* (owned and controlled by the United States) and some writings, inventions, and other works are in the *public* *domain* (available for use and reprinting by anyone). See also **eminent domain.**

Domestic   *1.* Relating to the home. *Domestic relations* is the law of **divorce, custody, support, adoption,** and so on. *2.* Relating to the state or country. A *domestic corporation* is created by the laws of the state or country in question.

Domicile   A person's permanent home, legal home, or main residence. "Abode," "citizenship," "habitance," and "residence" sometimes mean the same, but often do not. *Domiciliary* means relating to a person's permanent home. [pronounce: <u>dom</u>-i-sile]

Dominant   Possessing rights against another thing. A *dominant estate* is land that has rights (such as an **easement**) in other land. For *dominant cause,* see **proximate cause.**

Dominion   Legal ownership plus full actual control.

<u>Do</u>native   As a gift; relating to a gift.

Do<u>nee</u>   A person to whom a gift is made or to whom a **power** given. A *donee beneficiary* gets something from a **contract** between other persons.

Do<u>nor</u>   A person making a gift or giving another person a **power.**

Dormant   "Sleeping," inactive, silent, or concealed. A *dormant partner* is a **partner** who has a financial interest but takes no control over the business and is usually unknown to the public.

Double   *1. Double entry bookkeeping* is a system that shows every transaction as both a **credit** and a **debit** by using horizontal rows and vertical columns of numbers that must come to the same final totals. *2. Double hearsay* itself contains hearsay (for example, if John testified in court that he heard Mary say something that Mary heard from someone else). *3. Double indemnity* is insurance coverage that results in a double payoff if something happens in a certain way; for example, an accidental rather than a natural death. *4. Double insurance* is insurance from more than one company on the same **interest** in the same thing. (It is not usually possible to collect more than what a thing is worth in this way.) *5. Double jeopardy* is a second prosecution against the same person for the same crime or for a **lesser included offense** once the first prosecution is totally finished and decided. Double jeopardy is prohibited by the U.S. **Constitution.** *6. Double taxation* is either two taxes by the same government on the same property during the same time period for the same purpose (this is not legal), or generally taxing the same thing twice (this may be legal). *7.* A *double will* is **reciprocal.**

Doubt Uncertainty of mind about proof in a trial. See **beyond a reasonable doubt.**

Dower A wife's right to part of her dead husband's property. This right is now **regulated** by state **statutes.** This is *not "dowry,"* a nonlegal word for property a bride brings to marriage. Compare **curtesy.**

Down payment The cash that must be paid at the time that something is bought using credit.

Draconian law A law that is especially harsh or severe.

Draft A **bill** of exchange or any other **negotiable instrument** for the payment of money that one person **draws** on another. To use an ordinary personal **check** as an example: one person (the *drawer*) writes the check directing payment by a bank (the *drawee*) to another person (the *payee*). See **overdraft, sight draft,** and **time draft.**

Draftsman (or drafter) A person who writes a legal document.

Draw   *1.* Prepare a legal document. *2.* Write out and sign a **bill** *of exchange,* a **note,** a **check,** etc., or take money from a bank account. A *drawer* is a person who does one of these things; and a *drawee* is a person to whom a bill of exchange is addressed (who is requested to pay it), a bank that has money withdrawn, etc.

Droit   (French) *1.* "Right"; justice. *2.* A law; the law. [pronounce: drwah]

Dry   **Passive;** inactive; **formal;** or **nominal** only.

Duces tecum   (Latin) "Bring with you." A **subpoena** *duces tecum* commands a person to come to court and bring documents or other pieces of **evidence.**

Due   *1.* Owing; payable. *2.* Just, proper, regular, lawful, sufficient, or reasonable. For example, *due care* means proper or reasonable care for the situation. *3.* The *Due Process Clause* of the U.S. **Constitution** requires that no person be deprived of life, liberty, or property without *due process of law.* These *due process* requirements vary in detail by situation, but their core is that a person should always have **notice** and have a real chance to present his or her side in a legal dispute and that no law or government procedure should be **arbitrary** or unfair. *Due process* specifics include the right to a **transcript** of court proceedings, the right to question adverse witnesses, etc.

Dummy   Sham; make believe; set up as a "front." *Dummy incorporators* may legally set up a corporation under a state's laws, then drop out.

Duress   Unlawful pressure on a person to do what he or she would not otherwise have done. It includes force, threats of violence, physical restraint, etc.

Durham rule   The principle, used in some states, that a **defendant** is not guilty of a crime because of **insan-**

ity if he or she was "suffering from a diseased or defective mental condition at the time of the act and there was a causal connection between the condition and the act."

Duty *1*. Any obligation, whether legal, moral, or ethical, but in particular an obligation to obey a law or a legal obligation to another person. *2*. A tax on imports or exports.

Dying declaration See **declaration.**

EBT *Examination before trial* of a **party** to a lawsuit. It is a part of the **discovery** process.

ED Eastern **district.**

EEOC Equal Employment Opportunity Commission.

EIS Environmental Impact Statement.

EO Executive order.

EPA Environmental Protection Agency.

ERISA Employee Retirement Income Security Act.

ESOP (ESOT) Employee stock ownership plan (trust).

Earned income Money or other compensation received for work, as opposed to, for example, the profits gained from selling property.

Earnest money A **deposit** paid by a buyer to hold a seller to a deal and to show the buyer's **good faith.**

Easement The right of a specific non-owner of a piece of land (such as a next-door neighbor, the government, or a public utility) to use part of the land in a particular way; for example, to walk across a specific strip or to lay a sewer line. This right usually stays with the land when it is sold.

<u>E</u>dict A major law made by a king or other head of state.

Effects **Personal** property.

Efficient cause **Proximate cause.**

Eighth Amendment See **Bill of Rights.**

Ejectment The name for an old type of lawsuit to get back land taken away wrongfully. It was used primarily to establish **title** to land and was brought against a fictitious **defendant** called the "*casual ejector.*"

Ejusdem generis (Latin) "Of the same kind or type." Under the *ejusdem generis rule,* when a list in a document is followed by general words, those words should apply only to things of the same kind as the things on the list. [pronounce: ee-<u>use</u>-dem]

Election The act of choosing, such as choosing from among legal rights. For example, a wife might have to *elect* between what was left to her in the husband's **will** and what state law reserves for the wife as a minimum share of the husband's **estate.**

Electoral college The group of persons chosen by voters to elect the U.S. president and vice-president. This is now almost a formality, though an *elector* can technically vote differently from the way the majority of votes in the state were cast.

Eleemosynary Charitable. [pronounce: el-e-<u>mos</u>-e-nary]

Element A basic part. For example, some *elements* of a **cause of action** for **battery** are an intentional, unwanted, physical contact. Each part ("intentional," "unwanted," etc.,) is one *element.*

Emancipation Setting free. For example, a child is *emancipated* when old enough so that the parents have no further right to control nor obligation to support him or her.

Embargo   A government's refusal to allow things (certain goods, another country's ships, etc.) into or out of the country.

Embezzlement   The **fraudulent** and secret taking of money or property by a person entrusted with it. Usually, an employee taking money and faking business records or **account** books.

Emblements   Crops grown by a tenant farmer.

Embracery   An old word for attempting to bribe a jury.

Eminent domain   The government's right and power to take private land for public use by paying for it.

Emolument   Any financial or other gain from employment.

Empanel   Impanel.

Emphyteutic lease   A **lease** on land that is long-term and can be passed on to another person as long as the rent is paid.

Employee Retirement Income Security Act   A federal law that established a program to protect employees' pension plans by setting up a fund to pay when plans go broke, by setting rules for when a pension becomes **vested,** etc.

Employers' liability acts   Federal and state laws on when an employer must pay for an employee's injuries and illnesses. When they include payment funds, they are **workers' compensation laws.**

En   (French) "In." For *en banc*, see **banc.** *En ventre sa mère* means "in its mother's womb." [pronounce: ahn vahntre sa mare]

Enabling   Giving power. An *enabling clause* is the part of a **statute** that gives officials power to put it into effect and enforce it. An *enabling power* is a **power of appointment;** and an *enabling statute* is a law that grants new powers, usually to a public official, a county, or a city.

Enact Put a **statute** into effect; pass a statute through a **legislature;** establish by law.

Encroachment Unlawfully extending property onto another person's property; for example, by putting a fence on a neighbor's side of a boundary line.

Encumbrance A **claim, charge,** or liability on property, such as a **lien** or **mortgage,** that lowers its value. When you put a valid claim on a property, you *encumber* it.

Endorsement Indorsement.

Endowment *1.* Setting up a fund (or the fund itself), usually for a public institution. *2.* An insurance policy that pays a set amount at a set time or at death.

Enfeoffment Feoffment.

Enfranchise See **franchise.**

Engage Do more than once, and probably regularly.

Engagement Contract or obligation.

Engrossment (or engrossing) Making a final or "good" copy of a document, often prior to voting on a **bill** or signing a **deed.**

Enhancement Increasing something (good or bad).

Enjoin Require, command, or forbid. See **injunction.**

Enjoyment The use of a right; the ability to use a right.

Enlarge *1.* Make larger. *2.* Extend a time limit. *3.* Release a person from **custody.**

Enroll Register or **record** a formal document in the proper office or file. An *enrolled bill* is a **bill** that has gone through the steps necessary to make it a law, and the *enrolled bill rule* is that once a law has been *enrolled,* its wording may not be challenged by referring to prior versions.

Entail Restrict an **inheritance** in land so that it can be passed on only to children, then children's children, and so on. Create a **fee** *tail*.

Enter *1*. Go into (a building); go onto (land, to take possession); become part of (an agreement). *2*. Place formally on the **record.** To *enter an appearance* is to submit a piece of paper to the court saying that you are now formally a part of the case, either as a **party** or as a lawyer. *Entering judgment* is the formal act of recording a **judgment** in the court's permanent records.

Entirety As a whole; not divided into parts. See **tenant.**

Entitlement **Absolute** (complete) right to something (such as social security) once you show that you meet the legal requirements to get it.

Entrapment The act of government officials (usually police) or their agents inducing a person to commit a crime that the person would not have otherwise committed. *Entrapment* is a **defense** to a criminal charge.

Entry *1*. See **enter.** *2*. Going into a building unlawfully to commit a crime.

Enumerated Mentioned specifically; listed.

Enumeratio unius **Expressio unius.**

Enure **Inure.**

Equal protection of laws (clause) The part of the Fourteenth Amendment to the U.S. **Constitution** requiring that the government not treat equals unequally, set up illegal categories to justify treating persons unfairly, or give unfair or unequal treatment to a person based on race, religion, gender, and so on.

Equal Rights Amendment A proposed **constitutional amendment** forbidding discrimination based on sex.

Equitable Just, fair, and right for a particular situation. Also, when something *should* exist but does *not* exist under a strict interpretation of the law, a court may decide that it *does* exist. For example, an *equitable mortgage* is a court's decision that a deed transferring property was really given to **secure** a debt so that a **mortgage,** not a complete property transfer, exists. An *equitable action* is a lawsuit based on a court's **equity** powers.

Equity *1.* Fairness in a particular situation or a court's power to "do justice" when specific laws do not cover the situation. See **equitable.** *2.* The name for a system of courts that originated in England to take care of legal problems, like those mentioned in **equitable,** when existing laws and courts could not do justice. *3.* The value of property after all charges against it are paid. *4.* **Stock;** sometimes, **common stock** only. *5. Equity of redemption* is the right of a person to stop a mortgage **foreclosure** by paying all money owed plus interest and costs within a state-specified time period.

Erasure The procedure by which a person's criminal or juvenile delinquency **record** may be destroyed or at least sealed and made unavailable for public access.

Erratum (Latin) A mistake in printed material.

Error A mistake made by a judge in the procedures used at trial or in making legal **rulings** during the trial. Some errors must be objected to at the time in order to ask a higher court to review the case. An error that could have affected the outcome is called *reversible, plain,* or *fatal error* by the higher court; a trivial error is called *harmless error.*

Escalator clause A provision in a **contract** that allows a price to rise if, for example, costs rise, a government maximum is raised, etc.

Escape clause A provision in a **contract** that allows a person to avoid doing something, or to avoid **liability,** if certain things happen.

Escheat The state's getting of property because no owner can be found; for example, if no **heirs** can be found when a person dies.

Escobedo rule When a suspect in police **custody** has asked for and been denied a lawyer, nothing the suspect then says can be used in a criminal trial. See also **Miranda warning.**

Escrow Money, property, or documents belonging to person A and held by person B until person A takes care of an obligation to person C. For example, a mortgage company may require a home owner with a **mortgage** to make monthly payments into an **escrow** account to take care of the yearly tax bill when it comes due.

Esq. Esquire. A title given to lawyers.

Establish *1.* Settle or prove a point. *2.* Set up; create; found.

Establishment clause The part of the First Amendment to the U.S. **Constitution** that states, "Congress shall make no law respecting an *establishment* of religion, or prohibiting the free exercise thereof."

Estate *1.* The **interest** a person has in property; a person's right or **title** to property. For example, a *future estate* is a property interest that will come about only in the future if an uncertain event takes place. *2.* The property itself in which a person has an interest; for example, *real estate* (land and buildings) or a *decedent's estate* (things left by a dead **person**). *3.* An *estate tax* is paid on a dead person's property as a whole before it is divided up and handed out. Compare **inheritance** *tax.*

Est<u>opp</u>el *1.* A person's being stopped by that person's prior acts from claiming a right against someone else who has legitimately relied on those acts. For example, if a person signs a deed, that person may be *estopped* from later going to court claiming that the deed is wrong. *2.* A person's being stopped from proving something (even if true) in court because of something that person said before that shows the opposite (even if false). *3. Estoppel by judgment* is the inability to raise an issue against a person in court because a judge has already decided that precise issue between the persons. *4.* An *estoppel certificate* is a **mortgage** company's written statement of the amount owed on a mortgage as of a certain date.

Et (Latin) "And." *Et al.* is short for *et alii* ("and others"). *Et ux* is short for *et uxor* ("and wife"). *Et vir* means "and husband."

Ethical considerations General guidelines for proper behavior as a lawyer in the **Code of Professional Responsibility.** Compare **disciplinary rules.**

Ethics Standards of fair and honest conduct; in particular, professional standards for lawyers and judges.

Evasion Eluding or dodging. For example, *tax evasion* is illegal nonpayment or underpayment of taxes (as compared to *tax avoidance,* which is using all legal means to reduce your tax burden). Also, if a **pleading** is *evasive,* the other side may demand a *more definite statement.*

Eviction A landlord putting a tenant out of property, either by taking direct action (a "self-help" eviction, which is often illegal) or, more often, by going to court.

Evidence *1.* All types of information (observations, recollections, documents, concrete objects, etc.,) presented at a trial or other hearing. *2.* Any information that might be used for a future trial.

3. Evidence law is the rules and principles about whether evidence can be admitted (accepted as proof) in a trial and how to evaluate its importance. *4.* An *evidentiary fact* is a fact that is learned directly from **testimony** or other evidence. Conclusions drawn from these facts are called *ultimate facts*.

Ex (Latin) *1.* A prefix meaning many things, including out of, no longer, from, because of, by, and with. *2. Ex officio* means by the power of the office (official position) alone. [pronounce: ex o-fish-i-o] *3. Ex parte* means with only one side present. For example, an *ex parte order* is one made on the request of one side in a lawsuit when (or because) the other side is not present in court (because the other side failed to show up, because the other side did not need to be present, or because there *is* no other side). [pronounce: ex par-tee] *4. Ex post facto* means after the fact. An *ex post facto law* retroactively attempts to make an action a crime that was not a crime at the time it was done, or it is a law that attempts to reduce a person's rights based on a past act that was not subject to the law when it was done. *Ex post facto laws* are prohibited by the U.S. **Constitution.** *5. Ex rel.* is short for *ex relatione* ("on relation" or "from the information given by"). When a case is titled "*State ex rel. Doe v. Roe,*" the state is bringing a lawsuit for Doe against Roe.

Examination An investigation or questioning. For example, the questioning of a witness under **oath** proceeds from **direct** examination to **cross**-examination (to redirect, to recross, etc.).

Examiner **Hearing** officer or **administrative** judge.

Exception *1.* Leaving something or someone out intentionally. *2.* A formal disagreement with a judge's refusal of a request or **overruling** of an ob-

jection. This disagreement is formally saved for later, usually for **appeal.** *Exceptions* need not be taken to appeal judges' decisions in most courts.

Excise   A tax on the manufacture, sale, or use of goods, or on the carrying on of an occupation or activity.

Excited utterance   A statement made about an event, during or just after the event, by a person who is still emotional as a result of the event. In-court testimony about another's *excited utterance* is often admissible as **evidence** as an exception to the **hearsay rule.**

Exclusion   *1.* Money that may be given away each year without paying tax on giving it away. See also **deduction, exemption,** and **credit.** *2.* An *exclusionary clause* is a part of a **contract** that tries to restrict the legal **remedies** available to one side if the contract is broken. *3.* An *exclusionary rule* is a reason why even **relevant evidence** will be kept out of a trial. *"The"* *exclusionary rule* is that illegally gathered evidence may not usually be used in a **criminal** trial.

Exclusive   Shutting out all others; sole; one only. For example, if a court has *exclusive jurisdiction* over a subject, no other court in the same area can decide a lawsuit on that subject. For *exclusive agency* or *authorization,* see **listing.**

Exculpate   Provide an **excuse** or **justification;** show that someone has not committed a crime or a wrongful act. An *exculpatory clause* is a **trust** provision that relieves a **trustee** of all responsibility for things that go wrong or for losses if the trustee acts in good faith.

Excuse   A reason that will stand up in court for an unintentional action. For example, if someone kills another accidently and it is not his or her fault, it is *excusable homicide.* Compare **justification.**

Execute Complete, make, perform, do, or carry out. For example, to *execute a* **contract** is to sign it and make it valid, and to *execute an obligation* created by the contract is to carry it out or perform it. The process may be called *an execution;* for example, when an official carries out a court's **order** or **judgment.** If something is *executed,* it is completed. Compare with **executory.**

Executive *1.* The **administrative** branch of government that carries out the laws, as distinguished from the **judicial** and **legislative** branches. *2.* An *executive agreement* is a document, similar to a **treaty,** that is signed by the U.S. president but that does not require approval by the **Senate.** *3.* An *executive order* is a law put out by the president or a governor that does not need to be passed by the **legislature.** *4. Executive privilege* is the U.S. president's right to keep some information from public disclosure. *5.* An *executive session* is a closed meeting.

Executor A person selected by a person making a **will** to **administer** the will and to hand out the property after the person making the will dies.

Executory Still to be carried out; incomplete; depending on a future act or event. Compare with **executed.**

Exemplar **Evidence** of physical identification of a person, such as a fingerprint or a blood sample.

Exemplary damages **Punitive damages.**

Exemplification An official copy of a public document used as **evidence.**

Exemption *1.* Freedom from a general burden, duty, service, or tax. *2.* The substraction from income for tax purposes of a certain amount of money for each family member. See also **credit, deduction,** and **exclusion.** *3*. Property a **debtor** may keep when property is taken away by court **order,** such as in **bankruptcy.**

Exequatur (Latin) Having a U.S. lawsuit "*clothed with an exequatur*" means having it validated by the local court to have it recognized and enforced in a foreign country.

Exercise Make use of. For example, to "*exercise a purchase option*" is to make use of a right to buy something by buying it.

Exhaustion of remedies A person must usually take all reasonable steps to get satisfaction from an **administrative agency** before taking a problem with that agency to court (and to get satisfaction from a state government before going into federal court). This is called "exhaustion of administrative (state) remedies."

Exhibit *1*. Any object or document offered and marked as **evidence** in a **trial, hearing, deposition, audit,** etc. *2*. Any document attached to a **pleading, affidavit,** or other formal paper.

Exoneration *1*. Clearing of a crime or other wrongdoing; exculpation. *2*. Removal of a burden or **duty.** *3*. The right of a person who pays a debt for another person to be reimbursed by that other person. *4*. The right to be paid off on a **negotiable instrument.**

Expatriation The voluntary giving up of your citizenship. This includes such acts as joining another country's army.

Expectancy Something hoped for. For example, an **inheritance** under a **will** is an *expectancy* because the person making the will might change the will.

Expert witness A person with special knowledge or experience who is allowed to **testify** at a trial not only about facts (like an ordinary witness) but also about professional conclusions drawn from those facts.

Exploit *1.* Make use of. *2.* Take unfair advantage; use illegally.

Exports clause A U.S. **constitutional** ban on individual states imposing import or export taxes.

Expository statute A law **enacted** to explain a prior law.

Express Clear, definite, direct, actual, or known by explicit words. Usually the opposite of **implied.**

Expressio unius est exclusio alterius (Latin) "The mention of one thing rules out other things not mentioned." The phrase expresses a rule of thumb sometimes used to interpret documents.

Expropriation The taking of private property for public use.

Expunge Blot out, obliterate, completely remove, or strike out.

Extension *1.* A lengthening of time; for example in the **term** of a **lease**. *2. Extending a case* means a judge's applying the rule that decided it to another case that is only somewhat similar.

Extenuating circumstances Surrounding facts that make a crime less evil or blameworthy. They do not lower the crime to a less serious one, but they do tend to lower punishment.

Exterritoriality The freedom from a foreign country's local laws enjoyed by ambassadors and many subordinates living in that country. (*Not* **extraterritoriality.**)

Extinguishment The ending of a right, power, contract, or property interest. For example, a right of **tenancy** *extinguishes* if the tenant moves out or if the tenant buys the house.

Extortion Illegally compelling or forcing something; for example, forcing a confession by deprivation of food, getting something by threats of harm to person, property, or reputation, or getting something by misusing the power of public office.

Extra *1*. Outside of. *2*. In addition to.

Extradition One country (or state) giving up a person to a second country (or state) when the second country (or state) requests the person for a trial on a **criminal** charge or for punishment after a trial.

Extrajudicial *1*. Unconnected with court business, outside the court, or beyond the proper scope of court business. *2*. Not having legal effect, though said or done by a judge. See **dictum.**

Extraneous evidence Evidence **aliunde.** See **extrinsic evidence.**

Extraordinary remedy A group of actions a court will take only if more usual legal **remedies** will not suffice. These include **habeas corpus** and **mandamus.**

Extraterritoriality The operation of a country's laws outside of its physical boundaries; for example, the United States's right to bring to trial and punish its soldiers for crimes committed on a U.S. base in a foreign country. (*Not* **exterritoriality.**)

Extremis (Latin) Last illness or mortal injury.

Extrinsic evidence **Evidence** drawn from things outside a **contract** or other document. For example, the fact that a person was forced to sign a contract is *extrinsic* to the words (**face**) of the contract itself.

Eyewitness A person with firsthand knowledge of an event. Someone who can **testify** as to what he or she saw, heard, etc.

Eyre A court of traveling judges in old England.

F Federal Reporter (see **National Reporter System**). *F.2d* is the second **series** of the Federal Reporter.

FAA Federal Aviation Administration.

FAS Free alongside. The selling price includes shipping costs and delivery alongside the ship.

FASB Financial **Accounting** Standards Board.

FBI Federal Bureau of Investigation.

FCC Federal Communications Commission.

FDA Food and Drug Administration.

FDIC Federal Deposit Insurance Corporation.

FEPC Fair Employment Practices Commission.

FHA *1*. Federal Housing Administration. *2*. Farmers Home Administration. Also FmHA.

FHLB Federal Home Loan Bank.

FHLMC Federal Home Loan Mortgage Corporation (*Freddie Mac*).

FICA Federal Insurance Contributions Act (*Social Security*).

FLSA Fair Labor Standards Act (*Minimum Wage; Child Labor; etc.*).

FMCS Federal Mediation and Conciliation Service.

FMV Fair **market value.**

FNMA Federal National Mortgage Association (*Fannie Mae*).

FOB Free on board. The selling price of goods includes transportation to the FOB point, a place named in the contract.

FOIA Freedom of Information Act.

FPC Federal Power Commission.

FPR Federal Procurement Regulations.

FRAP Federal Rules of **Appellate** Procedure.

FRB Federal Reserve Board.

FRCP Federal Rules of **Civil Procedure.**

FRD **Federal Rules Decisions.**

FTC Federal Trade Commission. Enforces prohibitions against **unfair competition** and other business and consumer laws such as the **Consumer Credit Protection Act.**

FY **Fiscal** year.

F.Supp. **Federal Supplement.**

Face *1.* All things seen in normal inspection of a document, primarily the document's language. *2. Face value* is the formal cash-in value written on a **note** or other financial document. *Face value* does not include interest or other charges and does not depend on the note's fluctuating value in the marketplace.

Facsimile Exact copy.

Fact *1.* An act; a thing that took place; an event. *2.* Something that exists and is real, as opposed to opinion, supposition, or what *should* exist. A *question of fact* is about what happened. (A *question of law* is about how the law affects what happened and what should have happened according to the law.) *3.* A *fact situation* is a summary of the facts of a case without any comments or legal conclusions.

Factor A person who is given goods to sell and gets a **commission** for selling them.

Factum (Latin) Act; fact; central fact or act upon which a question "turns."

Failure of consideration The situation when something offered in a deal (the **consideration**) becomes worthless or ceases to exist before the deal is completely carried out.

Failure of issue Dying without children.

Fair *1. Fair comment* is the **common law** (pre**constitutional**) right to comment, within limits, upon the conduct of public officials without being **liable** for **defamation**. *2. Fair credit reporting acts* are federal and state laws **regulating** the organizations that investigate, store, and give out **consumer** *credit* information, organizations that collect bills, etc. *3. Fair hearing* is the word many **administrative agencies** use for their trial-like decision-making process, which is used when a person **appeals** an administrative decision. The **hearing** need not use full trial rules. *4. Fair market value* is **market value**. *5. Fair trade* is the fixing of a retail price for an item by the manufacturer. This may be illegal. *6. Fair use* is the limited use of another's copyrighted work (often for purposes such as news reporting or parody) permitted by **copyright** law even if no fee is paid and no permission is granted. *7.* The *fairness doctrine* is a former Federal Communications Commission rule that broadcasters must present, or let others present, all sides of major public issues if they present one side.

False *1.* Intentionally or knowingly untrue. *2.* Untrue in fact. *3. False arrest* or *false imprisonment* is any unlawful restraint or deprivation of a person's liberty, usually by a public official. It is a **tort**. *4. False pretenses* is a lie told to cheat another person out of money or property. It is a crime in most states. *5. False representation* is similar to *false pretenses*, but it is the basis for a lawsuit, rather than a crime, if a person is hurt financially by relying on a lie. *6. False swearing* is lying on an **affidavit** or under **oath**, but not in court. It is a less serious form of **perjury.**

Falsus in uno doctrine   (Latin) The principle that if a jury thinks a witness is lying about one thing, the jury may disregard everything.

Family   *1.* A broad word that can mean parents and children, any blood relatives, any persons living as a single group, etc. *2.* The *family car doctrine* (*or family purpose doctrine*) is the rule that a car's owner will usually be **liable** for damage done by a family member driving the car. The rule has been limited or rejected by most states. *3. Family court* is the name for different types of courts that may handle various cases including child **abuse** and **neglect, support, paternity, custody, juvenile delinquency, divorce, separation,** etc. *4.* For *family law*, see **domestic** relations law.

Fannie Mae   Federal National Mortgage Association.

Fatal   See **error.**

Fault   *1.* Lack of care; failure to do a duty; responsibility for a wrong; cause of harm. *2.* Defect or imperfection. *3.* Under the **Uniform Commercial Code,** "a wrongful act, omission, or breach."

Feasance   Doing an act; performing a duty. [pronounce: <u>fee</u>-zense]

Fed   *1.* Short for *Federal. 2.* Federal Reserve Bank System.

Federal   *1.* National, as opposed to state, government. For the various U.S. federal **agencies,** look under their initials at the start of the letter. *2. Federal common law* is federal judge-made law based on the U.S. **Constitution** and **statutes.** It is restricted to areas such as **interstate commerce.** *3. Federal courts* are created by the U.S. **Constitution** and by **Congress.** They are part of one system that has federal **jurisdiction** based on such things as **diversity of citizenship** and *federal question* (a legal issue directly involving the U.S. Constitution, federal statutes, or **treaties**). *4.* The *Federal Register* is the first place that the rules and **regulations** of U.S. **administrative agencies** are published. Abbreviated *Fed. Reg.* *5.* The *Federal Reporter* contains the **opinions** of many courts below the U.S. Supreme Court level. Those lower court opinions not published here are in the *Federal Supplement.* *6.* The *Federal Rules* are the federal courts' rules of **civil procedure**, **criminal** procedure, **appellate** procedure, and **evidence**. *Federal Rules Decisions* is a **reporter** that publishes federal court decisions about the courts' procedural rules. *7.* For *Federal Supplement,* see *Federal Reporter. 8.* The *Federal Tort Claims Act* abolished the federal government's **immunity** from lawsuits based on some types of **torts**. *9.* A *federal union* is a uniting of two or more states into one strong central government with many powers left to the states.

Federalism City, state, and national governments existing side by side in the same area with the lower levels having some independent powers.

Federation A formal group of persons, organizations, or governments loosely united for a common purpose.

Fee *1.* A charge for services. *2.* Any **estate** in land that can be transferred by gift, sale, and inheritance. "Fee" is often used to mean *fee simple absolute,* a full estate in land with no ownership limitations. *3. Fee tail* is an **estate** that can be passed on only to children (or only to those in a set line of **inheritance**).

Fellow servant rule A rule, abolished in most states by **employers liability acts,** that an employer is not responsible for the injury one employee does to another if both were carefully chosen.

Felon A person convicted of a **felony.**

Felonious *1.* Done with the intent to commit a major crime; concerning a **felony.** *2.* Evil; malicious; unlawful. [pronounce: fe-<u>lone</u>-ee-us]

Felony *1.* A serious crime. *2.* A crime with a **sentence** of one year or more. *3.* The *felony-murder rule* is the principle that if you (even accidently) kill another while committing a **felony**, then the killing is murder.

Feme couvert (Law French) A married woman; one who in the past could not perform some legal acts, such as make a **contract.** The opposite was *feme sole* (an unmarried woman). [pronounce: fem <u>coo</u>-vair]

Feoffment The old method of transferring full ownership of land in England. [pronounce: <u>feef</u>-ment]

Feudal law The law of property from the Middle Ages in England.

Fiat (Latin) "Let it be done"; a command, especially an authoratative, yet arbitrary command.

Fiction A *legal fiction* is an assumption that something that is (or may be) false or nonexistent is true or real. Legal fictions are assumed or invented to help do justice. For example, bringing a lawsuit to throw a nonexistent "John Doe" off one's property used to be the only way to establish a clear right to the property when legal **title** was uncertain.

Fictitious *1.* Fake (and usually in bad faith). *2.* Nonexistent; made up.

Fidelity bond Insurance on a person protecting against that person's dishonesty. A company must often buy this type of insurance when an employee is in a position of trust, handles large sums of money, and is seldom checked on by others.

Fiduciary *1.* A person who manages money or property for another person and in whom that other person has a right to place great trust. *2.* A relationship like that in #1. *3.* Any relationship between persons in which a person acts for another in a position of trust; for example, lawyer and client or parent and child.

Field warehousing An arrangement by which a lender takes formal control of goods stored in a borrower's possession.

Fifth Amendment See **Bill of Rights.** "Take the Fifth" means refuse to answer a question because it might implicate the person in a crime.

File *1.* The complete court record of a case. *2.* "To file" a paper is to give it to the court clerk for inclusion in the case record. *3.* A folder in a law office (of a case, a client, business records, etc.).

Filiation proceeding **Paternity suit.**

Final argument A last statement made to the jury (or to the judge when there is no jury) by each side in a trial. Each side presents what it thinks the facts are and how it thinks the law applies to those facts.

Final decision (or decree, determination, judgment, opinion, or order) Each of these words has opposite uses. *1.* The last action of a court; the one upon which an **appeal** can be based. *2.* The last decision of a court or a series of courts from which there are *no more appeals possible.*

Financial statement A summary of what a company or other organization owns and what it owes. It may be a **balance sheet,** annual report, profit and loss statement, etc.

Financing statement A paper, filed on the proper public records, that shows a **security** interest in goods.

Finding   A decision (by a judge, jury, hearing examiner, etc.) about a question of fact; a decision about **evidence.**

Firm offer   A written **offer** by a merchant to buy or sell goods that will be held open for a certain length of time. It is a type of **option** that requires no **consideration** to be valid.

First Amendment   See **Bill of Rights.**

First-degree murder   See **degree.**

First impression   New. A case or question is "of first impression" if it presents an entirely new problem to the court and cannot be decided by **precedent.**

First instance   A *court of first instance* is a **trial** court as opposed to an **appeals** court.

First mortgage (or lien)   The **mortgage** or **lien** that has the right to be paid off before all others. This is not necessarily the first in time.

Fiscal year   Financial records year, not necessarily January through December.

Fishing trip (or expedition)   *1.* Using the courts to find out information beyond the fair scope of the lawsuit. *2.* The loose, unfocused questioning of a **witness** or the overly broad use of **discovery.**

Fitness for a particular purpose   The **implied warranty** that if a merchant should know that an item is used for a particular purpose, the merchant is responsible to buyers for harm resulting from proper use for that purpose.

Fixation   See **fixed work.**

Fixed assets   A company's permanent land, machinery, etc.

Fixed charges (or costs)   Business costs, such as rent, that continue whether or not business comes in.

Fixed opinion A **juror**'s **bias** about guilt or liability.

Fixed work Under **copyright** law, a new work is "fixed" or "created," and thus protected, when it is put in stable, tangible form, such as written on paper or recorded on film.

Fixture Anything attached to land or a building. The word sometimes refers to attached things that *may* be removed by a tenant and sometimes refers to attached things that *may not*.

Flagrante delicto (Latin) In the act of committing the crime.

Floating *1.* Short-term (as in *floating debt*). *2.* Varying (as in *floating interest*). *3.* Open-ended (as in a *floating lien*, which includes later-purchased property under an earlier **lien**).

Flotsam The wreckage of a ship or its goods found floating in the water. Compare **jetsam**.

Followed A **case** is *followed* by a later case if it is relied upon as **precedent** to decide the later case.

For cause For a sound legal reason, not merely a stated reason.

Forbearance Refraining from action, especially action to enforce a right or to collect on an overdue debt.

Force *1.* Unlawful or wrongful violence. *2.* "In force" means in effect and valid. *3.* *Force majeure* (Law French) is an irresistible or unavoidable force of nature, such as an earthquake.

Forcible detainer The act of a person who refuses to give up occupancy of land or a building to the rightful owner or tenant. The summary (quick) court process to get this land back is also called *forcible (or unlawful) detainer.*

Foreclosure An action by a person who holds a **mortgage** to: (1) take the property away from the mortgagor (such as a home owner); (2) end the mortgagor's right in the property; and (3) sell the property to pay the mortgage debt.

Foreign Belonging to, coming from, or having to do with another country or state. For example, a Maine court would call a **corporation** incorporated and based in Ohio a *foreign corporation.*

Foreman The leader of a **jury,** who speaks for it.

Forensic Having to do with courts and the law.

Foreseeability The degree to which the consequences of an action should have been considered. *Not* hindsight.

Forfeit Lose the right to something because of an offense, a **breach** *of contract*, or the neglect of a duty. [pronounce: for-fit]

Forgery Making a fake document (or altering a real one) with intent to commit a **fraud.**

Form *1.* A model document to work from or a legal paper with blanks to be filled in. *2.* The language, arrangement, conduct, procedure, or legal technicalities of a document or **proceeding**, as opposed to its **substance (what it is about).**

Formal *1.* In form only, as opposed to real or substantial. For example, a *formal party* is involved in name only and has no real interest in the proceedings. *2.* Following full, proper procedure.

Formed design A deliberate, set intention to commit a crime.

Forms of action Special, individual, technical ways each different type of lawsuit formerly was brought to court. If a legal problem did not fit into one of these pigeonholes (such as **assumpsit, detinue, ejectment, replevin, trespass,** *trespass on the* **case,** or **trover**), it could not be brought to court.

Fornication Sexual intercourse between a man and woman who are not married to each other.

Forswear *1*. Swear to something one knows is untrue. This is broader than **perjury** but not as serious. *2*. Formally deny or deny under oath.

Forthwith Immediately; as soon as possible.

Fortuitous Happening by chance or accident; unexpected; unforeseen; unavoidable; *not* "lucky."

Forum non conveniens (Latin) "Inconvenient court." If two or more courts both have proper **venue** for a case, a judge may rule that the case must be brought in the *other* court for either the convenience of or fairness to one of the parties.

Forum shopping A person's choosing the one court, among two or more that may legally handle a lawsuit, that might look most favorably at that person's side of the case.

Foundation *1*. Basis. For example, the *foundation* of a trial is the group of issues in dispute between the sides, as set out in the **pleadings.** *2*. The preliminary questions to a **witness** that establish the admissibility (legal usability) of that person's **testimony** as **evidence** in a trial.

Four corners **Face** of a document.

Fourteenth Amendment The U.S. **constitutional** amendment that forbids the states from abridging the "privileges and immunities" of U.S. citizens, forbids the states from depriving persons of **due process** or **equal protection** of the laws, and changes the **apportionment** of congressional **representatives.**

Fourth Amendment See **Bill of Rights.**

Frame *1*. Draw up; put into words. *2*. Falsely incriminate.

Franchise A business arrangement in which a person buys the right to sell, rent, or otherwise control the products or services of a company, the right to a particular business territory, etc.

Fraud Any kind of trickery used by one person to cheat another.

Fraudulent Cheating. For example, a *fraudulent convey-ance* is a **debtor**'s transfer of property to someone else to cheat a **creditor** who might have a right to it.

Free and clear Unrestricted, doubt-free legal owner-ship (of property) with no liens or mortgages.

Freedom The right to do what you want, consistent with laws protecting others' rights. For example, *freedom of speech* is the constitutional right to say what you want as long as you do not interfere with others' rights protected by the laws of **defamation,** public safety, etc. Other freedoms protected by the **Constitution** include freedom of *association, contract, religion,* and *the press.*

Freehold Ownership of land, either unrestricted or limited by no more than a time limit.

Friend of the court **Amicus curiae.**

Friendly fire A fire that remains contained where in-tended but that may do damage anyway.

Friendly suit A lawsuit brought by agreement to settle a point of law that affects opposing persons.

Frisk A superficial running of hands over a person's body to do a quick search, usually for weapons.

Frivolous Legally worthless. For example, a **pleading** that clearly has no legal "leg to stand on," even if every fact it claims is true, is *frivolous.*

Frolic An employee's deviation from an employer's mission to do something for himself or herself.

Frozen Cannot be sold, moved, transferred, etc.

Fruit Product of; result of. For example, rental income is the *fruit* of renting out land, and stolen money is the *fruit of crime.*

Frustration *Frustration of contract* occurs when carrying out a bargain has become impossible because of some change or occurrence that is not the fault of the persons making the deal. *Frustration of purpose* occurs when, even if a bargain can be carried out, some change has wiped out the real reasons for the contract. In some cases, promises need not then be carried out.

Fugitive from justice A person accused of committing a crime who leaves the area or hides to avoid prosecution.

Full faith and credit The constitutional requirement that each state must treat as valid, and enforce when appropriate, the laws and court decisions of other states. This rule has exceptions, especially when the other state lacks **jurisdiction.**

Fundamental law A country's **constitution** or its basic governing principles.

Fungible Able to be easily replaced one for another; for example, pounds of a particular grade of rice. [pronounce: fun-jible]

Future *1.* For *future acquired property,* see **after-acquired property clause.** *2. Future advances* are money lent on the same **security** as a prior loan. *3. Future earnings* are estimated money that would have been made in the future if an injury had not occurred. *4. Future interests* are present rights in property that give the right to future possession or use; for example, the right to own property and use it after ten years go by. *5. Futures* are contracts promising to buy or sell standard commodities (such as rice) or **securities** at a future date and at a set price. These are "paper" deals, involving profit and loss on promises to deliver, not necessarily involving possession of the actual commodities.

GAAP *Generally Accepted Accounting Principles,* put out by the Financial Accounting Standards Board.

GAAS *Generally Accepted Auditing Standards,* put out by the American Institute of Certified Public Accountants.

GAO General Accounting Office. The agency that assists the U.S. Congress in financial matters, **audits** and investigates federal programs, etc.

GNMA Government National Mortgage Association (*Ginnie Mae*).

GPO Government Printing Office. The agency that publishes all the laws, **regulations,** etc. of the federal government.

GSA General Services Administration. The agency that manages U.S. property.

Gag order A judge's order that lawyers and witnesses not discuss the trial with outsiders.

Garnishment A legal process, taken by a **creditor** who has received a money **judgment** against a **debtor,** to get the debtor's money. This is done by **attachment** of a bank account or by taking a percentage of the debtor's regular income.

Gen. **General**.

General *1.* A whole group, as opposed to only a part or one individual; applying to all; broad or unlimited. For those *general* words (such as *general partner*) not found under the following, look under the main word (**partner**) or under the opposite (usually **special** or **limited**). *2.* A *general assembly* is either an entire

legislature or only the lower **house.** *3.* A *general assignment for creditors* is a transfer of all rights to a **debtor**'s property to a **trustee** who settles the debtor's affairs and distributes money to the **creditors**. *4. General assistance (or relief)* is local welfare aid to the poor, usually temporary and without federal funding. *5.* A *general average loss* is a loss at sea that will be shared by the ship owner and all owners of cargo shipped. This happens if the lost or damaged items (often thrown overboard) were intentionally lost to save the ship and the rest of the cargo. *6.* A *general building scheme* is the division of land into building lots that are sold with identical land use restrictions. *7.* A *general contractor* **contracts** for a whole job and may hire subcontractors to do parts. *8.* A *general creditor* is a person who is owed money but who has no **security** for the debt. *9.* For *General Digest*, see **American Digest System.** *10.* A *general execution* is a court **order** to a sheriff or another court official to take any personal **property** of a **defendant** to pay off a **judgment.** *11. General jurisdiction* is a court's power to hear and decide any of a wide range of cases that come up within its geographical area. *12.* A *general lien* is a right (arising from a **contract**) to hold *personal* **property** of another person until payment is made on a debt. *13.* A *general warranty deed* is a document used for the transfer of land that includes the promise to protect the buyer against all claims by others to ownership of the property transferred. Compare **quitclaim deed.**

Germane Close on point; relevant; pertinent.

Gerrymander Create unusually shaped (or otherwise unusual) political boundaries or districts to accomplish an improper purpose.

Gift Any willing transfer of money or property without payment close to the value of the thing transferred.

Ginnie Mae Slang for Government National Mortgage Association.

Gist The main point, issue, or argument.

Good Valid; legally sufficient.

Good faith *1.* Honest; honesty in fact. *2.* According to the **Uniform Commercial Code,** a *merchant's good faith* is "the observance of reasonable commercial standards of fair dealing in the trade." *3.* A *good faith purchaser* in commercial law is a person who buys something honestly, pays good value, and knows of no other person's claim to the thing bought.

Goods A general word with a meaning as broad as all property, excluding land and buildings, or as narrow as items for sale by a merchant.

Goodwill The reputation and patronage of a company. It can generally be valued as the amount a company would sell for over the value of its physical property, money owed it, and other **assets.**

Government instrumentality (or immunity) doctrine A legal rule that no organization run by the government may be taxed.

Grab law See **aggressive collection.**

Grace *1.* As a favor. *2.* Not automatic. *3.* A holding off on demanding a payment or enforcing a right. This may be as a favor, or it may be a legal requirement.

Graduated Going up by set formula.

Grand jury See **jury.**

Grand larceny A **theft** of money or property worth more than an amount set by law.

Grandfather clause   An exception to a restriction or requirement that allows all those already doing something to continue, even if they would otherwise be stopped by the restriction.

Grant   *1.* Give or confer. *2.* A transfer of land, usually by **deed.** *3.* A gift or subsidy. *4. Grantors* make grants to *grantees.*

Gratuitous   Without payment or other **consideration.** A *gratuitous licensee* is a nonbusiness visitor or social guest.

Gravamen   The basis or "heart" of a **charge, complaint,** etc.

Green card   Popular name for the *permanent resident* **visa** that is a requirement for noncitizens to hold many jobs in the United States. The card is no longer green.

Grievance procedure   An orderly, regular way of handling problems between workers and employers, prisoners and guards, etc.

Gross   *1.* Great or large. *2.* Flagrant or shameful. *3.* Whole or total. For example, *gross income* is all money taken in.

Ground rent   Rent for raw land.

Grounds   Basis, foundation, or points relied on. For example, *grounds* for **divorce** may include **adultery, cruelty,** etc.

Group legal services   Legal help for members of an organization or employees of a company, paid in advance like group health insurance.

Guaranty (or guarantee)   *1.* The same as a merchant's **warranty** that goods are of a certain quality, will be fixed if broken, etc. *2.* A promise to fulfill an obligation (or pay a debt) if the person who has the obligation fails to fulfill it. For example, John contracts with Ron that if Ron lends Don five dollars and Don fails to pay it back in a week, John will pay it. *3.* Any promise.

Guardian *1.* A person who has the legal right and duty to take care of another person or that person's property because that person (for example, a child) cannot. The arrangement is a *guardianship.* *2.* A *guardian ad litem* (usually a lawyer) is appointed by a court to take care of the interests of a person who cannot legally take care of himself or herself in a lawsuit involving that person.

Guest statute Laws in some states that do not permit a person who rides in another person's car as a *guest* (without payment or business purpose) to sue that person if there is an accident, unless that accident involves more than ordinary **negligence.**

Guilty *1.* Responsible for a crime. *2.* Convicted of a crime. *3.* Responsible for a civil wrong (**tort** or **breach of contract**).

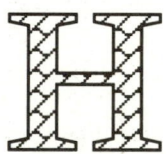

HB *House Bill.* A **bill** in the process of going through the **House of Representatives.**

HDC **Holder in due course.**

HOW **Home owners warranty.**

HR **House of Representatives.**

HUD The U.S. Department of Housing and Urban Development.

Habeas corpus (Latin) "You have the body." A judicial **order** to someone holding a person to bring that person to court; for example, to a warden who may be holding a prisoner illegally or to a father holding a child when the mother claims **custody.** [pronounce: <u>hay</u>-bee-as <u>core</u>-pus]

Habendum clause The part of a **deed** that describes the ownership rights being transferred.

Habitability The requirement that a rented house or apartment be fit to live in, primarily that it can pass building and sanitary code inspections.

Habitual *1.* Regular, common, and customary; more than just frequent. *2. Habitual intemperance* is regular drunkenness (and drug addiction in some states) that is serious enough to interfere with a normal home life or job. This may be **divorce grounds.**

Hand down Decide a case by filing or announcing the decision.

Handicap *1.* See **disability.** *2.* An impairment that substantially limits performance of an important life function. *3. Handicap* is defined differently in different **statutes.**

Harassment Words and actions that unlawfully annoy or alarm.

Harbor *1.* Shelter, house, keep, or feed. *2.* Conceal a person for an illegal purpose, such as to hide a criminal from police arrest.

Hatch Act A federal law prohibiting political activity such as holding public office by federal and some state employees.

Have and hold A common, but unnecessary, phrase in a **deed,** often the first phrase of a **habendum clause.**

Hazard Any risk, danger, or probability of loss or injury.

Headnote   A summary of a **case** placed at the beginning of the case when it is published.

Hearing   *1.* A court proceeding. *2.* A trial-like proceeding conducted by an **administrative agency** or in another noncourt setting. It may be held by a *hearing examiner, hearing officer, administrative law judge,* etc. *3.* A meeting of a **legislative committee** to gather information. *4.* A *public hearing* may be an agency's showing of a new plan or proposed action for public comment and criticism.

Hearsay   A statement about what someone else said (or wrote or otherwise communicated). Hearsay **evidence,** concerning what someone said outside of a court proceeding, is offered in the proceeding to prove the truth of what was said. The *hearsay rule* bars the use of hearsay as evidence in court to prove the hearsay's truth unless allowed by a *hearsay exception,* such as for an **excited utterance.**

Heart-balm acts   State laws eliminating or restricting lawsuits based on **breach of promise** to marry or seduction of an adult.

Heat of passion   A state of violent and uncontrollable provoked anger that may reduce the legal definition of a killing from **murder** to **manslaughter.**

Heir   A person who **inherits** property; a person who has a *right* to inherit property; or a person who has a right to inherit property only if another person dies without leaving a valid **will.**

Held   Decided. See **hold.**

Henceforth   An unnecessarily formal word meaning "from now on."

Herein, hereto, etc   Vague, unnecessary words often found in legal documents: *hereafter* (in the future); *herein* (in this document); *hereinabove* (earlier in this document); _hereinafter_ (later in this document); _hereto_ (to this); _heretofore_ (in times past); _hereunder_ (in, or in accordance with, this document); _herewith_ (in this or with this).

Hereditaments Anything that can be inherited. Inheritable objects are _corporeal hereditaments,_ and inheritable rights are _incorporeal hereditaments._

Hermeneutics The study of the rules and techniques used to interpret documents.

High crimes and misdemeanors The basis for **impeachment** in the U.S. Constitution. This may include **felonies;** it may include offenses against the United States with serious governmental consequences; or it may be whatever **Congress** decides it is.

Highest and best use Potential land use that will bring in the most money.

Hoc (Latin) This.

Hold _1._ To possess or own something lawfully and by good **title.** _2._ To decide. A judge who decides how law applies to a case or "declares **conclusions of law**" is said to "_hold that. . . ._ " _3._ Conduct or have take place; for example, to "_hold court._" _4. Hold harmless_ means to agree to pay certain claims that might come up against another person. _5. Hold over_ means either to keep possession as a **tenant** after a **lease** period is over or to stay in office after a **term** of office is over.

Holder _1._ A person who has legally received possession of a **negotiable instrument,** such as a **check,** and who is entitled to get payment on it. _2._ A _holder in due course_ is a holder who buys a negotiable instrument thinking it is **valid** and having no knowledge that any business involving it is "shady." The **Uniform Commercial Code** defines it as "a holder who takes the instrument for value, in good faith and without notice that it is overdue or has been dishonored or any defense against or claim to it."

Holding The core of a judge's **decision** in a case. It is that part of the judge's written **opinion** which applies the law to the facts of the case and about which it can be said, "the case means no more and no less than this." When later cases rely on a case as **precedent,** it is only the holding that should be used to establish the precedent. A holding may be less than a judge says it is. If the judge made broad, general statements, the holding is limited to only the part of the generalizations that directly applies to the facts of that one case. Compare **dicta.**

Holding company A company that exists primarily to control other companies by owning their **stock.**

Holograph A **will, deed,** or other legal document that is entirely in the handwriting of the signer.

Home owners policy Standard insurance that covers fire, water, theft, **liability,** and other losses.

Home owners warranty The protection of a new home against loss due to major defects for several years either under a **warranty/insurance** program run by a national builders' association or under state laws.

Home rule Local self-government.

Homestead exemption State laws allowing the head of a family to keep a home and some property safe from **creditors.**

Homicide Killing another person (not necessarily a crime).

Hon. Honorable. Often placed before a judge's name.

Honor To **accept** (or pay) a **negotiable instrument,** such as a **check,** when it is properly presented for acceptance (or payment).

Honorary trust A **trust** that gets no special tax advantages but that is not quite a private, ordinary trust; for example, a trust set up to "feed the pigeons in Clark Park." Few states allow these trusts.

Horizontal Among similar products, producers, merchants, etc.

Hornbook A book summarizing the basic principles of one legal subject, usually for law students.

Hostile _1_. A _hostile fire_ is either a fire that escapes from where it was contained or a fire that was never intended to exist at all. _2. Hostile possession_ means claiming possession of land against the whole world, including the owner in the land records, but not necessarily in an aggressive or emotionally "hostile" way. _3_. A _hostile witness_ is a **witness** called by one side in a trial who shows so much **prejudice** or hostility to that side that he or she can be treated as if called by the other side.

Hot cargo Goods produced or handled by an employer with whom a **union** has a **labor dispute.**

Hotchpot Mixing of property belonging to several persons to divide it equally.

House One of the branches of a **legislature;** sometimes, only the lower branch, called the _House of Representatives._

House counsel A lawyer who is an employee of a business and does its day-to-day legal work.

Housebreaking Breaking into and entering a house to commit a crime. Some states call it **burglary** if done at night.

Hung jury A **jury** that cannot reach a **verdict** (decision) because of disagreement among jurors.

Hypothecate _1_. To **pledge** or **mortgage** a thing without turning it over to the person making the loan.

2. To secure repayment of a loan by holding the stock, bonds, etc., of the debtor.

Hypothetical question A process of setting up a series of facts, assuming that they are true, and asking for an answer to a question based on those facts. In a trial, hypothetical questions may be asked of an **expert witness** only.

ICC *1.* Interstate Commerce Commission. A federal agency that **regulates** railroads, trucking companies, etc. *2.* Indian Claims Commission.

ILP Index of Legal Periodicals.

IMF International Monetary Fund. A United Nations agency that stabilizes currency exchange rates and promotes world trade.

INS Immigration and Naturalization Service.

IRA Individual Retirement Account.

IRC Internal Revenue Code. The U.S. tax laws.

IRS Internal Revenue Service. The U.S. tax agency.

Ibid. (Latin) The same; found on the same page, in the same book, etc.

Id. (Latin) The same; exactly the same thing or person. Short for *idem.*

Identity Exactly the same, so legally the same.

Illegal Contrary to the criminal law; breaking a law (not merely improper, a **tort,** or civilly wrong).

Illegitimate *1.* Contrary to the law; lacking legal authorization. *2. Illegitimate child,* as a word for a child born to an unmarried mother, may no longer be used as a legal description in some states and may not be used to limit a child's rights in many states.

Illicit   Prohibited; unlawful. [pronounce: il-_liss_-it]

Illusory promise   A statement that looks like a promise that could make a **contract** but that, upon close examination of the words, promises nothing real or legally binding.

Imbargo   See **embargo.**

Imbezzle   See **embezzlement.**

Immaterial   Not necessary; not important; trivial.

Immediate   _1._ Close, closest, or touching. _2._ As fast as reasonably possible.

Immediate cause   The last event in a series of events, which, without any further events, produced the result in question. This may be the same as, or different from, **proximate cause.**

Immediate issue   Children.

Imminent   Just about to happen; threatening. _Not_ "eminent."

Immoral   A vague word that, legally, usually means serious illegality.

Immovables   Land and things naturally and permanently attached.

Immunity   _1._ Any exemption from a legally imposed duty. _2._ Freedom from a duty; freedom from a penalty. _3._ The freedom from prosecution (based on anything the **witness** says) that is given by the government to a witness who is forced to **testify** before a _grand_ **jury,** a **legislature,** etc. _4._ See **government instrumentality** and **sovereign immunity.**

Impanel   Make up a list of possible **jurors** for a trial or select those who will actually serve.

Imparl Delay formal proceedings and discuss settlement.

Impeachment *1.* Showing that a **witness** is untruthful, either by **evidence** of past conduct or by showing directly that the witness is lying. *2.* The first step in the removal from public office of a high public official. For example, the U.S. House of Representatives may draw up accusations called "articles of impeachment" against the president, vote on them, and present them to the Senate for a trial.

Impediment A thing causing the legal inability to make a **contract.** For example, an *impediment to marriage* might be a prior, still valid marriage.

Impertinence Irrelevance in the sense that the proof offered may be relevant to an issue, but the issue itself is irrelevant to the trial.

Implead Bring into a lawsuit. For example, if A sues B and B sues C in the same lawsuit, B *impleads* C.

Implied Known indirectly. Known by analyzing surrounding circumstances or the actions of the persons involved. The opposite of **express.** For example, one *implied* **warranty** the law imposes on merchants is that unless goods are labeled "as is" or the equivalent, they must be fit for normal use.

Impossibility That which cannot be done. A contract is not binding and cannot be enforced if it is *physically impossible* (be in two places at once), *legally impossible* (make a contract at age four), or *logically impossible* (sell a hat for sixty dollars when the buyer pays ninety for it). These are all forms of *objective impossibility. Subjective impossibility,* however (such as not having enough money to pay for something you have contracted to buy), will not get you out of a contract.

Imposts Taxes; import taxes.

Impound _1_. Take a thing into the **custody** of the law until a legal question about it is decided. _2_. Take action, as a president or governor, to prevent the spending of money that the **legislature** has ordered spent.

Impracticable A stuffy word meaning less than impossible but more than inconvenient; too difficult to require in fairness.

Imprimatur (Latin) Government permission to publish (not required in the United States).

Imprisonment _1_. Putting a person in prison. _2_. Depriving a person of personal liberty in any physical way.

Improvement An addition or change to land or buildings that increases the value. More than a **repair** or replacement.

Imputed _1_. Treated "as if"; carried over to; attributed to. _2_. _Imputed income_ is **income** that will be taxed to a person whether or not the money was actually received. _3_. _Imputed knowledge_ is facts that a person should know because the facts are available and it is the person's legal duty to know them. _4_. _Imputed negligence_ exists, for example, if David is **negligent** and Paul is responsible for David's actions, because David's negligence is imputed (carried over) to Paul.

In blank See **blank indorsement.**

In camera (Latin) "In chambers." In a judge's private office; also describes a **hearing** in court with all spectators excluded.

In common With others; by all without division; together. Describes something shared on equal terms. For example, if two persons own a house "in common," they both own all of it.

In forma pauperis (Latin) "As a pauper." Permission to sue in court without paying court costs.

In kind By the same type of thing.

In limine (Latin) Preliminary. A **motion** *in limine* is often a pretrial **protective order.**

In loco parentis (Latin) Acting in the place of a parent for the care and supervision of a child.

In pais (Law French) *1.* "In the countryside"; outside the courtroom; having to do with facts rather than with law. *2.* Done informally rather than by legal action or document. [pronounce: in pay]

In pari delicto (Latin) In equal fault; equally guilty.

In pari materia See **pari materia.**

In perpetuity Forever.

In personam (Latin) Describes a lawsuit brought to enforce a right against another person, as opposed to one brought to enforce rights in a thing or against the whole world (**in rem**). For example, a suit for automobile accident injuries is *in personam* because it is against the driver or owner only. A suit to establish **title** to land is *in rem* because, even if a person is fighting the claim, a victory is binding against the whole world and a "thing" is primarily involved.

In posse (Latin) Not now or yet existing, but possible.

In re —— (Latin) "In the matter of ——." The name of a case concerned with a thing, rather than a lawsuit directly between two persons. For example, *"in re Brown's Estate"* might be a case in **probate** court to dispose of a dead person's property, and *"in re Mary Smith"* might be a child **neglect** proceeding against the parents of Mary Smith. [pronounce: in ray]

In rem See **in personam** for the contrasting definition of *in rem.*

In specie (Latin) *1.* In the same or similar form or way. *2.* Exactly the same; *specific* **performance.**

In terrorem (Latin) "By threat." An _interrorem clause_ in a will "threatens" a **beneficiary** with **revocation** of that person's **bequest** if the beneficiary contests the will.

Inadmissible Describes facts or things that cannot be admitted into **evidence** in a trial.

Inadvertence _1._ Lack of attention or carelessness. _2._ Excusable mistake or oversight.

Inalienable Describes that which cannot be given, taken, or sold away.

Inc. Incorporated. _Pink Ink, Inc._ is the Pink Ink Corporation.

Incapacity See **capacity.**

Incarceration Confinement in jail or prison.

Incest Sexual intercourse between a man and a woman who, according to state law, are too closely related by blood.

Inchoate Partial, unfinished, unripened. For example, an _inchoate instrument_ is a document, such as a **deed,** that is **valid** between the **parties** but that will not give the holder full rights or protections against most others until it is registered or recorded with the proper officials. [pronounce: in-ko-ate]

Incidental Depending on something else more important. For example, _incidental damages_ are the "side costs" of a broken **contract,** such as storing the goods you thought were sold.

Incite Urge, provoke, strongly encourage, or stir up.

Income _1._ Money gains from business, work, or investment. _2._ All financial gain. _3. Income averaging_ (now available only for certain pension plan distributions) is reducing taxes by showing that income in prior years was far lower and by paying taxes on the basis of average income for several years. _4. In-_

come splitting is reducing total family taxes by giving income-producing property to a family member who pays taxes at a lower rate. *5. Income tax* is a tax on profits from business, work, or investments but not on the growth in value of investments.

Incompatibility *1.* Describes two or more ideas or things that cannot logically, physically, or legally coexist. *2.* The inability of a husband and wife to live together in marriage; this is **grounds** for **divorce** in some states without either person being at fault.

Incompetency The lack of legal ability to do something; the condition of persons who lack the mental ability to manage their own affairs and who have someone appointed by the state to manage their finances.

Incompetent evidence Facts, objects, **testimony,** etc., that may not be used as **evidence** in a legal proceeding.

Inconsistent Contradictory, so that if one thing is **valid** (or one thing can happen), another thing cannot be valid (or another thing cannot be allowed to happen).

Inconvenience A broad word meaning anything from "trivial problem" to "serious hardship or injustice."

Incorporate *1.* Formally create a **corporation.** The persons who do this are *incorporators*. *2.* To *incorporate by reference* is to make something a part of something else by mere mention; for example, if in document A it says that "document B is incorporated by reference," then document B becomes a part of document A even though the words in document B are not rewritten into document A.

Incorporeal Without body. The opposite of **corporeal.**

Increment One piece or part of a piece-by-piece increase; anything gained or added; the process of adding to something.

Incriminate   Implicate in a crime or show involvement in a crime. *Incriminatory* is tending to show guilt.

Incroachment   See **encroachment.**

Inculpate   *1.* Accuse of a crime. *2.* Involve in guilt or crime.

Incumbent   *1.* A person who presently holds an office. *2.* Required.

Incumbrance   See **encumbrance.**

Incur   Get. Get something bad, such as a debt or **liability,** because the law requires it. For example, you *incur a liability* when a court gives a money **judgment** against you.

Indebitatus assumpsit   See **assumpsit.**

Indecent   Offensive to public morality.

Indefeasible   Describes a right that cannot in any way be defeated, **revoked,** or taken away.

Indefinite   See **indeterminate.**

Indemnify   Compensate or promise to compensate a person who has suffered a loss or who may suffer a future loss.

Indemnity   A contract to compensate or reimburse a person for possible losses of a particular type. It is a type of **insurance.**

Indenture   Many different types of agreements, such as: a **deed,** with identical copies for each person signing; a written **bond** sales agreement; a **mortgage** that includes a **lien;** etc.

Independent contractor   A person who contracts with another person or a business to do a particular piece of work by his or her own methods and under his or her own control.

Indeterminate   With the exact time period not set. For example, an *indeterminate sentence* is a jail or prison term with a maximum or minimum set but not the exact amount of time.

Indicia (Latin) Indications; pointers; signs; circumstances that make a certain fact probable but not definite. For example, *indicia of title* are documents (such as photocopies), other than original legal proofs, that something is owned. [pronounce: in-dish-ee-a]

Indictment A formal accusation of a crime, made against a person by a *grand* **jury** upon the request of a **prosecutor.** [pronounce: in-dite-ment]

Indirect cost Fixed charges.

Indirect evidence Circumstantial evidence.

Indispensable party A person who has such a stake in the outcome of a lawsuit that the judge will not make a final decision unless that person is formally joined as a **party** to the lawsuit.

Indorsement *1.* Signing a document "on the back," or merely signing it anywhere. *2.* Signing a **negotiable instrument,** such as a check, in a way that causes the piece of paper, and the rights it stands for, to transfer to another person.

Inducement *1.* A statement or promise by a person that convinces another person to make a deal. A benefit or advantage of a deal. *2.* A thing that convinces someone to do something. The motive for an action.

Industrial union A labor union whose members may have different skills but who work for the same type of industry.

Infamy The loss of a good reputation because of a **conviction** of a major crime, and the loss of certain legal rights that accompanies that loss.

Infancy A general word for being a very young child. In some states, this means the same as being a **minor.**

Infant _1._ A person under the age of adulthood. _2._ A very young child.

Inference A fact (or proposition) that is _probably_ true because a true fact (or proposition) leads you to believe that the _inferred_ fact (or proposition) is also true. For example, if the first four books in a set of five have green covers, it is a reasonable _inference_ that the fifth book has a green cover.

Inferior court _1._ Any court but the highest one in a court system. _2._ A court with special, limited responsibilities; for example, a **probate** court.

Infeudation An obsolete word for granting a **freehold.**

Infirmity A defect. For example, if the papers that transfer a **title** are defective, the title transferred has an _infirmity._

Information _1._ A formal accusation of a crime made by a public official such as a prosecuting attorney. _2._ A sworn, written accusation of a crime that leads to an **indictment.** _3._ Personal knowledge of something. _"Information and belief,"_ however, may mean no more than a person's opinion.

Informed consent A person's agreement to allow something to happen (such as surgery) that is based on full disclosure of the facts needed to make the decision intelligently.

Infra (Latin) _1._ Below, under, or within. _2._ Later in this book.

Infraction A violation or **breach** of a contract, a duty, or a minor law.

Infringement A **breach** or violation of a right; for example, the unauthorized making, using, selling, or distributing of something protected by a **patent, copyright,** or **trademark.**

Ingross See **engrossment.**

Inherent Derived from and inseparable from the thing itself. For example, *inherent danger* is the danger some objects have by merely existing (probably a bomb, but not a hammer); and an *inherent vice* is a basic defect.

Inherit Receive property from a dead person, either by effect of **intestacy** laws or by means of a **will.** An *inheritance tax* is the tax a person who inherits pays. It is *not* an **estate tax.**

Initiative The procedure for the people to directly enact laws by voting, without the need for the laws' passage by the **legislature.**

Injunction A judge's order to a person to do or refrain from doing a particular thing. For example, a court might *issue an injunction* to **enjoin** (prevent) a company from dumping wastes into a river. An injunction may be *preliminary* or *temporary* (until the issue can be fully tried in court), or it may be *final* or *permanent.*

Injure *1.* Harm. *2.* Violate another person's legal rights. *3.* An *injury* is any wrong, hurt, or damage done to another person's rights, body, reputation, or property.

Innocent *1.* Not guilty. *2.* Not responsible for an action or an event. *3.* Honestly; without knowledge.

Inns of Court Associations that govern the education and **admission** to the **bar** of prospective trial lawyers in Great Britain.

Inoperative Not now in effect.

Inquest *1.* A **hearing** by a **coroner** into the cause of a person's death, when the death was either violent or suspicious. *2*. Any formal inquiry; for example, into a person's sanity or into the validity of a **title.**

Inquisitorial system A method of trial in which the judge actively participates in fact-finding and in prosecution for the government. The *inquisitorial system* is different from the **adversary system** used in the United States.

Insanity A legal, not a medical, word that is no more precise than "crazy." It has different meanings in different situations, such as, for example, in a criminal **prosecution,** a hearing on a **will's** validity, a **defense** to a **contract** lawsuit, a proceeding to put a person away in a mental hospital, etc. Even within each situation, there are several competing, often vague, definitions. See **capacity, Durham rule,** and **M'Naghten rule.**

Insecurity clause A section of a note or **contract** that gives a **creditor** the right to make an entire debt come due if there is a good reason to think that the **debtor** cannot or will not pay. Compare **acceleration** *clause.*

Insolvency Inability to pay debts as they come due or having fewer **assets** than **liabilities.**

Inspection Looking at things, documents, etc., often during the **discovery** process; looking at a work site to determine such things as worker safety or the cleanliness of food service.

Installment A separate delivery or payment. *Installment credit* is an arrangement in which a borrower agrees to pay off a debt (plus interest and finance charges) by making regular (often monthly) payments. See **Consumer** *Credit Protection Act.*

Instance *1*. Forceful request. *2*. Situation or occurrence.

Instant Present or current. The *"instant case"* means the current lawsuit.

Instigate Push into action (especially illegal action); **abet.**

Institutes An old word for various legal textbooks.

Instructions Directions given by the judge to the jury explaining how they should go about deciding the case. This may include a summary of the questions to be decided and the laws that apply plus an explanation of the **burden of proof.**

Instrument *1.* A written document; a formal or legal document such as a **contract** or **will.** *2.* **Negotiable instrument.**

Instrumentality An organization totally controlled by another one.

Insurable interest A person's real financial interest in another person or in an object. An **insurance** contract must involve an *insurable interest* or it may be unenforceable because it is a form of gambling.

Insurance *1.* A **contract** in which one person pays money and the other person promises to reimburse the first person for specified types of losses if they occur. The person agreeing to compensate is the *insurer* or *underwriter;* the person paying is the *insured;* the payment is a *premium;* the contract is a *policy;* the person or thing protected is the *life (object) insured;* and the types of harm protected against are *risks* or *perils.* *2.* There are hundreds of types of insurance and dozens of ways of arranging it. A few of the more common types (and the situations they cover) are: *automobile liability* (injury to other persons or their property from an accident involving a car one owns or drives); *casualty* (accidents and injuries); *credit life* (paying off a major purchase if a person dies while owing payments); *group* (insurance provided at lower rates through an employer or other defined group); *home owners* (a package of fire, theft, liability, and other insurance); *self* (putting aside money in an account to pay possible claims or merely being *prepared* to pay possible claims); *straight life* (life insurance with continuing payments); *term* (insurance that ends at the end of a certain time period); *title* (protection against claims made on the title to land one owns); *unemployment* (a government program through a person's job); and **workers' compensation.**

Insured   Either a person who buys insurance or a person whose life is insured.

Intangibles   Property that is really a right rather than a physical object; for example, bank accounts or **copyrights.**

Integrated   *1.* Made whole or complete. The process is called *integration. 2.* An *integrated agreement* is a written contract in which the persons making the contract state that it is their full, complete, and final agreement. All previous discussions, etc., are said to be *merged* into the agreement. See **parol evidence rule.** *3.* An *integrated bar* is a system in which all lawyers who practice before the courts of a geographical area must belong to one organization (the "bar"), which is supervised by the area's highest court.

Intendment   *1.* True, correct meaning. *2.* Intention.

Intent   The resolve or purpose to use a particular means to reach a particular result. *Intent* usually explains *how* a person wants to do something and *what* that person wants done; **motive** explains *why.*

Inter   (Latin) "Among or between." For example, *inter alia* means "among other things"; *inter se* [pronounce: say] means "among or between themselves only"; and *inter vivos* means "between the living." A *gift inter vivos* is an ordinary gift, as opposed to a *gift* **causa** *mortis,* and an *inter vivos trust* is an ordinary **trust,** as opposed to one set up under a **will.**

Interest *1.* A broad term for any right in property. For example, both an owner who **mortgages** land and the person who lends the owner money on the mortgage have an *interest* in the land. *2.* The extra money a person receives back for lending money to another person.

Interference In **patent** law, a hearing between two (or more) persons, each claiming the same invention or discovery, to determine who has *priority of invention.*

Interlocutory Provisional; temporary; while a lawsuit is still going on.

Internal Revenue Code The U.S. tax laws.

International Court of Justice A branch of the United Nations that settles voluntarily submitted disputes between countries and gives **advisory opinions** to other branches of the United Nations.

International law *1. Public international law* is the customary law that applies to interactions between countries. *2.* For *private international law,* see **conflict of laws.**

Interpellation *1.* Questioning. *2.* Short-term agreement. *3. Not* **interpolation.**

Interpleader *1.* A procedure in which persons having potentially conflicting claims against a third person may be forced to resolve the conflict before seeking **relief** from the third person. For example, if A is sued by B for a debt and A thinks that C might have a legitimate claim against A for the same debt, A may *interplead* C (bring in or "join" C as a **party**) to the suit. *2.* The settling or deciding of claims between **defendants** to then settle or decide claims between the **plaintiff** and the defendants.

Interpolation *1*. The insertion of words into a completed document. *2. Not* **interpellation.**

Interpretation *1*. The process of discovering or deciding the meaning of a written document by studying only the document itself and not the circumstances surrounding it. But see #2. *2*. Studying the document *and* surrounding circumstances to decide the document's meaning. See **construction.**

Interrogatories *1*. Written questions sent from one side to the other in a lawsuit, attempting to get written answers to factual questions or seeking an explanation of the other side's legal contentions. They are a part of the formal **discovery** process and usually take place before the trial. *2*. Any written questions.

Interstate Commerce Act A federal law that **regulates** the surface transportation of persons and goods between states. See **ICC.**

Interstate compact An agreement among states that has been passed as law in the states and has been approved by the U.S. Congress.

Intervening cause A cause of an accident or other injury that will remove the blame from the wrongdoer who originally set things in motion. It is also called *intervening act, intervening agency, superseding cause, supervening negligence,* etc.

Intervenor A person who voluntarily **enters** (becomes a **party** in) a lawsuit between other persons by joining the **plaintiff,** joining the **defendant,** or making separate claims. The process is called *intervention.*

Intestate *1*. Without a **will.** *Dying intestate* is dying without a valid will or without a will that covers all of the dead person's property. *2.* A person who dies without having a valid will. *3. Intestate succession* is the distribution of **inheritances** to **heirs** according to a state's laws about who should collect. This is done when the property is not covered by a valid will.

Intra   Within. For example, *intrastate* (as opposed to *interstate*) *commerce* is business carried out within one state.

Intrinsic evidence   Facts learned from a document itself, not from outside information about it.

Introduction of evidence   The submission of **evidence** for possible acceptance in a trial.

Inure   Take effect; result, usually by **operation of law.** For example, if benefits *inure* to Mr. Smith, they will come to him whether or not he does anything to get them.

Invalid   *1.* Inadequate; useless. *2.* Not binding; lacking legal force.

Inventory   A detailed list of articles of property; often, of articles held for sale.

Investment   *1.* Using money to make money; for example, by buying stock. *2.* An *investment banker* helps sell a corporation's new stocks and bonds to the public. *3.* The *investment tax credit* is a subtraction from income tax of a percentage of the price of some major business purchases.

Invitation   Asking someone to come onto property for a purpose involving your benefit, or keeping land or a building in such a way as to make persons think that you want them to come in. For example, a store owner *invites* the public to come in by actions, signs, and ads.

Invited error doctrine   The principle that when one side in a lawsuit gets away with using **inadmissible evidence,** the other side may use similar evidence to refute it.

Invitee A person who is at a place by **invitation.** Note: A social caller may be a **licensee,** not an *invitee*.

Invoice A list sent by a merchant that details goods sent to another person (often a purchaser) and usually gives prices item by item.

Involuntary manslaughter The unintentional, but still illegal, killing of another person. This crime is defined differently in different states.

Ipse dixit (Latin) "He himself said it." Describes a statement that depends for its persuasiveness on the authority of the person who spoke.

Ipso facto (Latin) By the fact itself; by the mere fact that.

Ipso jure (Latin) By **operation of law** alone.

Irreconcilable differences **Grounds** for **divorce** in some states because the marriage has simply broken down. Compare **no–fault.**

Irregularity The failure to proceed properly. The failure to take the proper formal steps in the proper way while involved in a lawsuit or while doing some official act. This is not illegal, but it may invalidate what a person is trying to accomplish.

Irrelevant evidence Proposed **evidence** that will neither help prove nor help disprove any point that matters in a lawsuit.

Irreparable injury Probable harm that cannot properly be remedied by money alone and that is serious enough to justify an **injunction.**

Irresistible impulse The loss of control due to **insanity** that is so great that a person cannot stop from committing a crime.

Irrevocable Incapable of being called back, stopped, or changed. See **revocation.**

Issuable *1.* Describes a **security** that can be offered for sale legally. *2.* Can be litigated, especially referring to a legal **issue** that is stated with enough specificity to allow its **adjudication.**

Issue *1.* To send forth, put out, or **promulgate** officially. For example, when a court *issues* a **writ** or other legal paper, it gives it to a court officer to be served on (delivered to) a person. *2.* One single point in dispute between two sides in a lawsuit. An issue may be *"of law"* (a dispute about how the law applies to the case) or *"of fact"* (about the truth of a fact). *3.* Descendants (children, grandchildren, etc.). *4.* A group of stocks or bonds that are offered or sold at the same time. *5.* The first transfer of a **negotiable instrument** such as a check. *6. Issue preclusion* is either **collateral estoppel** or **res judicata**.

Itemize List by separate articles or items; break down something by listing its separate parts.

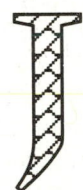

J *1.* Judge. *Johnson, J.* means Judge Johnson. *2.* Journal.

JAG Judge advocate general. See **military law.**

JD *Juris Doctor* or *Doctor of Jurisprudence*. This is now the basic law degree, replacing the LLB in the late 1960s. Many different law degrees are offered in other countries, and many advanced law degrees are offered in the United States and elsewhere.

JP Justice of the peace. A local judge.

Jactitation False boasting or false claims.

Jail A place of longer-term confinement than a police station lockup and shorter-term confinement than a

prison. It is usually to hold either persons convicted of **misdemeanors** (minor crimes) or persons who cannot get out on **bail** while awaiting trial.

Jailhouse lawyer A popular name for a prisoner who helps other prisoners with legal problems such as getting **sentences** reduced.

Jeopardy _1._ Danger; hazard; peril. _2._ The risk of **conviction** and punishment faced by a **defendant** in a criminal trial. [pronounce: jep-er-dee]

Jetsam Goods thrown off a ship, usually to lighten it in an emergency. Compare **flotsam.**

Job action A strike or work slowdown by public employees.

Jobber Either a person who buys and sells for other persons or a wholesaler.

John Doe A made-up name used in some types of lawsuits in which there is no real **defendant,** in a legal proceeding against a person whose name is not yet known, to protect a person's identity and so on, or as a name for a person in an example used to teach law.

Joinder Joining or uniting together. For example, _joinder of parties_ is the bringing in of a new person who joins together with the **plaintiff** as a plaintiff or the **defendant** as a defendant; _joinder of issue_ is when a lawsuit gets by the preliminary stages and issues are clearly laid out, with one side asserting the truth of each point and the other side asserting its falsity; _nonjoinder_ is the failure to bring in a person who is necessary as a **party** to a lawsuit; and _misjoinder_ is improper or mistaken joinder.

Joint _1._ Together; as a group; united; undivided. _2._ A _joint venture (or adventure)_ is a "one-shot" grouping of persons in a business. A continuing joint venture may be a **partnership.** _3. Joint and several_ means both together and individually. If a **liability** is *joint and several,* the **creditor** may seek repayment for the whole debt from one, some, or all of the persons responsible. *4.* A *joint estate* is property ownership by more than one person in which if one dies, the others get that share. *5. Joint lives* refers to a right that lasts only as long as all the persons in a certain group of persons live. *6.* A *joint stock company* is similar to a **corporation,** but all owners are **liable** for company debts, as in a **partnership.**

Joker A clause or phrase in a document that is superficially harmless but that destroys the document's legal effectiveness.

Journal *1.* A book that is written in regularly, such as an **account** book, in which all expenses paid and all money taken in are written down as they occur. *2.* A magazine such as a *law journal.*

Journalists' privilege **See fair comment** and **shield laws.**

Judge *1.* The person who runs a courtroom, decides all legal questions, and sometimes decides entire cases. *2.* Decide. *3.* A *judge advocate* is a military legal officer who may act as a judge or a lawyer.

Judgment *1.* The official decision of a court about the rights and claims of each side in a lawsuit. A *judgment on the merits* is a final decision based on the facts of the case and made at the end of the trial. *2.* Some other types of *judgments* include: *consent judgment* (putting a court's approval on an agreement between the sides about what the judgment should be); *default judgment* (given to one side because the other side does not show up in court or does not take proper procedural steps); and *interlocutory judgment* (given on either a preliminary or a side issue during the course of a lawsuit). *3.* A *judgment creditor* is a person who has proven a debt in court and is entitled to use court processes to collect it. The person owing the money is a _judgment debtor_. _4_. A _judgment note_ is the paper a debtor gives to a creditor to allow **confession of judgment.** _5. Judgment proof_ means that a judgment will have no effect against this person (no money, protected by wage protection laws, etc.).

Judicare Publicly financed legal services, usually free, and often allowing choice of lawyer.

Judicature Relating to the judicial branch of government; the judicial branch itself.

Judicial _1_. Having to do with a court, with a judge, or with the branch of government that interprets the law and resolves legal questions. _2. Judicial discretion_ is the right of a judge to have great leeway in making decisions so long as the law is followed and no arbitrary action is taken. _3. Judicial notice_ is the act of a judge in recognizing the existence or truth of certain facts without bothering to make one side in a lawsuit prove them. This is done when the facts are undisputed common knowledge or easily looked up. _4_. A _judicial question_ is an issue that the courts may decide, as opposed to a **political question,** which only the **executive** branch may decide, and a _legislative question,_ which only the **legislature** can decide. _5. Judicial review_ is a court's power to declare a law **unconstitutional** and to interpret state laws. The term also refers to an **appeal** from an **administrative agency.**

Judiciary The branch of government that interprets the law; the branch that judges.

Junior Describes an **interest** or right that collects after, or is subordinate to, another interest or right.

Jural *1.* Having to do with the basic law of rights and obligations. *2.* Describes legal, rather than moral, rights and obligations.

Jurat Name for the written statement on an **affidavit** about where, when, and before whom it was sworn to.

Juridical *1.* Having to do with the court system or with a judge. *2.* Regular; conforming to law and court practice.

Juris Doctor See **JD.**

Jurisdiction *1.* The geographical area within which a court (or a public official) has the right and power to operate. *2.* The persons about whom and the subject matters about which a court has the right and power to make binding decisions.

Jurisdictional *1.* Having to do with **jurisdiction.** *2.* Essential for jurisdiction. For example, the *jurisdictional amount* is the value of a claim made in a case. Some courts take only those cases that have claims above or below a certain money limit. *Jurisdictional facts* are those things a court must know before taking and keeping a case (such as whether the **defendant** has received proper **service** of court papers, etc.). *3.* A *jurisdictional dispute* is a conflict between unions either about worker representation or about which workers may do a type of work.

Jurisprudence The study of law and legal philosophy.

Jurist Either a judge or a legal scholar.

Juristic act Something done that is intended to have (and capable of having) a legal effect.

Juristic person A person for legal purposes, including both natural persons (individuals) and **artificial persons** (corporations).

Juror A person who is a member of a **jury.**

Jury _1._ A group of persons selected by law and sworn in to consider certain facts and determine the truth. The two most common types of juries are the _grand jury_ (persons who receive complaints and accusations of crime, hear preliminary evidence on the complaining side, and make formal accusations or **indictments**) and the _petit jury_ or _trial jury_ (usually twelve, but sometimes as few as six, persons who decide questions of **fact** in many trials). _2._ The _jury box_ is where the jury sits during a trial. _3._ A _jury commission_ is a committee of private citizens that picks **jurors** in some places. _4._ A _jury list_ is a list of those jurors selected to try a case, a list of all jurors commanded to be in court to be selected for various cases, or a list of all possible jurors.

Jus (Latin) _1._ Right or justice. _2._ Law, or the whole body of law. For example, _jus gentium_ is the "law of nations," or **international law.** _3._ A particular right. For example, _jus disponendi_ is the "right to dispose," or the right to do what one wants with his or her own property.

Just _1._ Legal or lawful. _2._ Morally right; fair. Words like _"just cause"_ and _"just compensation"_ include meanings #1 and #2.

Justice _1._ Fairness in treatment by the law. _2._ A judge, especially an **appellate** judge. _3._ The Department of Justice, the U.S. **cabinet** department that manages the country's legal business.

Justice of the peace One type of local judge.

Justiciable Proper to be decided by a court. For example, a _justiciable controversy_ is a real, rather than a hypothetical, dispute that a court may handle. [pronounce: jus-tish-able]

Justification A legally valid reason for an intentional action that would otherwise be unlawful. For example, **self-defense** may be *justification* to kill. Compare **excuse.**

Juvenile *1.* Not yet an adult for the purposes of the criminal law. *2.* Not yet an adult. This may be a different age than #1. *3.* A *juvenile court* is a court set up to handle cases of either **delinquent** or neglected children.

K Abbreviation for **contract.**

KB **King's Bench.**

Kangaroo court A popular expression for a mock court with no legal powers and only the power of force behind it.

Keep Carry on or manage (a hotel); tend or shelter (a dog); maintain continuously (a record book); store (a box); continue without change (a ship's course); or protect (a child).

Keogh Plan **(HR10 Plan)** A tax-free retirement account for persons with self-employment income. [pronounce: key-oh]

Key numbers A reference system that classifies legal subjects by specific topics and subtopics, with a Key number (☞) attached to each topic. Key numbers help you find cases by subject in the **American Digest System** and the **National Reporter System.**

Kicker An extra charge or penalty.

Kidnapping Taking away and holding a person illegally, usually against the person's will or by force.

Kin (or kindred)   *1.* Persons with a blood relationship. *2.* Persons with any relationship by blood or marriage.

Kind   See **in kind.**

King's Bench (or Queen's Bench)   An English court that developed most of the **common law** that has become the basis for U.S. law.

Kiting   Writing checks on an **account** before money is put in to cover them.

Knock down   An auctioneer's acceptance of a **bid** as final.

Knowingly   With full knowledge and intentionally; **willfully.**

LJ   *1.* Law Journal. *2.* Law judge.

LLB   Bachelor of Laws. Replaced by **JD** as the basic law degree in the late 1960s. *LLM* and *LLD* (masters and doctorate) are two advanced law degrees.

LR   *1. Law reports.* *2.* Law review (see **Law journal**).

LRI   Legal Resources Index.

LS   (Latin) *Locus sigilii;* "the place of the seal." These letters were once placed next to a signature to make a **contract** formally binding.

LSAT   Law School Admissions Test; "law boards."

L.Ed.   *Lawyer's Edition* of the U.S. Supreme Court Reports.

Labor contract   A **collective bargaining agreement.**

Labor dispute   A controversy between an employer and employees or between an employer and a union, involving wages, hours, working conditions, or the question of who has the right to speak for the employees.

Labor union   See **union.**

Laches   The legal doctrine that a delay (in pursuing or enforcing a claim or right) can be so long that the person against whom you are proceeding is unfairly hurt or **prejudiced** by the delay itself. This may keep you from winning. [pronounce: latch-es]

Land   Not only the surface of the earth, but also everything below and the airspace above; usually the same as property or **real estate.**

Land sales contract   A **contract** for the sale of real estate (often not recorded in the land records) in which the seller keeps **title** to the property until an agreed future time.

Land use planning   A general term that can mean **zoning** laws, real estate development and use laws, environmental impact studies, state and local master plans, etc.

Landlord   The owner of land or a building that is rented or leased to a **tenant.**

Landrum-Griffin Act   A federal law, passed in 1959, that gave several new rights to individual union members (such as the requirement that unions must have a fair **constitution**). It also changed the **Taft-Hartley Act** in several ways—some pro-union, some pro-employer. See **secondary boycott** and **hot cargo.**

Lapse   *1.* The end or failure of a right because of the neglect to enforce or use it within a time limit. *2.* The failure of a gift by **will.**

Larceny Stealing of any kind.

Last clear chance doctrine A legal principle that a person injured in (or having property harmed by) an accident may win **damages** even when **negligent** if the person causing the damage, while also negligent, could have avoided the accident after discovering the danger and if the person injured could not have. This rule is not accepted in every state and, where accepted, has many different names.

Last resort A _court of last resort_ is one from which no **appeal** is possible.

Latent _1._ Hidden; not easily discovered; the opposite of **patent.** _2._ Dormant, **passive,** or "put away." _3._ Slang for a fingerprint found in an investigation.

Lateral support The sideways support of land provided by adjoining land, and the right to such continued support.

Law _1._ That which must be obeyed. _2._ A **statute;** an act of the **legislature.** _3._ The whole body of principles, standards, and rules put out by a government. _4._ The principles, standards, and rules that apply to a particular type of situation; for example, _juvenile law. 5._ A _law day (or date)_ is a court-set day after which a **mortgagor** can no longer pay off a debt on real estate and get the land back from **foreclosure.** _6. Law French_ is the Norman French language used in the law in England for several centuries. Many words survive. _7._ A _law journal (or review)_ is a publication (usually by a law school) with articles on legal subjects such as court decisions and legislation. _8. Law Latin_ is the changed form of Latin that developed in the English courts. Many words survive. _9._ The _law merchant_ is the generally accepted customs of merchants that have standardized over the years and become a part of the formal law. *10*. For *law of nations,* see *public* **international law.** *11*. The *law of the case* is any **decision** or **ruling** in a case by a trial or **appeals** court. The *law of the case* may not usually be changed in any later phase of that same case, except by review of a higher court. Compare **res judicata.** *12*. *The law of the land* may be a rule that is in force throughout a geographical area; a country's customs that gradually become as important legally as written law; or basic ground rules of **due process** and **equal protection.** *13*. The *law of the road* is safety customs, such as "keep to the right," that have become law. *14*. *Law reform* is using a case in court to make basic changes in a law, often by bringing a **test case.** *15*. *Law reports* are published books in a series that contain the written **opinions** in cases decided by various courts. *16*. *Law Week (U.S. Law Week)* is a **loose-leaf service** with "hot off the press" news from the U.S. Supreme Court, other courts, and some **legislatures.**

Lawful   Legal; authorized by law; not forbidden by law.

Lawsuit   A **civil action.** A court proceeding to enforce a right between persons (rather than to **convict** a criminal).

Lawyer   A person licensed to practice law. Other words for *lawyer* include **attorney, counsel, solicitor,** and **barrister.**

Lay   *1*. Nonprofessional. A lawyer would call a non-lawyer a *layperson,* and a doctor would call a nondoctor a *layperson.* *2*. A *lay advocate* is a **paralegal** who specializes in representing persons in administrative **hearings.**

Laying foundation   Establishing the preliminary **evidence** needed to make later, more important evidence **relevant** and **admissible.**

Leading case   An important **case,** usually because it established a legal principle.

Leading question   A question that shows a **witness** how to answer it or suggests the preferred answer; for example, "Isn't it true that you were in Boston last week?" These questions are usually permitted on **cross** *examination,* but not on **direct examination.**

Lease   A **contract** for the use of something but not its ownership. In the case of land or buildings, the **lessor** is called the **landlord** and the **lessee** is the **tenant.**

Leaseback   A sale of property with a **lease** of the same property from the buyer back to the seller.

Leasehold   Property rights that a **tenant** has in land or buildings held by **lease.**

Least-fault divorce   **Comparative rectitude.**

Leave   *1.* Give by **will.** *2.* Permission. *Leave of court* is permission from a judge to take an action in a lawsuit that requires permission.

Ledger   A business **account** book, usually recording day-to-day transactions and usually showing **debits** and **credits.**

Legacy   *1.* A gift of money by **will.** *2.* A gift of personal property (anything but real estate) by will. *3.* Any gift by will. *4.* A *legacy tax* is a tax on the privilege of inheriting something. It may be an **inheritance tax** or a flat fee.

Legal   *1.* Required by law; permitted by law; not forbidden by law; concerning the law. The meaning is not always clear from the context. *2.* Concerning an old *court of law* as opposed to a *court of* **equity.** *3.* *Legal age* is the age at which a person becomes old enough to make contracts to which the person can be held, buy alcoholic beverages, legally consent to sexual intercourse, or perform some other action. It varies from state to state and from action to action. *4. Legal aid* provides free legal help to poor persons. *5.* For *legal assistant,* see **paralegal.** *6. Legal cap* is long legal stationery with a wide left-hand margin and a narrow right-hand margin. *7.* For *legal cause,* see **proximate cause.** *8. Legal detriment* is a **liability,** duty, or change in financial position that results from making a contract or relying on a promise. See **promissory estoppel.** *9.* A *legal entity* is a living person, a **corporation,** or any organization that can sue and be sued or otherwise function legally. *10. Legal ethics* is the study of the moral and professional duties owed by lawyers to their clients, to other lawyers, to the courts, and to the public. The subject is made concrete in the **Code of Professional Responsibility** of the **ABA.** *11.* A *legal executive* is a highly trained **paralegal** in England. *12.* For *legal fiction,* see **fiction.** *13.* For *legal investments (or list),* see **prudent person rule.** *14. Le-gal proceedings* are any actions taken in court or connected with a lawsuit. *15. Legal realism* is a philosophy of law that takes psychology, sociology, economics, politics, etc., into account to explain how legal decisions are made. *16.* A *legal representative* is a person who takes care of another person's business involving courts; legal representatives include **executors, administrators** of wills, family members entitled to bring a **wrongful death action,** etc. *17.* A *legal residence* is the place where one actually lives and intends to stay. See **domicile.** *18. The Legal Services Corporation* is the organization that runs the federally funded program of *legal aid. 19. Legal tender* is official money (dollar bills, coins, etc.). *20.* For *legal value,* see **par value, book value,** and **face** *value. 21.* For *legal worker,* see **paralegal.**

Legalese   Legal jargon or overly complicated language in laws, regulations, contracts, etc.

Legalism   *1.* A judge's adherence to the exact wording or narrowest interpretation of a law, rather than basing a decision on what would be fair or on what was probably intended by the law's passage. *2.* **Legalese.**

Legatee   A person who **inherits** something by **will.**

Legislate   To enact or pass laws. A *legislator* (person who makes laws) works in a *legislature* (lawmaking branch of government) on *legislation* (laws, **statutes, ordinances,** etc.). This work of *legislation* (considering and passing laws) is a **legislative** function.

Legislation   See **legislate.**

Legislative   *1.* Lawmaking, as opposed to **executive** (carrying out or enforcing laws) or **judicial** (interpreting or applying laws). *2. Legislative courts* are established by a **legislature** rather than by a **constitution.** *3. Legislative facts* are general facts that help an **administrative agency** to decide general questions of law and policy and to make rules. They are different from **adjudicative facts.** *4. Legislative history* is the background documents and records of **hearings** held on a **bill** as it becomes a law. *5. Legislative immunity* is the constitutional right of a member of Congress to say almost anything while performing an official function and to be free from most lawsuits based on what was said. *6.* The *legislative intent rule* is that a court should decide what the lawmakers meant or wanted when they passed a **statute** by looking at the *legislative history.* It is one of several possible ways of interpreting statutes. See #7. *7.* The *legislative purpose rule* is that a court should look at what the law was before the present statute was passed and decide by looking at the statute itself what it was trying to change. See #6.

Legislator (and Legislature)   See **Legislate.**

Legitimate   *1.* Lawful or legal. Also see **illegitimate.** *2.* Make lawful.

Lessee   A person who **leases** or rents something *from* someone. A lessee of land is a **tenant.**

Lesser (included) offense   A crime that is a part of a more serious crime, as **manslaughter** is of **murder.**

Lessor   A person who **leases** or rents something *to* someone. A lessor of land is a **landlord.**

Let   *1.* **Award** a contract (such as for construction work) to one of several bidders. *2.* Lease.

Letter   *1.* The strict, precise, literal meaning of a document. The exact language (of, for example, a **statute**) rather than the spirit or broad purpose. *2.* A formal document. *3.* A *letter of attorney* is a document giving a **power of attorney.** *4.* A *letter of credit* is a written statement by a bank or other financer that it will back up or pay the financial obligations of a merchant involved in a particular sale. It is sometimes a **negotiable instrument.** *5.* A *letter of intent* is a preliminary written understanding that is meant to be the basis for a **contract.** *6.* A *letter ruling* is a written answer by the **IRS** to a taxpayer about how the tax laws apply to a specific set of facts.

Letters   *1.* Formal, written permission to do something. *2.* *Letters of administration (or letters testamentary)* are court papers allowing a person to take charge of the property of a dead person in order to distribute it. *3.* For *letters of marque and reprisal,* see **marque.** *4.* *Letters rogatory* are a request made by one court to another in a different **jurisdiction** that a **witness** answer the **interrogatories** sent with the letter.

Leverage   *1.* The power of a small amount of money to buy things of far greater value through borrowing. *2.* Any borrowing to buy an asset.

Levy *1.* To **assess,** raise, or collect; for example, to *levy a tax* is to either **pass** one in the **legislature** or collect one. *2.* To seize or collect; for example, to *levy on a debtor's property* is to put it aside by court **order** to pay **creditors.** *3.* The **assessment** or seizure itself in #1 or #2.

Lex *1.* (Latin) Law (or a collection or body of laws). For example, *lex mercatoria* is the **law merchant.** *2. Lex loci* is the "law of the place." For example, *lex loci delictus* is the law of the place where the crime took place. These words may be abbreviated without the "*loci.*" *3. Lex fori* is the law of the forum (court); it is the law of the state or country where the case is decided. **Conflict of laws** rules help a judge choose between *lex fori* and *lex loci* (#2).

Lexis A computerized legal research source.

Leze majesty (Law French) **Treason** or rebellion.

Liability A broad word for legal obligation, responsibility, or debt.

Liable Responsible for something (such as harm done to another person); bound by law; having a duty or obligation enforceable in court by another person. *Not* **libel.**

Libel *1.* Written **defamation;** published, false written statements that injure a person's reputation. *2.* Formerly the name for the **complaint** in an admiralty (maritime or ocean-ship) court; sometimes still a specialized type of **complaint,** such as a *divorce libel. 3. Not* **liable.**

Libelant **Plaintiff.**

Libelous Defamatory; tending to injure a reputation.

Liberty *1.* Freedom from illegal personal restraint. *2.* Personal rights under law.

License *1.* Formal permission to do something specific; for example, a state driver's license. *2.* Acting without any legal restraint; disregarding the law entirely.

Licensee *1*. A person who holds a **license.** *2*. A person who is on property with permission but without any enticement by the owner and with no financial advantage to the owner. In **negligence** law, an invited personal guest may be a *licensee* rather than an **invitee** in many situations.

Licentiousness *1*. Doing what one wants with total disregard for ethics, law, or others' rights. *2*. Moral and sexual impurity.

Lien *1*. A claim against specific property that can be enforced in court to secure payment of a **judgment,** duty, or debt. *Lien* is sometimes defined to *exclude* claims due to contracts or mortgages. A *mechanic's lien* is the right of a worker to hold property worked on until the worker is paid for the service. *2*. For *lien creditor,* see **secured creditor.** *3*. A *lien theory state* is a state in which a **mortgage** is considered a **lien** on property, and the **title** does not transfer to the lender. [pronounce: leen]

Lieu (French) *In lieu of* means *instead of.*

Life estate (or interest or tenancy) An ownership interest in property (an **estate**) that lasts until a named person or persons die.

Life in being The lifetime of a specific person already born, or the lifetime of a person who *will* be alive when a **deed** or **will** takes effect.

Lift Remove an obstacle or obligation; stop the effect of something, such as a court **order.**

Limine See **in limine.**

Limitation *1*. A restriction. *2*. A time limit. For example, a *statute of limitations* is a law that sets a maximum amount of time after something happens for it to be taken to court, such as a "three-year statute" for lawsuits based on a *breach of contract*. *3*. *Limitation* of a **case** is a judge's refusal to apply the rule that decided it to deciding another case.

Limited   *1.* Partial or restricted.   *2.* For *limited divorce,* see *legal* **separation.**   *3.* A *limited partnership* is a special form of unincorporated business association, available under state laws, that allows the business to be run by *general partners* and financed partly by *limited partners,* who may take no part in running the business and have no liability for business losses, lawsuits, and so on, beyond the money they put in or promise to put in. This is similar to the *limited liability* of a corporation's shareholders. *4.* "Limited" (*Ltd.*) is the British word for *incorporated.*

Lindberg Act   A federal law prohibiting the transportation of a kidnapped person across a state line.

Line of credit   The promise to lend money up to a maximum, usually for an ongoing series of transactions.

Line of descent   A **direct** *line of descent* includes grandparents, parents, children, etc., and a **collateral** *line of descent* includes brothers, aunts, nieces, etc.

Lineal   In a line; in a direct **line of descent.**

Liquid   *1.* Having enough money to carry on a normal business. *2.* Easily turned into cash. *3.* A company's ability to carry on business or to turn **assets** into cash is called *liquidity.*

Liquidate   *1.* Pay off or settle a debt. *2.* **Adjust** or settle the *amount* of a debt. *3.* Settle up affairs and distribute money, such as that of a dead person or an out-of-business company. *4.* Processes #1, #2, and #3 are *liquidations.*

Lis pendens (Latin)   *1.* A pending lawsuit. *2.* A warning notice that **title** to property is in **litigation** and that anyone who buys it gets it with legal "strings attached."

Listing   A **real estate** agent's right to sell **land.** An *open* (or *general*) *listing* is the right to sell that may be given to more than one agent at a time. An *exclusive agency listing* is the right of one agent to be the only one other than the owner who may sell the property during a period of time. An *exclusive authorization to sell listing* is a written **contract** that gives one agent the sole right to sell the property during a time period. This means that even if the owner finds the buyer, the agent gets a **commission.** *Multiple listing* occurs when an agent with an exclusive (or exclusive agency) listing shares information about the property with many members of a real estate association and agrees to share the sales commission with the agent who finds the buyer. A *net listing* is an arrangement in which the seller sets a minimum price he or she will take for the property, and the agent's commission is the amount the property sells for over that price.

Literary property   A written work, such as a novel or screenplay, protected by **copyright.**

Litigant   A **plaintiff** or **defendant** in a lawsuit.

Litigate   *1.* Actively carry on a lawsuit. *2.* Carry on the **trial** part of a lawsuit.

Litigation   A lawsuit or series of lawsuits.

Litigious   *1.* Prone to bringing lawsuits; bringing too many lawsuits. *2.* Disputable; subject to disagreement.

Littoral   Having to do with a shore, bank, or side of a body of water.

Livery   An old word for the formal transfer and either actual or symbolic delivery of something, especially land.

Living trust   See **inter vivos** *trust.*

Loan shark   A person who lends money at an interest rate higher than the legal maximum or who uses **extortion** to force repayment.

Lobbying Attempting to persuade a **legislator** either to vote a certain way on a **bill** or to introduce a bill.

Local _1_. A _local action_ is a lawsuit that may be brought in only one place. _2_. A _local agent_ is a state-required company representative who must **register** to accept **service** of **process** for lawsuits against the company. _3_. A _local assessment_ is a tax on only those properties benefiting from an improvement, such as a sidewalk.

Locative calls The description of land in a **deed** or other document by using landmarks, physical objects, etc.

Lockout An employer's refusal to allow employees to work. It is a tactic in an employer-union dispute.

Loco parentis See **in loco parentis.**

Locus (Latin) _1_. "Place." For example, _locus contractus_ means "the place where the contract was made." See also **lex** _loci_. _2_. See **LS.**

Lodger A person who pays to live in part of a dwelling managed by another person and who does not have total control over those rooms.

Logging in Recording the names of persons as these persons are brought to a police station. It may be combined with **booking.**

Long-arm statute A state law that allows the courts of that state to claim **jurisdiction** over (decide cases directly involving) persons outside the state if the person has certain _minimum contacts_ with the state.

Loophole _1_. A technical way to avoid the intent or main thrust of a law or contract. _2_. Someone else's way of legally avoiding taxes. (See **deduction, credit, exclusion,** etc., for _your_ way.)

Loose-leaf service A set of books in loose-leaf binders that gives up-to-the-minute reports on one area of the law, such as federal taxes. As the law changes, new pages replace old ones.

Loss A broad word that can mean anything from *total loss* (dropping a coin accidently in the ocean) through *partial loss* (a drop in the value of a **stock**) to *technical loss* ("loss of an eye" might mean "not able to see well enough to work." In general, the legal use of the word is close to its ordinary use.

Lot *1.* An individual piece of land. *2.* A thing or group of things that is part of one separate sale or delivery.

Ltd. Limited.

Lucrative title An old phrase for rights to property received by gift or **inheritance.**

Lump-sum settlement *1.* Payment of an entire amount of owed money at one time rather than in installments. Such settlement may be far less than the entire amount owed or in dispute. *2.* Payment of a fixed amount of money to take care of a continuing obligation that might otherwise have gone on forever. For example, *lump-sum alimony* might be a payment of one large sum to avoid the possibility of having to pay a changeable, potentially greater, amount of money on a regular basis for a long time.

Lunacy See **insanity.**

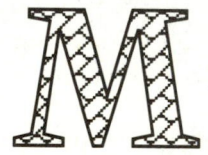

MD Middle **district.**

MJ Military Justice Reporter.

Magistracy A broad term ranging from all public officials, through all judges, to judges of limited **jurisdiction** only.

Magistrate   A judge, usually with limited functions and powers.

Magna Charta   A document, signed by the English king in 1215, that defined and gave some individuals many basic personal, property, and religious rights for the first time.

Magnuson-Moss Act   A federal law that set standards for **warranties** on **consumer** products.

Mail-order divorce   A **divorce,** not valid in the United States, granted by a country in which neither person lives nor has traveled to for the divorce.

Mailbox rule   The rule that when the practice is reasonable, *sending* (not receipt of) an **acceptance** of an **offer** forms a valid **contract.**

Maintenance   *1.* Carrying on; keeping from **lapse** or failure; doing repeatedly. *2.* Meddling with a lawsuit that does not concern you; for example, by paying a person to continue a lawsuit he or she would have dropped. See also **champerty.** *3.* Supplying the necessities of life. See also **separate maintenance**.

Majority   *1.* Full legal age to manage your own affairs. *2.* More than half.

Make whole   Put a person who has suffered a loss due to another's wrong back into the financial position he or she was in before the wrong was done.

Maker   A person who initially signs a **negotiable instrument,** such as a **note,** and by doing so promises to pay on it.

Mala fides   (Latin) Bad faith. [pronounce: mal-a feed-eze]

Mala in se (or prohibitum)   See **malum in se (or prohibitum).**

Malfeasance   Wrongdoing, especially a public official doing something illegal.

Malice   *1.* Ill will. *2.* Having no moral or legal justification for intentionally harming someone. *3.* *Malice* *aforethought* is an intention to seriously harm someone or to commit a serious crime. *4.* In **defamation** law, knowledge of falsity or reckless disregard for whether or not something is false.

Malicious mischief The crime of intentionally destroying another person's property.

Malicious prosecution Bringing unjustified criminal charges to harm someone. This is a **tort.**

Malpractice Professional misconduct or unreasonable lack of professional skill.

Malum in se (Latin) "Wrong in and of itself"; morally wrong; describes **common-***law* crimes.

Malum prohibitum (Latin) "Prohibited wrongs"; describes **statutory** crimes.

Mandamus (Latin) "We command." A court **order** that tells a public official or government department to do something. It may be sent to the **executive** branch, **legislative** branch, or a lower court. [pronounce: man-<u>day</u>-mus]

Mandate *1.* A judicial command to act; see **mandamus.** *2.* An authorization to act. *3.* Require. See **mandatory.**

<u>Mandatory</u> Required; must be followed or obeyed. *Mandatory authority* is **binding authority.**

Mann Act A federal law prohibiting the transport of women across state lines for immoral purposes, usually prostitution.

Manslaughter An unlawful killing without **malice.** It is a crime less severe than **murder.**

Marbury v. Madison The **Supreme Court** case that established the courts' right of **judicial review** of acts of Congress.

Margin *1.* A boundary or boundary line. *2.* The percentage of the cost of a stock (or other **security**) that a buyer must pay in cash. _3_. For _marginal rate_, see **tax** _rate_.

Marital _1_. Having to do with a marriage. _2_. The _marital deduction_ is the amount of money a wife or husband can inherit from the other without paying **estate** or gift taxes. _3_. The _marital communications privilege_ is either the right of a husband and wife to keep some things secret between them or the right of a husband or wife to keep the other from testifying against him or her in some criminal trials.

Maritime law   The law of ships, sailors, and ocean commerce.

Market price   _1_. The price at which something has just sold in a particular market. _2_. **Market value**.

Market value   The price to which a willing seller and a willing buyer would agree for an item in the ordinary course of trade. It has many other names, such as "actual value," "clear value," "fair market value," "just compensation," etc.

Marketable   _1_. Easily sold for cash. _2_. Commercially valid; for example, _marketable title_ to land is ownership that can be freely sold because the ownership is clear of any reasonable doubt.

Markup   The meeting in which a **committee** of a **legislature** goes through a **bill** section by section to revise and finalize it.

Marque and reprisal   The request made to the ruler of one country to seize the citizens or goods of another country until some wrong done by that country is righted.

Marshal   A person employed by a federal court to keep the peace, deliver legal orders, and perform duties similar to those of a state **sheriff**.

Marshaling   Arranging, ranking, or disposing of things in order. For example, _marshaling assets and_ *claims* is collecting them up and arranging the debts into proper order of priority and then dividing up the assets to pay them off.

Martial law Government by the military; control of the domestic civilian population by the military in wartime or during a breakdown of civilian control. [pronounce: <u>mar</u>-shal]

Martindale-Hubbell A set of books that lists many lawyers by location and type of practice. Other volumes contain summaries of each major area of the law in each state and most foreign countries.

Massachusetts trust A **business trust.**

Master *1.* An employer who has the right to control the actions of employees. *2.* A person appointed by a court to carry out the court's **orders,** such as sales of property or information gathering. *3.* Overall or controlling; for example, a city might have a *master plan* coordinating housing, business, zoning, etc.

Material *1.* Important; probably necessary; having effect; going to the heart of the matter. *2.* A *material allegation* in a **pleading** is a statement that is essential to the legal effect of the **claim** or **defense** being used. *3.* A *material* **fact** is either a basic reason for a contract, without which it would not have been entered into, or a fact that is central to winning or deciding a case. *4.* A *material issue* is a question that is formally in dispute between persons properly brought before the court and that is important in determining the outcome of the lawsuit. *5.* A *material witness* is a person who can give **testimony** no one else can give. A *material witness* may sometimes be held by the government against his or her will in an important criminal case.

Materialman Supplier. A person who supplies building materials for a construction or repair project.

Matter *1.* A central, necessary, or important fact. *2.* An event, occurrence, or transaction. *3.* The subject of a lawsuit. *4.* See **in re.** *5.* A *matter of fact* is a question that can be answered by using the senses or deduced from **testimony** or other **evidence.** *6.* A *matter of law* is a question that can be answered by applying the law to the facts of the case. *7.* A *matter of record* is anything that can be proved by merely checking a court record; sometimes, the word is broadened to include anything that can be proved by checking any official record.

Maturity The time when a debt or other obligation becomes due or a right becomes enforceable.

Maxim A general statement about the law that works when applied to most cases.

Mayhem The crime of violently, maliciously, and intentionally giving someone a serious permanent wound.

Mechanic's lien A worker's legal claim to hold property (such as a car) until repair charges are paid or to file formal papers securing a right to property (such as a car or house) until charges for work done are paid.

Mediation Outside help in settling a dispute. The person who does this is a *mediator.* A mediator can only persuade, not force a settlement. Compare **arbitration.**

Medical examiner A public official who investigates violent or unexplained deaths, performs autopsies, and helps prosecute homicide cases. Compare **coroner.**

Meeting of minds Agreement among all persons entering into a deal on the basic meaning and legal effect of the **contract.**

Membership corporation A nonprofit, non**stock** corporation created for social, charitable, political, or other similar purposes.

Memorandum *1.* An informal note; a written summary of a meeting or **contract.** *2.* A written document proving that a contract exists. *3.* A **brief** of law submitted to a judge. *4.* A *memorandum decision* is a court's decision that gives the **ruling** (what it decides and orders done) but no **opinion** (reasons).

Mens rea (Latin) "Guilty mind"; wrongful purpose; criminal intent. A state of mind that, when combined with an **actus** *reus,* produces a crime.

Mensa et thoro See **a mensa et thoro.**

Mental cruelty See **cruelty.**

Mercantile Commercial; having to do with buying and selling.

Merchantable Fit to be sold; of the general type and quality described and fit for the general purpose for which bought.

Merger *1.* The union of two or more things, usually with the smaller or less important thing ceasing to exist once it is a part of the other. Companies, rights, contracts, etc., can *merge.* *2.* A *merger clause* in a contract may end all prior oral agreements by making the written contract the entire agreement.

Merits *1.* The central part of a case; the "meat" of one side's legal position. *2.* The substance or real issues of a lawsuit, as opposed to the form or the legal technicalities it involves. *3.* See **judgment** for *judgment on the merits.*

Mesne Middle; intermediate. For example, *mesne process* includes the legal papers and court **orders** *in between* the start and end of a lawsuit. [pronounce: men]

Metes and bounds Boundary lines and fixed points and angles used to describe and measure the perimeter of land.

Military law The law that **regulates** the armed forces and its members. It is contained in the **Code of Mil-**

itary Justice,** administered by a **judge** *advocate general* of each service, and decided by a system of *military courts,* primarily **courts-martial.**

Mind and memory A phrase describing adequate mental **capacity** to make a **will** (knowledge of what you are doing, what you are giving away, and to whom).

Mineral right A right either to take minerals out of the ground or to receive payment for minerals taken out.

Ministerial *1.* Done by carrying out orders rather than by personally deciding how to act. In this sense, a police *chief's* actions would be "discretionary" and a police *officer's* "ministerial." But see #2. *2.* Done by carrying out a general policy (whether or not there is much choice of action) rather than by setting or making **policy.** In this sense, a police *chief's* actions would be "ministerial" and the police *board's* "discretionary." But see #1.

Minor *1.* A person who is under the age of full legal rights and responsibilities. *2.* Less or lower.

Minority opinion **Dissent**ing opinion.

Minute book The record kept by the **clerk** of some courts that lists a summary of all **orders** by case and case number.

Miranda warning The warning that must be given to a person **arrested** or taken into **custody** by a police officer or other official. It includes the fact that what the person arrested says may be held against him or her and informs the person of the rights to remain silent, to contact a lawyer, and to have a free lawyer if the person arrested is poor.

Misadventure An accident or unintentional injury, often with no one legally at fault.

Misappropriation Taking something wrongfully but not necessarily illegally.

Miscarriage of justice Unfair harm done to a person by legal proceeding or other official action.

Misconduct **Malfeasance, misfeasance,** or **nonfeasance.**

Misdemeanor A criminal offense less serious than a **felony** that is usually punishable by a fine or less than a year in jail.

Misfeasance The improper doing of an otherwise proper or lawful act.

Misfortune An accident that could not be guarded against.

Misjoinder See **joinder.**

Misprision The failure to carry out a public duty, such as to report a crime or to properly carry out a high public office.

Misrepresentation A false statement. It is *innocent misrepresentation* if not known to be false, *negligent misrepresentation* if the person should have known better, and *fraudulent misrepresentation* if meant to be misleading.

Mistake An unintentional error or act. A *mistake of fact* is a mistake about facts that is not caused by a **negligent** failure to find out the truth. A *mistake of law* is knowledge of the true facts combined with a wrong conclusion about the legal effect of the facts.

Mistrial A trial that the judge ends and declares will have no legal effect because of a major defect in procedure or because of the death of a **juror,** a deadlocked jury, or other major problem.

Mitigating circumstances Facts that do not justify or **excuse** an action but that can lower the amount of moral blame and thus lower the **criminal penalty** or **civil damages** for the action.

Mitigation of damages *1.* Facts showing that the size of a claim for **damages** is unjustified. *2.* The principle that a person suing for **damages** must have taken reasonable steps to minimize the harm done, or the amount of money awarded will be lowered.

Mittimus   The name for a court **order** sending a convicted person to prison or transferring records from one court to another.

Mixed question   A legal question involving both **fact** and **law** or involving both **local** and **foreign** law.

M'Naghten rule   A person is "not guilty because of **insanity**" if, at the time of the offense, "a defect of reason produced by a disease of the mind" caused the person to "not know the nature of the act" or to "not know right from wrong." One of many different definitions of insanity used to determine whether a person will be held criminally responsible for an act.

Model acts   Proposed laws put out by the National Conference of Commissioners on Uniform State Laws (but not those proposed as **uniform acts**); for example, the _Model Public Defender Act_.

Money market   The institutions that deal with short-term loans and near-term fund transfers.

Money-purchase plan   A pension plan in which an employer contributes a fixed amount each year. The ultimate value of the **benefits** paid will vary, depending on investment earnings.

Monition   A judge's order or warning.

Monopoly   Control by one or a few companies of the manufacture, sale, distribution, or price of something.

Moot   _Moot_ has conflicting and overlapping definitions: _1._ No longer important or no longer needing a decision because _already decided_. A federal court will not take a case if it is _moot_ in this sense. _2._ For the sake of argument or practice. _Moot court_ is a practice court for law students. *3.* Abstract. Not a real case involving a real dispute. *4.* A subject for argument; undecided; unsettled.

Moral <u>tur</u>pitude Describes any crime, such as **larceny,** that involves immorality or dishonesty.

Mora<u>to</u>rium A deliberate delay or suspension, usually enforced.

Mortgage The putting up of land or buildings (or, in the case of a **chattel mortgage,** personal **property**) in exchange for a loan. The property is **collateral** for repayment of the loan. A mortgage usually takes one of three forms: (1) The ownership of the property actually transfers in whole or part to the *mortgagee* (lender). (2) The ownership stays with the *mortgagor* (borrower), and the mortgage has the same effect as a **lien.** (3) The property is put into a **trust** with an independent person until the debt is paid off.

Mortmain statutes Laws, now mostly invalidated, that limit deathbed gifts to charity.

Most favored nation An agreement between two countries that each will treat the other as well as the country it treats best.

Motion A request that a judge make a ruling or take some other action. For example, a *motion to dismiss* is a request that the judge throw the case out.

Motive The reason *why* a person does something. *Not* **intent.**

Mouthpiece Slang for lawyer.

Movables Personal **property.**

Movant Person who makes a **motion.**

Move Make a **motion.**

Mugshot A picture taken during a police **booking.**

Multifariousness Several unconnected claims combined in one lawsuit or several unconnected subjects combined in one legislative **bill.**

Multilateral Among several persons, companies, or governments.

Multiple listing See **listing.**

Multiplicity of actions Two or more lawsuits against the same defendant about the same issues. The suits should usually be combined into one.

Municipal Having to do with a government, usually with a local government. For example, a *municipal corporation* (or *municipality*) is a local government that has been set up according to state requirements. Abbreviated Mun.

Muniments Documents such as **deeds** that are **evidence** of **title.**

Murder The unlawful killing of another human being that is premeditated (planned) or is done with **malice aforethought.**

Mutatis mutandis (Latin) With necessary changes in detail.

Mutilation *1.* Cutting, tearing, erasing, or changing a document in a way that changes or destroys its legal effect. *2.* **Mayhem.**

Mutual *1.* Done together; **reciprocal.** *2.* A *mutual company's* customers are also its owners who get the profits. *3.* A *mutual fund* is an investment company that sells its own **shares** to the public, pools its investors' money, and buys shares of stock in many other companies. *4.* A *mutual mistake* is a mistake, made by both sides in a contract, about a subject that was important to both in their decisions to make the deal. A mutual mistake may make a contract **voidable.**

Mutuality of contract (or obligation)   The principle that each side must do something, or promise to do something, to make a **contract** binding and valid.

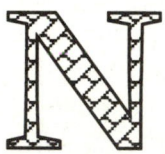

NA   Nonacquiescence; not allowed; not available; not applicable; etc.

NALA   National Association of Legal Assistants.

NALS   National Association of Legal Secretaries.

NB   (Latin) *Nota bene.* Mark well; note well; pay special attention to.

NCD   (Latin) *Nemine contra dicente.* No one dissenting.

ND   Northern **district.**

NE   North Eastern Reporter (see **National Reporter System**).

NLADA   National Legal Aid and Defender Association.

NLRB   National Labor Relations Board. A federal agency that **regulates** labor-management activities such as **collective bargaining,** union elections, **unfair labor practices,** etc.

NOV   **Non obstante veredicto.**

NOW   *Negotiable order of withdrawal.* A type of interest-paying checking account.

NP   **Notary public.**

NR   New reports; not reported; nonresident; etc.

NS   New series.

Naked   Incomplete; without force; unjustified.

National Labor Relations Act   A combination of the **Wagner, Taft-Hartley,** and **Landrum-Griffin** Acts.

National Reporter System   A system of sets of books that collects all cases from state supreme courts and other courts by region. (For example, the North Eastern Reporter covers Illinois, Indiana, Massachusetts, New York (Court of Appeals only), and Ohio. It is abbreviated *N.E.*, with a series number such as *N.E.2d* for "second series.") The Reporter System also has sets for all federal cases, some lower court cases state by state, and a **digest** for each region. It has become the official place for some states to publish their decisions.

Nationality   The country of which a person is a citizen (but some persons, such as residents of a U.S. *territory,* may be U.S. *nationals* but not citizens).

Natural   *1. Natural affection* is love or family ties between persons directly related (parent-child, husband-wife, sister-brother). This alone may be **consideration** for a contract. *2.* A *natural heir* can mean a child, close relative, or anyone who would **inherit** if there were no will. *3. Natural law* is either the rules of conduct that are thought to be the same everywhere because they are basic to human behavior, or basic moral law. *4.* A *natural object* is a person who would have inherited property given in a **will** even if there were no will.

Naturalization   Becoming a **citizen** of a country.

Ne exeat   (Latin) "Do not leave." A court paper forbidding a person from leaving the area.

Necessary (or necessity)   *1.* Physically, logically, or legally required. *2.* Appropriate or helpful.

Neglect *1.* See **negligence.** *2.* Lack of proper care for a child.

Negligence The failure to exercise a reasonable amount of **care** in a situation that causes harm to someone or something. It can involve doing something carelessly or failing to do something that should have been done. Negligence can vary in seriousness from **criminal** (so extreme that it turns noncriminal conduct into a crime) through **gross** (recklessness or willfulness), *ordinary* (failing to act as a reasonably careful person would), and *slight.*

Negotiable instrument A signed document that contains an unconditional promise to pay an exact sum of money, either when demanded or at an exact future time. Further, it must be marked **payable** "to the **order** of" a specific person or payable "to **bearer**" (the person who happens to have it). *Negotiable instruments* include **checks, notes,** and *bills of exchange.* A whole branch of law concerns this area, which has a special vocabulary of ordinary sounding words (such as **"holder"**) that have specialized meanings. You can, however, understand a lot about negotiable instruments by looking at what is printed on a check, thinking about the reasons for each phrase or blank, and reading the bank's rules for cashing the check.

Negotiate *1.* Discuss, arrange, or bargain about a business deal or discuss a compromise to a situation. *2.* Transfer a **negotiable instrument** from one person to another.

Nemo (Latin) No one; no person.

Net The amount remaining after subtractions. For example, *net assets (or net worth)* are what is left after subtracting what a person owes from what he or she has.

Next friend A person who acts formally in court for a child without being the child's legal **guardian.**

Next of kin Either persons most closely related to a dead person or all persons entitled to **inherit** from a person who has not left a **will.**

Nice question A question that is hard to decide.

Nihil (or nil) (Latin) Nothing.

Nineteenth Amendment The U.S. **constitutional** amendment that gave women the right to vote.

Ninth Amendment See **Bill of Rights.**

Nisi *1.* (Latin) "Unless." A judge's **rule, order,** or **decree** that will take effect *unless* the person against whom it is issued comes to court to "show cause" why it should not take effect. *2. Nisi prius,* in U.S. law, describes a **trial** court. [pronounce: ni-si pri-us]

No contest *1.* See **nolo contendere.** *2.* For *no contest clause,* see **in terrorem.**

No-fault *1.* A type of automobile **insurance,** required by some states, in which each person's own insurance company pays for injury or damage up to a certain limit no matter whose fault it is. *2.* A *no-fault divorce,* available in most states, is granted upon proof that a husband and wife have lived apart without marital relations for a period of time, usually six months or one year.

Nolle prosequi (Latin) The ending of a criminal case because the **prosecutor** decides or agrees to stop prosecuting. When this happens, the case is "*nollied,*" "*nolled,*" or "*nol. prossed.*" (This is *not* **nolo contendere** or **non prosequitur.**)

Nolo contendere (Latin) "I will not contest it." A **defendant's plea** of "*no contest*" in a **criminal** case. It means that he or she does not directly admit guilt but submits to sentencing or other punishment. (This is *not* **nolle prosequi** or **non prosequitur.**)

Nominal In name only; not real; slight; token.

Nominee A person chosen as another person's representative.

Non compos mentis (Latin) "Not of sound mind." This includes idiocy, **insanity,** severe drunkenness, etc.

Non obstante veredicto (Latin) "Not withstanding the verdict." A judge's giving **judgment** (victory) to one side in a lawsuit even though the jury gave a **verdict** (victory) to the other side.

Non prosequitur (or non pros.) (Latin) "He does not follow up." Describes a **judgment** given to a **defendant** because the **plaintiff** has stopped carrying on the case. This is now usually replaced by a **motion** *to dismiss* or by a **default** *judgment.* (This is *not* **nolle prosequi** or **nolo contendere.**)

Non sui juris (Latin) "Not of his own law or right." Describes a **minor,** an insane person, etc.

Non vult contendere **Nolo contendere.**

Nonage Not yet of legal age; still a **minor.**

Nonconforming 1. *Nonconforming goods* are goods that fail to meet **contract** specifications. *2.* A *nonconforming lot* is a piece of land with a size or shape that would not be permitted by current **zoning** laws. *3.* A *nonconforming use* is the use of a piece of land that is permitted, even though that type of use is not usually permitted in that area by the zoning laws. This can happen because the use (building size, etc.,) existed before the zoning law or because a **variance** was granted.

Noncontestable clause An insurance policy provision that prohibits the insurance company from refusing (on the basis that there was a **mistake** or **fraud** in the insurance application) to pay a claim if a certain amount of time has passed since the application was made.

Nonfeasance   The failure to perform a required duty, especially by a public official.

Nonrecourse loan   Any loan for which the borrower is not *personally* **liable** and for which the lender may only take and sell the **collateral** (if any) if the loan is not repaid.

Nonsuit   The ending of a lawsuit because the **plaintiff** has failed to take a necessary step or accomplish a necessary action. In most places, this is now a **dismissal,** a **default judgment,** or a **directed verdict.**

Norris-La Guardia Act   A 1932 federal law to prevent many types of **injunctions** against strikers and to prohibit **yellow dog contracts.**

Notary public   A person given power by a state to administer **oaths,** to certify the authenticity of signatures, to witness wills, and so on within the state.

Note   See **promissory note.**

Notes of decisions   References to cases that discuss the laws printed in an **annotated statutes** book.

Notice   *1.* Knowledge of certain facts. See also **constructive notice.** *2.* Formal receipt of the knowledge of certain facts. This may be by delivery (*personal*) or delivery to an **agent (imputed).** *3.* For *notice* laws in real estate, see **recording acts.** *4.* A *notice to quit* is the written notice from a landlord to a tenant that the tenant will have to move.

Novation   The substitution by agreement of a new **contract** for an old one, with all the rights under the old one ended. The new contract is often the same as the old one, except that one or more of the **parties** is different.

Nude   Lacking something basic to be legally valid.

Nudum pactum (Latin) "Nude pact" or bare agreement. A promise or action without any **consideration** (payment or promise of something of value) other than good will or affection. [pronounce: <u>new</u>-dum <u>pack</u>-tum]

<u>**Nugatory**</u> Invalid; without force or effect.

Nuisance Anything that annoys or disturbs unreasonably, hurts a person's use of his or her property, or violates the public health, safety, or decency. A *nuisance* may be subject to private lawsuit or public prosecution.

Null No longer having any legal effect or validity.

Nunc pro tunc (Latin) "Now for then." Describes something done "now" that has the same effect as if done "then," so it has retroactive effect. For example, a judge may issue an **order** to have legal effect that starts at an earlier date, in effect *backdating* it.

<u>**Nuncupative will**</u> An oral **will.** It is valid in a few states.

OMB The U.S. Office of Management and Budget.

OPM The U.S. Office of Personnel Management.

OR Short for "own recognizance" (see **recognizance**).

OSHA The U.S. Occupational Safety and Health Administration.

Oath A formal swearing that you will tell the truth or that you will do something.

Obiter dictum   See **dictum.**

Object   *1.* Purpose. *2.* Claim that an action by your adversary in a lawsuit (such as the use of a particular piece of **evidence**) is improper, unfair, or illegal, and ask the judge for a **ruling** on the point. *3.* Formally state a disagreement with a judge's ruling, usually to preserve a right to **appeal** based on that ruling.

Obligation   A broad word that can mean any **duty,** any legal duty, a duty imposed by **contract,** a formal written promise to pay money, a duty owed to the government, a tax owed, etc.

Obligee   A person to whom a **duty** is owed.

Obligor   A person who owes a **duty** to another person.

Obliteration   Erasing, lining out, or writing over words.

Oblivion   An act of forgiving and forgetting, such as granting a **pardon.**

Obscene   Lewd and offensive to accepted standards of decency.

Obstructing justice   Interfering by words or actions with the proper working of courts or court officials; for example, trying to keep a **witness** from appearing in court.

Occupancy   Physical possession of land or buildings, either with or without legal right or **title.**

Of counsel   *1.* A person employed as a lawyer in a case. *2.* A lawyer who helps a primary lawyer in a case. *3.* A lawyer who advises a law firm or is a temporary member.

Of course   As a matter of right. Actions that a person may take in a lawsuit, either without asking the judge's permission or by asking and getting automatic approval.

Of record Entered on the proper formal records. For example, *counsel of record* is the lawyer whose name appears on the court's records as the lawyer in a case.

Off Postponed indefinitely.

Offense A **felony, misdemeanor,** or other violation of the law.

Offer *1.* To make a proposal; to present for acceptance or rejection. An *offer* in **contract** law is a proposal to make a deal. It must be communicated from the person making it to the person to whom it is made, and it must be definite and reasonably certain in its terms. *2.* To attempt to have something admitted into **evidence** in a trial; to introduce evidence.

Officer of the court *1.* A **judge, clerk, sheriff, marshal, bailiff, constable,** or other court employee. *2.* Lawyers are also *officers of the court* and must obey court rules, be truthful in court, and generally serve the needs of justice.

Official notice The same as **judicial notice,** but for an **administrative agency,** not a judge.

Offset Any claim or demand made to lessen or cancel another claim. When done in a lawsuit, it may be a **setoff,** a **counterclaim,** or a **recoupment.**

Olograph **Holograph.**

Ombudsman (Swedish) A person who acts as the government's "complaint bureau" and who has the power to investigate official misconduct, help fix wrongs done by the government, and, sometimes, prosecute wrongdoers.

Omnibus (Latin) *1.* Containing two or more separate and independent things. For example, an *omnibus bill* is a legislative **bill** concerning two or more entirely different subjects. *2.* An *omnibus clause* is a provision of a **will** that gives out all property not specifically mentioned.

Omnis (or omne, omni, omnia, etc.)   (Latin) "All"; as in the phrase "*omnis definitio in lege periculosa*" (all legal definitions are dangerous).

On account   As part payment for something bought or owed.

On all fours   See **all fours.**

On demand (or on call)   Payable immediately when requested.

On or about   Approximately. A phrase used to avoid being bound to an exact date.

On point   A law or prior case is *on point* if it directly applies to the facts of the present case.

On the merits   See **merits.**

One   A useless word when put in front of a word that needs no number; for example, "one Marcie Evans testified that. . ."

Onerous   *1.* Unreasonably burdensome. *2.* In exchange for something (not a U.S. use of the word).

Onus probandi   **Burden of proof.**

Open   *1.* Begin; make visible or available; visible or apparent; remove restrictions; with no limit as to time or amount; etc. *2.* To *open a judgment* is to keep a **judgment** from going into effect until a court can reexamine it. *3.* An *open bid* is an offer to do work or supply materials that reserves the right to lower the bid to meet the competition. *4.* For *open listing,* see **listing.** *5.* An *open mortgage* is a **mortgage** that can be paid off without penalty at any time. (See also #9.) *6.* An *open price term* is an unspecified price in a contract. *7.* An *open shop* is a business where non-union persons may work. *8.* An *open-end contract* is a **requirements contract.** *9.* An *open-end mortgage* is a

mortgage allowing future borrowing against the same **collateral.** See also #5.

Opening statement The introductory statements made at the start of a trial by lawyers for each side, who typically explain the version of the facts best supporting their side of the case, how these facts will be proved, and how they think the law applies to the case.

Operation of law Describes the automatic effect some laws have on rights and responsibilities. For example, the wife of a man who dies without a will may gain ownership of her husband's property by *operation of law* without taking any action.

Operative words That part of a document by which rights are actually created or transferred.

Opinion *1.* A judge's statement of the decision he or she has reached in a case. *2.* A judge's statement about the conclusions of that judge and of others who agree with the judge in a case. A *majority opinion* is written when over half of the judges in a case agree with both the result and the reasoning used to reach the result. A *plurality opinion* is written when a majority of the judges agree with the result but not with the reasoning. A *concurring opinion* agrees with the result but not the reasoning. A *dissenting* or *minority opinion* disagrees with the result. (Concurring, dissenting, and minority opinions are all *separate opinions*.) A *per curiam opinion* is unanimous and anonymous, and a *memorandum opinion* is unanimous and briefly states only the result. *3.* A document prepared by a lawyer for a client that gives the lawyer's conclusions about how the law applies to a set of facts in which the client is interested. *4. Opinion evidence* is evidence about what a **witness** thinks, believes, or concludes about facts, rather than what the witness saw, heard, etc. It is usually accepted only from an **expert witness.**

Oppression Unconscionability.

Opprobrium Shame or disgrace.

Option A **contract** in which one person pays money for the right to buy something from, or sell something to, another person at a certain price and within a certain time period.

Optional writ A **show cause** order.

Oral argument The presentation of each side of a case before an **appeals** court, with the judges usually interrupting to ask questions.

Oral contract (or will) A **contract** (or **will**) that is not entirely in writing or not in writing at all.

Order *1.* A written command or direction given by a judge. For example, a *restraining order* is a judicial command to a person to temporarily stop a certain course of action. *2.* A command given by a public official. *3.* "*To the order of*" is a direction to pay something. These words (or "pay to the **bearer**") are necessary to make a document a **negotiable instrument.** A document with these words is called *order paper. 4.* Instructions to buy or sell something.

Ordinance A local law, rule, or **regulation.**

Organic Basic or fundamental. For example, an *organic act* is a law giving self-government to a geographic area, and *organic law* is the basic law of a government, such as its **constitution.**

Original jurisdiction The power of a court to take a case, try it, and decide it (as opposed to *appellate jurisdiction,* the power to hear and decide an **appeal**).

Ostensible Apparent or visible. For *ostensible authority,* see **apparent authority.**

Ouster Throwing someone off land who has a right to possess it. [pronounce: <u>ow</u>-ster]

Out-of-court settlement   A private compromise or agreement that ends a lawsuit without official help from, or orders by, the judge.

Out-of-pocket   Describes a loss measured by the difference between the price paid for an item and the (lower true) value of that item.

Output contract   An agreement in which a manufacturing company agrees to sell everything it makes to one buyer, and the buyer agrees to take it all. This is a valid **contract** even though the amounts are indefinite. Compare **requirements contract.**

Over   *1.* Continued (on the next page, in the next session of court, etc.).   *2.* Shifting or passing from one person, thing, or time to another.

Over-the-counter   Describes **securities** (such as **stock**) sold directly from **broker** to broker or to customer, rather than through an exchange.

Overbreadth   A law will be declared **void** for overbreadth if it tries to punish speech or conduct protected by the **Constitution** and if it is impossible to eliminate the unconstitutional part of the law without invalidating the whole law.

Overdraft (or overdraw)   Taking out more money by check from an account than you have in the account.

Overhead   **Fixed charges** and any costs that cannot be allocated to a particular product or department.

Overreaching   Taking unfair commercial advantage by **fraud** or by **unconscionability.**

Overrule   *1.* To reject or supercede. For example, a case is *overruled* when the same court, or a higher court in the same system, rejects the legal principles on which the case was based.   *2.* To reject (as the judge) an **objection** made during a trial.

Overt   Open; clear. For example, an *overt act* in **criminal** law is more than mere preparation to do something criminal; it is at least the first step of actually attempting the crime.

Oyer and terminer (Law French) "Hear and decide." Describes some higher state **criminal** courts. [pronounce: oy-yay / term-i-nay]

Oyez (Law French) "Hear ye." The word cried out by a court official in some courtrooms to get attention at the start of a court session. [pronounce: oy-<u>yay</u>]

P _1_. Pacific Reporter (see **National Reporter System**). _2_. **Plaintiff.**

PBGC Pension Benefit Guaranty Corporation.

PC _1_. Professional corporation. A special type of **corporation** set up by doctors, lawyers, etc. _2_. Also patent cases; penal code; and many British phrases, such as Pleas of the Crown and Privy Council.

PCR **Postconviction remedies.**

P-H Prentice-Hall (**see loose-leaf service**).

PHV **Pro hac vice.**

PJ Presiding judge.

PL Public law; public laws; pamphlet laws.

PLI Practicing Law Institute. A nonprofit organization that publishes books and holds seminars to educate lawyers.

PLS A professional legal secretary who has passed the **NALS** exam.

POD Payable on death (to another person if the first one dies).

PS Public **statute.**

PTI Previously taxed income.

PUC Public Utilities Commission. State agencies that regulate power companies, railroads, etc.

PUD Planned unit development.

Package Including many different things; a complete deal.

Packing Trying to get a favorable decision by improperly including specific persons among the decision makers.

Pact A bargain or agreement.

Paid-in Supplied by the owners.

Pais See **in pais.**

Palimony Payments, usually resembling **alimony,** based on an **express** or **implied** contract between unmarried persons who lived together in a sexual relationship.

Palpable Plain, clear, easily seen, or notorious; usually refers to an **error,** an **abuse** of authority, or something else wrong.

Panel *1.* A jury list. *2.* A group of judges, smaller than the entire court, that decides a case.

Paper *1.* "The papers" are all the documents concerned with a lawsuit. *2.* "Paper" may be short for **commercial paper** or for a **negotiable instrument.** *3.* "Paper" may mean "only paper." For example, a *paper title* is a **document of title** that may or may not be valid. *4.* When a **prosecutor** "papers" a case, it means, in some places, that it *will* be formally prosecuted and, in other places, that it will *not* be formally prosecuted further.

Par Face *value.* If a $100 **bond** sells in the bond market for $100, it sells *at par.*

Paralegal A nonlawyer who needs legal skills to do a job. Most persons who work for lawyers (such as legal secretaries or legal assistants) are *paralegals,* as are many persons who work for agencies and do law-related work.

Parallel citation An alternate reference to a case (or other legal document) that is published in more than one place.

Paramount title *1*. Best right of ownership. A **holder in due course** has *paramount title* to a document (and to all the money and property it stands for. *2*. In real estate law, *paramount title* previously meant original title, but it has come to mean "better title" or "superior title."

Parcener (or coparcener) A **joint heir** who inherits property along with another person, each inheriting the whole thing.

Pardon A president's or governor's release of a person from punishment for a crime.

Parens patriae (Latin) The right of the government to take care of minors and others who cannot legally take care of themselves. The use of this power to deprive a person of freedom has been limited. [pronounce: pa-rens pat-ri-eye]

Parent corporation A **corporation** that fully controls or owns another.

Pari (Latin) *1*. Equal; the same. *2. Pari causa* means with (or by) equal right or equal cause. *3. Pari materia* means "on the same subject"; interdependent. For example, two laws *in pari materia* must be read together as if one law. *4. Pari passu* means equally; without preference.

Pari delicto (Latin) *1*. Equal fault. *2*. The *doctrine of pari delicto* in **contract** law is the principle that a court should not help enforce an illegal or invalid contract unless one side is much less at fault than the other. *3.* There are several *doctrines of pari delicto* in **tort** law. One is the principle that in cases of approximately equal fault, the **defendant** should win.

Parity Equality; equivalence; comparability.

Parliamentary law Rules and customs by which **legislatures,** and other types of meetings, are run.

Parliamentary system A government, such as that in England, in which an elected **legislature** selects a *prime minister* and **cabinet.**

Parol Oral; not in writing. For example, *parol evidence* is oral **evidence** (the evidence a **witness** gives). The *parol evidence rule* is the principle that the meaning of a written agreement, in which the parties have expressly stated that it is their complete and final agreement, cannot be contradicted or changed by using prior oral or written statements or agreements as **evidence.** Exceptions to the rule include situations in which there was **duress, fraud,** or **mistake.** *Not* **parole.**

Parole A release from prison, before a **sentence** is finished, that depends for its continuation on good behavior while out. *Parole officers* supervise these *parolees* released by a *parole board. Not* **parol.**

Part performance See **performance.**

Particular average loss A loss of property at sea that is the result of **negligence** or accident and that must be borne by the owner of the property.

Particulars The details of a legal **claim** or of separate items on an **account** or for sale. See also **bill of particulars.**

Parties See **party.**

Partition Dividing land owned by several persons into smaller parcels owned by each person individually.

Partner A member of a **partnership.** A *full* or *general* partner participates fully in running the company and sharing the profits and losses. A *dormant, silent,* or *sleeping* partner is a person who is in a partnership but who is not known as a partner by the public, does not take an active hand in the business, and, if also a *special* or *limited* partner, puts in a fixed amount of money, gets a specified amount of profit, and is usually not **liable** for anything beyond the investment itself. Finally, a *nominal* or *ostensible* partner is *not* a partner but appears to be one.

Partnership A type of business association that involves a **contract** between two or more persons to carry on a business together and to share money and labor put in and profits or losses taken out. It is *not* a **corporation.** See **partner.**

Party *1.* A person concerned with or taking part in any matter, affair, or proceeding. *2.* A person who is either a **plaintiff** or a **defendant** in a lawsuit. A *real party* is a person who actually stands to gain or lose something from being part of the case and a *formal* or *nominal party* is one who has only a technical or "name only" interest. *3.* A *third party* is a person who is not directly involved in a **contract,** lawsuit, or other matter, but who is or might be affected by it. *4.* A *party wall* is a wall on a property line that is part of the structure of adjoining buildings. *5. Party of the first part* is an unnecessary phrase used instead of repeating the name of a party to a document.

Pass *1.* Say or pronounce. For example, a judge *passes sentence* on a convicted criminal. *2.* Enact successfully. For example, a **bill** *passes* when a **legislature**

votes "yes." *3*. Examine and determine. For example, a jury *passes upon* the issues in a lawsuit. *4*. Transfer or become transferred. For example, property *passes* from one person to another when a **deed** is properly written, signed, and delivered. *5*. Approve. *6*. Offer a fake as real.

Passage Enactment or approval of a **bill** by one **house** of a **legislature;** enactment by both houses; or enactment plus signature by the president, governor, or the like.

Passim (Latin) Found in various places (in the book).

Passive *1*. Inactive. *2*. Submissive or permissive rather than actually agreeing to or participating in something.

Patent *1*. Open, evident, plainly visible. *2*. A right (given by the federal government to a person) to control the manufacture and sale of something that person has discovered or invented. *3*. A **grant** of land by the government to an individual.

Paternity suit A court action to prove that a person is the father of a child and to get **support** for the child from the father.

Patronage *1*. All the customers of a business; giving a company business. *2*. The privilege of some public officials to give out jobs on their own **discretion,** without going through **civil service.**

Pawn Give personal **property** to a commercial lender as **security** for a loan.

Payable *1*. Owing and to be paid in the future. *2*. Owing and due for payment now.

Payee The person to whom a **negotiable instrument** is made out; for example, if a check is made payable "to the order of John Doe," then John Doe is the payee.

Peace bond   A court-ordered **bond** to guarantee good behavior for a time period.

Peculation   **Embezzlement.**

Pecuniary   Related to money.

Pederasty   Anal intercourse between males, especially between men and boys. It is a crime in many states.

Peers   Equal persons. A trial "by a jury of **peers,**" however, does not mean by persons exactly equal to the **defendant** but by citizens chosen fairly.

Penal   *1*. Concerning a penalty. In this sense, a *penal action* is a **civil** lawsuit to make a wrongdoer pay a fine or penalty to the person harmed, and a *penal bond* is a **bond** put up as a promise to pay money if a certain thing is not done. *2*. Criminal. In this sense, a *penal action* is a **criminal** prosecution, and a *penal code* is a collection of state or other criminal laws. *3*. For *penal damages,* see *punitive* **damages.**

Penalty   *1*. A punishment imposed by law. *2*. A sum of money promised by one person to another, to be paid if the first person fails to do something.

Pendency   While **pending.**

Pendent jurisdiction   A federal court's right to decide a claim based on a nonfederal **issue** if this claim depends on the same set of facts as does the federal issue.

Pendente lite   (Latin) "Pending the suit"; while a lawsuit is in progress. [pronounce: pen-<u>den</u>-te lee-te]

Pending   As yet undecided; begun but not finished.

Penology   The study of prisons and criminal punishment.

People   *1*. A nation or state. *2*. All **persons** in a nation or state as one whole group. *3*. *Not* the plural of **person** in the law.

Peppercorn Something of actual, but very insignificant, value.

Per (Latin) *1.* By; through; by means of; during. *2.* For *per autre vie,* see **autre vie.** *3. Per capita* (by heads) means by the number of individual persons, each equally. Compare #6. *4. Per curiam* (by the court) means an **opinion** backed by all the judges in a particular court and usually with no one judge's name on it. [pronounce: per cure-i-am] *5. Per se* means in and of itself; taken alone; inherently. [pronounce: per say] *6. Per stirpes* (by the roots) is a method of dividing a dead person's **estate** by giving out shares equally "by representation" or by family groups. For example, if John leaves $3,000 to Mary and Sue, and Mary dies, leaving two children (Steve and Jeff), a *per stirpes* division would give $1,500 to Sue and $750 each to Steve and Jeff. A *per capita* division would give $1,000 each to Sue, Steve, and Jeff. [pronounce: per stir-pees]

Peremptory *1.* Absolute; conclusive; final; or arbitrary. *2.* Not requiring any explanation or cause to be shown. For example, a *peremptory challenge* to a potential **juror** is the automatic elimination of that person from the jury by one side before trial without needing to state the reason for the elimination. *3.* A *peremptory ruling* is a judge's ruling that takes the final decision away from the jury; for example, a **directed verdict** or *judgment* **non obstante veredicto.**

Perfect *1.* Complete; enforceable; without defect. Also called "*perfected.*" *2.* To tie down or "make perfect." For example, to *perfect a title* is to record it in the proper place so that your ownership is protected against all persons, not just against the person who sold you the title. This is called "perfection."

Performance Carrying out a **contract,** promise, or other **obligation** according to its terms so that the obligation ends. *Specific performance* is being required to do exactly what was agreed to. A court may require specific performance if one side to a contract fails to perform and **damages** (money) will not properly compensate the other side for harm done. *Part performance* is carrying out some, but not all, of a contract, or doing something in **reliance** on another's promise. Part performance makes certain agreements enforceable.

Perjury Lying while under **oath,** especially in a court proceeding. It is a crime.

Permissive *1.* Allowed or endured, as opposed to actively approved of. *2.* By right.

Perpetual succession The continuous existence of a **corporation** as the same "being" even though its owners and **directors** change.

Perpetuating testimony A procedure for taking and preserving **testimony** (usually by **deposition**) of persons who are in very bad health, very old, about to leave the state, etc.

Perpetuating evidence Making sure that **evidence** is available for a possible trial later.

Perpetuity *1.* Forever. *2.* An investment that gives equal future payments essentially forever. *3.* Any attempt to control the **disposition** of property by **will** that is meant to last longer than the life of a person alive when you die (or at least conceived by then) plus twenty-one years. Most states prevent such control by a law called the *rule against perpetuities.*

Perquisites Benefits of a job in addition to salary; for example, a company car for personal use.

Person *1.* A human being (a *natural person*). *2.* A **corporation** (an *artificial person*), treated as a person in most legal situations. *3.* Any other "being," such as a group of **trustees,** entitled to sue as a legal entity. *4.* The plural is "persons," *not* **people.**

Personal *1.* Having to do with a human being. *2.* Having to do with movable **property,** as opposed to land and buildings. *3. Personal injury* often refers to **negligence** lawsuits, such as for auto accidents.

Personalty **Personal** property; movable property.

Persuasive authority All sources of law that a judge might use, but is not required to use, in making up his or her mind about a case; for example, legal encyclopedias or related cases from other states. A case might be strongly persuasive if it comes from a famous judge or a nearby, powerful court.

Pertinent **Relevant** to an **issue** that is itself relevant to the outcome of a trial.

Petit (or petty) jury A *trial* **jury.**

Petition *1.* A written request to a court that it take a particular action. In some states, the word is limited to requests when there is no other side in the case (**ex parte** cases), and in some states, a **complaint** is called a *petition. 2.* A request made to a public official. *3.* A *petition in bankruptcy* is a paper filed in **bankruptcy** court by a debtor, requesting relief from debts, or by **creditors** asking that a person be put into involuntary bankruptcy.

Petitioner **Plaintiff.**

Petitory action A lawsuit to establish **title** to land, as opposed to a lawsuit to gain physical possession of the land.

Pettifogger An old word for an incompetent lawyer or one who tries to drown an **issue** in trivia.

Philadelphia lawyer Originally, a skillful lawyer; now, a sly or tricky lawyer.

Physical fact *1*. An indisputable law of nature or a scientific fact. *2*. Something visible, audible, or otherwise "graspable" by the senses.

Picketing Persons gathering outside a place to disturb its activities or to inform persons outside of grievances, opinions, etc., about the place.

Piercing the corporate veil A judge's holding individual owners, **directors,** officers, and so on, **liable** for a **corporation**'s debts or wrongdoing. This is done only in unusual circumstances.

Plagiarism Taking all or part of the writing or idea of another person and passing it off as one's own. See also **infringement.**

Plain error rule The principle that an **appeals** court can **reverse** a **judgment** because the trial court made a major **error** in its proceedings, even if the error was not objected to at the time.

Plain meaning rule *1*. The principle that if a law seems clear, you should take the simplest meaning of the words and not read anything into the law. This is one of several possible ways of interpreting **statutes.** *2*. The principle that if a document seems clear, its meaning should be determined from the document alone, not from other **evidence** (such as **testimony**).

Plain view doctrine The rule that if police officers see or come across something while acting lawfully, that item may be used as **evidence** in a **criminal** trial even if the police did not have a **search warrant.**

Plaintiff A person who brings (starts) a lawsuit against another person. *Plaintiff in error* means **appellant.**

Planned unit development Land to be developed as a whole with different types of uses, approved even if

zoning requirements for one piece might not allow that particular building.

Plat A map showing how a piece of land will be subdivided and built upon, by lot, street, and block number.

Plea *1.* The **defendant's** formal answer to a criminal **charge: guilty,** not guilty, or **no contest.** *2.* See **pleading.** *3.* An older word for several types of civil **motions,** such as a *plea in abatement,* that have largely been replaced by a *motion to* **dismiss.** *4. Plea bargaining* is negotiations between a **prosecutor** and a criminal **defendant's** lawyer, attempting to resolve a criminal case without trial. For example, during plea bargaining, the defense lawyer may suggest that the defendant **plead guilty** in exchange for the prosecutor's agreeing to accept a *plea* to a less serious **charge,** to drop some charges, or to promise not to request a heavy **sentence** from the judge.

Plead *1.* Make or file a **pleading** or a **plea.** *2.* Argue a case in court.

Pleading The process of making formal, written statements (*pleadings*) of each side of a **civil** *case.* First the **plaintiff** submits a paper with "facts" and claims **(complaint);** then the **defendant's** paper submits "facts" and countercharges **(answer);** then the plaintiff may respond; and so on, until all issues and questions are clearly posed for a trial. *Pleadings* may include **counterclaims, cross-claims,** etc. "*The pleadings*" is the sum of all these papers. Modern legal *pleadings* may be amended freely to fit facts as they develop. In contrast, old **common-law** *pleadings* (such as a *declaration, defendant's plea, replication, rejoinder, surrejoinder, rebutter, surrebutter,* etc.,) were so rigid that one technical mistake could lose a lawsuit. (See **theory of pleading doctrine.**)

Plebicite   A vote by the people for or against a proposed new major law or expressing an opinion on a major public issue.

Pledge   Handing over physical possession of a piece of personal **property** (such as a radio) to another person, who holds it as **security** for a debt.

Plenary   Full; complete; of every person or every thing.

Pocket part   An addition to a lawbook that updates it until a new edition comes out. It is usually found inside the back cover, secured in a "pocket," and should always be referred to when doing legal research.

Point   _1_. An individual legal proposition, argument, or question raised in a lawsuit. _Points and authorities_ is the name for a document prepared to back up a legal position taken in a lawsuit (for example, to support or oppose a **motion**). _2_. One percent (or one standard unit of measure).

Police power   The government's right and power to set up and enforce laws to provide for the safety, health, and general welfare of the people; for example, to **license** doctors.

Policy   _1_. The general operating procedures and goals of an organization. _2_. The general purpose of a law. _3. Public policy_ is the general good of the state and its people. _4._ See **insurance.**

Political question   A question that the courts will not decide because it concerns a decision properly made by only the **executive** or **legislative** branches of government.

Polling the jury   Individually asking each member of a **jury** what his or her decision is.

Polls   A _challenge to the polls_ is an objection to the selection of a particular **juror,** made before the jury convenes.

Polygamy Having more than one wife or husband; a crime in the United States.

Polygraph A lie detector.

Popular name tables Reference charts that cross-reference the common name of a **statute** with its official name and number; for example, you could find the official name and **citation** of the "Sherman Act."

Positive evidence Direct evidence.

Positive law Law that has been enacted by a **legislature.**

Posse comitatus (posse) (Latin) "The power of the state." The group of citizens who may be gathered by the **sheriff** or other law officer to help enforce the law, usually on an emergency basis.

Possession Control of **property.** For example, a **tenant** may have *possession* of land, and someone with an illegal drug in a pocket has *possession.*

Possessory action A lawsuit (for example, an **eviction**) to gain control of property, as opposed to one that attempts to get legal ownership to property.

Postconviction remedies Procedures for prisoners to challenge their **convictions** or **sentences.**

Posting Writing down or transferring an **entry** (such as the amount of money spent for a lamp) into an **account** book.

Postmortem (Latin) "After death." An examination of a body to determine the cause of death.

Postponement *1.* **Subordination.** *2.* **Continuance.**

Pourover A **will** that gives money or property to an existing **trust** is a *pourover will,* and a similar trust is a *pourover trust.*

Power *1.* The right to do something. *2.* The ability to do something. *3.* A combination of #1 and #2. *4.* A *power of appointment* is a part of a **will, deed,** or separate document that gives someone the power to decide who gets the money or how it will be used. *5.* A *power of attorney* is a document authorizing a person to act as **attorney** for the person signing the document. *6.* A *power of sale* is the right of a **mortgage** holder or **trustee** to sell the real estate **secured** by the mortgage if payments are not made.

Practicable A stuffy word meaning "feasible"; can be done.

Practice *1.* Custom, habit, or an act regularly repeated. *2.* Formal court procedure; the way a lawsuit is taken to and through court, as opposed to what it is about. For example, a *practice manual* is a book of forms and procedures used in **pleading** and court procedure. *3.* Engage in a profession, such as law. *4.* Do things that are only permitted to be done by a member of a profession. For example, giving legal advice is *practice of law.*

Praecipe (Latin) A formal request that the court **clerk** take some action. A **motion** that can be granted by the signature of a court clerk without a judge's approval. A lawyer can "**enter** *an appearance*" in a case by praecipe. [pronounce: <u>pres</u>-i-pee]

Praedial Having to do with the use of the ground, such as growing crops. [pronounce: <u>pred</u>-i-al]

Prayer Request. That part of a legal **pleading** (such as a **complaint**) that asks for **relief** (help, money, specific court action, an action from the other side, etc.).

Preamble An introduction, usually saying why a document, such as a **statute,** was written.

Preappointed evidence Specific proof required by law.

Precatory Expressing a wish; advisory only; not legally binding in most situations. [pronounce: <u>prek</u>-a-tory]

Precedent *1.* A court decision, on a *question of law,* that is **binding authority** (see those words) on lower courts in the same court system (for cases in which those courts must decide a similar question of law involving similar facts). The U.S. court system is based on judges making decisions supported by past precedent rather than by logic alone. See also **stare decisis.** *2.* Something that must happen before something else may happen. **See condition** *precedent.* [pronounce: <u>press</u>-i-dent]

<u>Precept</u> A command by a person in authority or a rule of conduct.

<u>Precinct</u> A police or election district within a city.

Precipe Praecipe.

Preclusion order A judge's **order** forbidding one side in a lawsuit from making arguments based on something that side fails to produce after it is requested by **discovery.**

Precognition The examination of a **witness** before trial.

Predial Praedial.

Pre-emption *1.* The first right to buy something, such as stock. *2.* The first right to do anything. For example, when the federal government *pre-empts the field* by passing laws in a subject area, the states may not pass conflicting laws and sometimes may not pass laws on the subject at all.

Preference *1.* A **creditor**'s right to be paid before non-preferred creditors. *2.* The act of an **insolvent** (broke) **debtor** in paying off a **creditor** more than a fair share of what is left.

Preferential shop A place of business where **union** members will be hired first and laid off last.

Preferred stock See **stock.**

Prejudice *1.* Bias; a preconceived opinion. A *judge's prejudice* refers not to an opinion about the subject of the case but to the judge's bias for or against one of the *persons* in the dispute. *2.* If a case is *dismissed with prejudice,* it cannot be brought back into court again. *3.* Substantially harmful to rights. For example, *prejudicial error* by a judge is serious enough, and wrong enough, to be the basis for an **appeal.**

Preliminary hearing *1.* The first court proceeding on a **criminal** *charge* to decide whether there is enough evidence for the government to continue with the case. *2.* A court session for pretrial **motions.**

Premeditation Thinking in advance about how to do something (usually how to do a crime).

Premium *1.* An **insurance** payment. *2.* Extra purchase money paid.

Preponderance of evidence The greater weight of **evidence,** not as to *quantity* (number of witnesses or facts) but as to *quality* (believability and greater weight of important facts proved). This *standard of proof* is generally used in **civil** lawsuits.

Prerogative *1.* A special privilege. *2.* Special official power. *3.* *Prerogative writs* are **writs** a court will **issue** only under special circumstances. These include, for example, **mandamus** and **habeas corpus.** These **writs** have been replaced by regular **motions** or **complaints** in most courts.

Prescription *1.* A method of getting legal ownership of *personal* **property** (everything but land) by keeping it in a person's possession openly, continuously, and with a claim that it belongs to that person. This must be done for a time period set by state law. *2.* The right of access to a path, a waterway, light, etc., gained by long-time continuous use. *3.* An order or direction.

Present *1.* Immediate. *2.* See **presentment.** *3.* For *present recollection revived,* see **recollection.** *4.* A *present sense impression* is a statement made during or immediately after an event by a participant or observer. Present sense impressions can usually be testified to under an exception to the **hearsay rule.**

Presentence investigation   An investigation by a court-appointed social worker, **probation** officer, etc., into a criminal's background and prospects for rehabilitation.

Presentment (or presentation)   *1.* A *grand* **jury's** charging a person with a crime that it has investigated itself (not by an **indictment** given to it by a prosecutor). In some states, it is an informal statement, not a charge. *2.* Offering for payment a **negotiable instrument** such as a check.

Presents   An obsolete word for "legal document."

Presumption   A conclusion or inference drawn. A *presumption of fact* is a conclusion that because one fact exists (or one thing is true), another fact exists (or another thing is true). If no new facts turn up to prove the presumption wrong, it is **evidence** as good as any direct proof of the fact. A *presumption of law* is a rule of law that whenever a certain set of facts shows up, a court must automatically draw certain legal conclusions. For example, the *presumption of innocence* is that all persons are innocent of all crimes unless proven guilty **beyond a reasonable doubt.** Presumptions can be *rebuttable* (good until destroyed by more facts) or *conclusive, absolute, or irrebuttable* (an inference that must be drawn from a set of facts "no matter what").

Presumptive   May be inferred. For *presumptive evidence,* see **presumption** *of fact.*

Pretermitted heir   A child (or sometimes any descendant) either unintentionally left out of a **will** or born after the will is made.

Prevailing party   The person who wins a lawsuit, even if not satisfied with the result.

Preventive detention   Holding persons against their will because they are likely to commit a crime. This practice is **constitutional** only in certain situations.

Preventive law   Legal help and information designed to help persons avoid future legal problems rather than to solve existing legal problems.

Prima facie   (Latin) At first sight; on the face of it; presumably. Describes something that will be considered to be true unless disproved by contrary **evidence.** A *prima facie case* is a lawsuit that will win unless the other side comes forward with evidence to disprove it. [pronounce: pry-ma fay-she]

Primary authority   *1.* **Binding authority.** *2.* Laws, court decisions, regulations, and other similar sources of law rather than interpretive information from encyclopedias, **treatises,** etc.

Prime   Either original or most important. For *prime contractor, see* **contractor.**

Primogeniture   First child. A no-longer-followed rule that the first son inherited everything.

Principal   *1.* Chief; most important; primary. *2.* A sum of money invested, as opposed to the profits made (often **interest**) on that money. *3.* An employer or anyone else who has another person (an **agent**) do things for him or her. *4.* A person directly involved with committing a crime, as opposed to an **accessory.** *5. Not* **principle.**

Principle   A basic truth, doctrine, or generalization.

Prior hearing   A **hearing** by an **administrative agency** that sometimes must be given to a person before taking any action that harms the person.

Priority   The right to be first; often, the right to have a claim paid first and completely.

Prison A place of long-term incarceration for a crime. Compare **jail.**

Prisoner Anyone deprived of liberty by the government, either because of an accusation of a crime or a **conviction** of a crime.

Privacy Describes the right to be left alone. The right to privacy is sometimes "balanced" against other rights, such as freedom of the press.

Private *1.* Concerning individuals, not the general public and not the government. In this sense, *private law* is the law of relationships among persons (such as **contract** law), as opposed to **public law,** which concerns relationships between persons and the government or the operation of government. *2.* A *private attorney general* is an individual who goes to court to enforce a public right for all citizens. *3.* For *private international law,* see **conflict of laws.** *4.* A *private law (or bill)* is a **statute** passed to affect only one person or group, rather than the general public.

Privies See **privity** and **privy.**

Privilege *1.* An advantage; a right to preferential treatment; or an exemption from a duty others must perform. *2.* A basic right that cannot be taken away. But see #3. *3.* A special advantage, as opposed to a right; an advantage that can be taken away. *4.* The right to speak or write defamatory (personally damaging) words because the law specially allows it. *5.* The **right** and the **duty** to withhold information because of some special status or relationship of **confidentiality.** These privileges include husband-wife privilege, doctor-patient privilege, etc.

Privileges and immunities Describes the **constitutional** requirement that a state must treat a person from another state as fairly as it treats its own citizens.

Privity *1.* Private or "inside" knowledge. *2.* A close, direct financial relationship. For example, *privity of contract* exists among those who directly took part in making a deal with each other and have special rights and duties because of it. (If a manufacturer sells to a retailer who sells to a customer, the manufacturer and customer are not "in privity.")

Privy *1.* A person in **privity** with another. The plural is *privies.* *2.* **Private.**

Prize A ship taken from a country with which one is at war.

Pro (Latin) *1. Pro bono publico* means "for the public good." When abbreviated *pro bono,* it means free legal work for a charitable or public purpose. *2. Pro forma* means as a matter of form or a mere formality. A *pro forma* financial **statement** is one that is *projected* on the basis of certain assumptions. *3. Pro hac vice* means for this one particular time or purpose only. [pronounce: pro hock <u>vee</u>-chay] *4. Pro interesse suo* means "according to his interest" and is a court process by which a person who claims a right to property that has a **mortgage, judgment, lease,** etc., may ask a court to decide how much of the property is his or hers. *5. Pro rata* means proportionately; by percentage; by a fixed rate; by share. For example, if Tom, Dick, and Harry are owed two, four, and six dollars, respectively, by John, but John has only six dollars to give out, their *pro rata* share would be one, two, and three dollars, respectively. *6. Pro se* means for himself or herself in his or her own behalf. For example, *pro se representation* means that a person will handle his or her own case in court without a lawyer. [pronounce: pro say] *7. Pro tanto* means for that much; to the extent of; or partial payment. *8. Pro tem* is short for *pro tempore;* for the time being.

Probable cause The likelihood that a crime has been committed by the person whom a law enforcement officer seeks to arrest (or that the object sought by the officer will be found in the place to be searched). An officer's *probable cause* to conduct an arrest (or a search) depends on what the officer knew *before* taking action. Without probable cause, a judge will not issue an arrest (or search) **warrant,** and a warrantless emergency arrest (or search) may not be **constitutional.**

Probate *1.* The process of proving that a **will** is genuine and giving out the property in it. *2.* The name in some states for a court that handles the **distribution** (giving out) of dead persons' property and other matters, such as **civil** *commitments.*

Probation *1.* Staying out of jail, under conditions supervised by a *probation officer,* although convicted of a crime. *2.* A trial period, such as when a new employee lacks full job rights.

Probative Tending to prove or actually proving something. *Probative facts* are **evidentiary facts.**

Procedural law The rules of carrying on a civil lawsuit or a criminal case (how to enforce **rights** and **duties** in court) as opposed to **substantive law** (the law of the rights and duties themselves).

Procedure The rules and methods of carrying on a civil lawsuit or a criminal case (**pleading,** making **motions,** presenting **evidence,** etc.).

Proceeding *1.* A **case** in court, its orderly progression, or its recorded history. *2.* Any official action taken by a governmental body.

Proceeds Money or property gained from a sale or other transaction.

Process *1.* A court's ordering a **defendant** to show up in court or risk losing a lawsuit; a **summons.** *2.* Any court **order** that *"takes jurisdiction over"* (brings formally under the court's power) a person or property.

Prochein ami (Law French) **Next friend.** [pronounce: pro-shen ah-mee]

Proctor *1.* Someone appointed to manage another person's affairs. *2.* A lawyer, **agent,** or representative.

Procuration *1.* Either the process of making someone a **proctor** or doing something as someone's proctor. *2.* Pimping.

Procurement Government purchasing, usually by special rules.

Produce Bring forward; show; yield up. For example, a *motion to produce* or a *motion for production* is a request that the judge order the other side to show you specific documents.

Profer (or profert) **Proffer.**

Professio juris A made-up Latin word for an agreement in a **contract** to have the law of one particular state or country decide all questions involved in the contract.

Proffer *1.* To offer or present. *2.* **Avowal.**

Profits à prendre (French) The right to take the growing crops of another person's land. [pronounce: ah prahn-dr]

Profits à rendre (French) That which must be given or paid; usually rent. [pronounce: ah rahn-dr]

Progressive tax A tax that is proportionately greater on higher incomes or greater assets.

Prohibition An order to stop certain actions or a warning not to engage in them. A *writ of prohibition* is an order from a higher court telling a lower court to stop proceeding with a lawsuit.

Promise *1.* A statement that morally, legally, or in some other way binds the person who makes it to do something. *2.* In **contract** law, an oral or written statement from one person to another, given in exchange for something of value (which can be another promise). It may bind the person making the promise to do something and may give the other person the legal right to demand that it be done.

Promissory estoppel The principle that when Person A makes a promise and expects Person B to do something in **reliance** upon that promise, then Person B does act in reliance upon that promise, the law will usually help Person B enforce the promise.

Promissory note A document that contains an acknowledgment of a debt and a promise to pay the debt. A promissory note is **negotiable** if by its terms it can be sold. *2.* A *negotiable promissory note* typically requires the borrower to pay an exact sum of money immediately, when asked for, or by a certain date either "to the **order** of " a specific person or "to **bearer**" (the person who actually has it).

Promulgate Publish; announce officially; put out formally.

Pronounce Say formally and officially.

Proof *1.* **Evidence** supporting a contention. Those facts from which a conclusion can be drawn. In this sense, *proof* can be convincing or unconvincing. But see #2. *2.* The result of convincing **evidence.** The conclusion that the evidence shows that something is true or that an argument about facts is correct. In this sense, proof is always convincing. *3.* There are various **standards** *of proof,* including: *beyond a reasonable doubt* (how convincing evidence must be in a **criminal** trial); *by clear and convincing evidence;* and *by a preponderance (greater weight) of the evidence.*

Proper Fit, suitable, or appropriate. For example, a *proper party* to a lawsuit is a person who has a real, substantial interest in the suit's outcome, who can conveniently be added to the suit as a **party,** but without whom the suit *can* be decided.

Property *1.* Ownership of a thing; the legal right to own a thing. *2.* Anything that is owned or can be owned, such as land, automobiles, money, stocks, the right to use a famous actor's name, etc. Property is either **real** (land and things on it) or **personal** (everything else), but some property is hard to categorize as *real* or *personal.*

Proponent The person who offers or proposes something.

Proposal *1.* An **offer** that can be accepted to make a **contract.** *2.* A preliminary idea for discussion that is *not* an **offer.**

Propound Offer or propose something. To *propound a will* is to request that a **probate** court accept it as valid.

Proprietary Having to do with ownership.

Proprietorship *1.* Running a business. *2.* **Sole** *proprietorship.*

Prorate Divide or share proportionately. **See pro rata.**

Prorogation *1.* An agreement in a **contract** to allow the courts of one particular state or country to decide all disputes concerning the contract. *2.* A delay, putting off, or **continuance.**

Prosecute *1.* Formally start and pursue a **civil** lawsuit. *2.* Charge a person with a crime and bring the person to trial. The process is *prosecution,* the person harmed by the crime or who made the complaint is either a *prosecuting witness* or a *private prosecutor,* and the public official who presents the government's case is a *prosecutor.*

Prosecutorial discretion The power of the *prosecutor* to decide whether to **prosecute** a person, how serious a charge to press, how large a penalty to request, what kind of **plea bargaining** deal to accept, etc.

Prospective Looking forward; concerning the future; likely or possible. A *prospective law* applies to situations that arise after it is enacted. Most laws are *prospective* only.

Prospectus An offer put out to interest persons in a financial deal; for example, a document put out to describe a **corporation** and interest persons in buying its **stock.**

Prostitution A person offering her (in many states, his or her) body for sexual purposes in exchange for money. It is a crime in most places.

Protective (or protection) order *1.* A court **order** that temporarily allows one side in a lawsuit to hold back from showing the other side documents or other things that were (or might be) requested. *2.* Any court order protecting a person from harassment, **service** *of process,* etc. *3.* A court order putting a person in *protective* **custody** (jail, a mental hospital, a hiding place, etc.,) for the person's safety.

Protest *1.* A written statement that you do not agree with the legality, justice, or correctness of a payment but are paying it while reserving the right to get it back later. *2.* A formal certificate of the **dishonor** of a **negotiable instrument** that a person has presented for payment. It is signed by a **notary public** and is meant to give **notice** to all persons **liable** on it that they may have to pay.

Prothonotary Head clerk of some courts.

Protocol *1.* A first draft, preliminary document, or short summary. *2.* Formalities, especially of international diplomacy.

Province Duty, or area of responsibility.

Provisional Temporary or preliminary. A *provisional remedy* is a court **order** (or an action permitted by a court) that helps enforce the law on a temporary basis; for example, an **attachment.**

Proviso A **condition, qualification,** or **limitation** in a document.

Provocation An act by one person that triggers a reaction of rage in another. It may reduce the severity of a crime.

Proximate cause The "legal cause" of an accident or other injury, which may have several actual causes. The proximate cause of an injury is not necessarily the closest thing in time or space to the injury and not necessarily the event that set things in motion. It is a general word for a general idea. Some other names for the same idea are *dominant, efficient, immediate, legal, moving, next,* or *producing cause.*

Proxy A person who acts for another person, usually to vote in a meeting the first person cannot attend, or a piece of paper giving that right.

Prudent person rule The principle that a **trustee** may invest **trust** funds only in traditionally safe investments or risk being personally responsible for losses.

Public *1.* Having to do with a state, nation, or the community as a whole. *2.* Open to all persons. *3.* A *public defender* is a lawyer, paid directly or indirectly by government funds, who represents poor persons accused of crimes. *4. Public domain* refers to land owned by the government, to something free for anyone to use, or to something unprotected by a **patent** or **copyright.** *5. Public interest* is a broad term for anything that can affect the general public's finances, health, rights, and so on. *Public interest law* is nonprofit legal practice for a public cause. *6. Public law* is either a name given at time of enactment to most U.S. laws (and to some state laws), or the study of law that has to do with the operation of government and the relationship between the government and persons. *7. Public policy* is a vague word that can be as broad as "what is good for (or will not harm) the general public" or "the law." *8.* A *public service (or utilities) commission* **regulates** private businesses that have a state **charter,** perform a necessary public function, and need special government help.

Publication Making public. For example, in **copyright** law, *publication* is offering a book, a movie, etc., to the public by sale or other distribution; in the law of **defamation,** *publication* usually means communicating defamatory information to a person other than the one defamed; in the law of **wills,** *publication* is telling a **witness** that one intends a document to be his or her will; in the law of court **procedure,** *publication* is printing a legal notice in a newspaper; and in banking law, *publication* is trying to collect money on a forged check, dollar bill, etc.

Puffing *1.* Salesmanship that is mere general bragging rather than definite promises or intentionally misleading information. *2.* Secret bidding for an auction seller to raise the price.

Puis (or puisne) Lower ranking or **junior.**

Punitive damages See **damages.**

Pur autre vie **Autre vie.**

Purchase *1.* Buy. *2.* According to the **Uniform Commercial Code,** "any voluntary transaction creating an interest in property, including a gift." *3.* A *purchase money mortgage* is a buyer's financing of part of a purchase by giving a **mortgage** on the property to the seller as **security** for the loan. *4.* A *purchase money resulting trust* holds **title** to property in favor of a person putting up money to buy something in another person's name. *5.* A *purchase order* is a buyer's document that authorizes a person or company to deliver goods or perform services. It promises to pay for them.

Purge *1.* Cleanse, clear, or exonerate from a charge, from guilt, or from a **contract.** *2.* In the law of **wills,** *purge* means to omit a gift to a person named in a will (because the person is legally prohibited from getting anything) without destroying the rest of the will.

Purport *1.* Imply, profess outwardly, or give an impression (sometimes, a false impression). *2.* The meaning, intent, or purpose of something.

Pursuant In accordance with; in carrying out.

Purview The purpose, scope, and design of a **statute.**

Putative **Alleged,** supposed, or commonly known as.

Pyramid sales scheme A type of sales plan under which, once you become a "distributor," you get **commissions** not only for products you sell, but also for products sold by persons you bring into the business. It is also known as a *referral sales plan, chain referral plan,* and *multilevel distributorship.* It is illegal in some forms.

Q *1.* Quarterly. *2.* Question.

QB Queen's Bench (see **King's Bench**).

QV (Latin) *Quod vide.* "Look at." A direction to look in another specific place for more information.

Qua (Latin) As; considered as; in and of itself. For example, "the *trustee qua trustee* is **liable**" means that the **trustee** is liable as a trustee (but might not be liable as an individual).

Quaere (Latin) A **question,** query, or doubt. When used before a phrase, *quaere* means that what follows is an open question. *Not* **quare** [pronounce: quee-ree]

Qualification *1.* Possessing the personal qualities, property, or other necessary things to be eligible to fill a public office or take on a particular duty. *2.* **Limitation** or restriction.

Qualified *1.* Limited or restricted. *2.* A *qualified acceptance* in **contract** law is a **counteroffer** (see that word) that resembles an **acceptance** of another's offer. *3.* A *qualified indorsement* is signing a **negotiable instrument** "without recourse" to limit **liability** for payment.

Quantum meruit (Latin) "As much as he deserved." An old form of **pleading** a lawsuit for compensation for work done. The *theory* of quantum meruit (fair payment for work done) is still used in modern contract law. Also see **quasi** *contract.*

Quantum valebant (Latin) "As much as they were worth." An old form of **pleading** used in a lawsuit for payment for goods sold and delivered.

Quare (Latin) "Wherefore." For example, *quare clausum fregit* (wherefore he broke the close) is an old form of **pleading** a lawsuit for **damages** against someone who **trespasses** on another's land. *Not* **quaere.** [pronounce: kwa-re]

Quash Overthrow; **annul;** completely do away with; a court's stopping a **subpoena, order,** or **indictment.**

Quasi (Latin) "Sort of"; analogous to; "as if." For example, a *quasi contract* is an obligation "sort of like" a **contract** that is created not by agreement but by law.

The principle of quasi contract is used by courts to bring about a fair result when a person's actions or the relationship between persons makes it clear that one person *should* owe an obligation to the other that is similar to a contract.

Quasi judical (legislative) function The case-deciding (rule-making) function of an **administrative agency;** when it acts like a court (like a legislature).

Queen's Bench See **King's Bench.**

Query See **question** and **quaere.**

Question A subject or matter to be looked into or de-bated; a point in dispute in a lawsuit; an issue for decision by judge or jury; etc. For **leading, hypo-thetical, fact,** and **law** questions, see those words.

Qui (Latin) He or she (who). A *qui tam action* is a gov-ernment lawsuit based on an informer's tip.

Quia timet (Latin) "Because of fears." Describes a re-quest to a court similar to a request for an **injunction.**

Quick assets A company's cash plus its **assets** that are easily turned into cash.

Quid pro quo (Latin) Something for something; this for that. The giving of one valuable thing for an-other. **Consideration** that makes a contract **valid.**

Quiet Free from interference or disturbance. For ex-ample, an *action to quiet title* is a way of establishing clear ownership of land, and a *covenant for quiet en-joyment* is, among other things, a promise in a **deed** that the seller will protect the buyer from claims or lawsuits based on prior ownership rights.

Quietus A final **discharge** from a debt or obligation.

Quit *1.* Leave and give up possession of a place. *2.* Free or clear of a debt, of a criminal charge, etc.

Quitclaim deed A **deed** that passes on to the buyer all those rights or as much of a **title** as the seller has. A *quitclaim deed* does not **warrant** (promise) that the seller actually has any rights in the land to pass on.

Quo animo (Latin) "With what intention or motive?" See **animo.**

Quo warranto (Latin) "With what authority?" A proceeding in which a court questions the right of a person (usually a public official) to take a certain action or to hold a certain office.

Quod *1.* (Latin) That which; that. *2.* For *quod vide,* see **QV.**

Quorum The number of persons who must be present to make the votes and other actions of a group (such as a **board**) valid.

Quota *1.* An assigned goal or minimum requirement. *2.* A maximum limit. *3.* A share of a **liability.**

Quotation (or quote) A selling or asking price of a **security** or a **commodity.**

R ® is the symbol for federally **registered** as a **trademark, service** *mark,* or **certification** *mark.*

REIT Real estate investment trust.

RESPA Real Estate Settlement Procedures Act.

RFP Request for proposals.

RICO Racketeer Influenced and Corrupt Organizations Act.

RIF Reduction in force. A layoff by eliminating specific jobs.

RIL **Res ipsa loquitur.**

ROI **Return** on investment. See **yield.**

ROR Release on own **recognizance.**

RS Revised **statutes.**

Race statute See **recording acts.**

Rap sheet A police document listing a person's **arrest** and **conviction** record.

Rape The crime of a man imposing sexual intercourse by force or otherwise without legally valid consent. The definition of what precise acts constitute rape, and whether a man can be raped or a woman rape, differs from state to state.

Ratable *1*. Proportional; adjusted by some formula or percentage. *2*. A proportional, but usually unequal, division. *3*. Taxable.

Rate An amount fixed by mathematical formula or adjusted according to a standard.

Ratification Confirmation and acceptance of a previous act done by you or another person. For example, when the president signs a **treaty,** the Senate must *ratify* it to make it valid. Compare with **reaffirmation.**

Ratio decidendi (Latin) "Reason for decision." The core of a judge's **decision;** the basic ideas that a judge uses to decide a case. [pronounce: ra-shi-o des-i-den-di]

Ratio legis (Latin) Either the *reason* for passing a law (the problem that made it necessary) or the *reasoning* behind a law (the legal theory on which it is based).

Rational basis (or purpose) test The legal theory that a court should not second-guess a **legislature** or an **administrative agency** if the law or administrative decision has some *rational basis.*

Re (Latin) Concerning. See **in re.**

Readjustment A voluntary **reorganization** involving no court or other intervention.

Reaffirmation Agreement to something previously agreed to, especially if the prior agreement is not enforceable. Compare with **ratification.**

Real *1.* Having to do with land and things permanently attached to land, such as buildings. *2.* Having to do with a thing rather than with a person. *3.* A *real defense* is a **defense** that challenges the validity of a document rather than challenging the circumstances surrounding it; for example, **forgery.** *4. Real evidence* is objects seen by the jury, such as fingerprints.

Realized Actual; "in hand;" cashed in. For example, a *realized profit* is a cash-in-hand gain, as opposed to a *paper profit,* which is the increase in value of unsold property.

Realty Land and buildings; real estate.

Reapportionment Changing the boundaries of a **legislative** *district* to reflect population changes.

Reasonable A broad, flexible word used to make sure that a decision is based on the *facts* of a particular situation rather than on abstract legal principles. It has no exact definition but can mean *fair, appropriate, moderate, rational,* etc. Its definition tends to be circular. For example, *reasonable care* has been defined as "that degree of care a person of ordinary prudence (the so-called *reasonable person*) would exercise in similar circumstances."

Reassessment The government's reestimating the value of property and changing it for tax purposes.

Rebate A discount, deduction, or refund.

Rebut Dispute, defeat, or take away the effect of facts or arguments. *Rebuttal* is contradicting statements made by an adversary, and *rebuttable* means disputable. For example, a *rebuttable presumption* is a conclusion that will be drawn unless **evidence** is presented that counters it.

Rebutter A *common-law* **pleading,** the third by the **defendant.**

Recall *1.* Remove an elected official from office by a vote of the people. *2.* Notify product owners of a safety defect and offer to fix or take back the product. *3.* **Revoke,** cancel, or **vacate** a **judgment** because facts originally relied upon to grant it are found to be wrong.

Recaption Taking something back that has been taken away.

Recapture Taking something back, either by the terms of an agreement or by legal right.

Receipt *1.* Written acknowledgment that something has been received or put into your hands. *2.* The act of receiving.

Receipts Money that comes into a business, usually through sales.

Receivables See **account** *receivable.*

Receiver An outside person appointed by the court to manage money and property during a lawsuit. A *receivership* is often created by a court to manage a business because **creditors** suspect **fraud** or gross mismanagement.

Receiving stolen goods The crime of getting or concealing property known to be stolen by another.

Recess *1.* A brief break taken by a court, usually lasting an hour or two at most. *2.* A break in a **legislative** session, sometimes lasting many weeks.

Recidivist Either a repeat or a **habitual criminal.**

Reciprocal Mutual; bilateral (two-sided or two-way). For example, *reciprocal wills* are **wills** made by two persons and enforceable against each other because each person put something in his or her will that the other asked for.

Reciprocity *1*. Two states or countries giving identical privileges to citizens of the other. *2*. See **reciprocal.**

Recision   Rescission.

Recital   A formal listing of facts, such as a formal statement in a document that explains the reasons for the document or for the transaction involving it.

Reckless   Anything from "careless and inattentive" to "a willful disregard for the life of others."

Recognition   *1*. Designation of a gain or loss due to a *taxable event* (such as a sale of property) as "taxable" in the current tax year. A gain may be **realized,** but not *recognized,* if the tax law allows a person to put off payment of tax to another year. *2*. Acknowledgment that something done in one person's name by another person was authorized by the former. *3*. The purpose of *recognition* **picketing** is to force an employer to **bargain** with a particular **union.**

Recognizance   A formal obligation to do a certain act that is recorded in court. For example, a person accused of a crime may be allowed to go free before trial without putting up a **bail bond.** The person gives the court a formal written statement that failure to show up will mean payment to the court of a certain amount of money. This is called getting out on your *own recognizance.*

Recollection   The act of remembering. This may be done by a **witness** who *refreshes the memory* by using an object or document.

Reconciliation   *1*. The renewal of a broken relationship with forgiveness on both sides. *2*. Bringing two differing **accounts** into agreement; for example, the **balance** in a checkbook and the bank's monthly **statement.**

Reconveyance The return of **title** to property; for example, the return of title to a car when the bank loan is paid off.

Record _1._ A formal, written account of a case, containing the complete formal history of all actions taken, papers filed, **rulings** made, **opinions** written, and so on. The _record_ can also include all the **evidence (testimony,** physical objects, etc.,) as well as the evidence _refused_ **admission** by the judge. A _court of record_ includes all courts for which permanent records of proceedings are kept. _2._ A _public record_ is a document filed with, or put out by, a government agency and open to the public for inspection. For example, a _title of record_ to land is an ownership interest that has been properly filed in the public land records. The _recorder of deeds_ keeps these records, and the process is _recordation._

Recording acts State laws establishing rules for **priority** among persons who claim the same **interest** in **land** (and sometimes other property). _Race statutes_ favor the person who **records** (files) the claim first. _Notice statutes_ favor the person with the _later_ valid claim (whether or not recorded) over an earlier unrecorded claim unless that person knew about the earlier claim. _Race-notice statutes_ favor the person who records first with no knowledge of a prior unrecorded claim.

Recoupment _1._ Keeping or holding something back that you owe because there is a fair, just reason to do so. _2._ Taking or getting something back, especially money lost. _3._ A **counterclaim.**

Recourse _1._ The right of a person who holds a **negotiable instrument** to get payment on it from anyone who indorsed (signed) it. **Recourse** is available unless the signer signs it "no recourse" or "without recourse." _2._ The means to enforce a **right.**

Recovery *1.* The thing received when a lawsuit is decided in your favor. *2.* The amount of money given by a **judgment** in a successful lawsuit.

Recrimination *1.* The principle that if a person seeking a divorce is guilty of the same conduct on which **grounds** for the divorce are based, no divorce will be granted. *2.* An accusation made by an accused person against the accuser.

Recross See **examination.**

Recusation The process by which a judge is disqualified (or disqualifies himself or herself) from hearing a lawsuit because of **interest** or **prejudice.**

Red herring A preliminary **prospectus** used during the "waiting period" between filing a *registration statement* with the **S.E.C.** and approval of the statement.

Redaction A deletion, revision, or editing.

Reddendum A **clause** in a **deed** that reserves (keeps) a **reversion** right.

Redeem *1.* Buy back. Reclaim property that has been **mortgaged.** The process is *redemption. 2.* Turn in for cash.

Redirect See **examination.**

Redlining A refusal to make mortgage loans in an area, "because" of deteriorating conditions, which results in racial discrimination.

Redraft *1.* A second **note** or **bill** offered for payment after the first has been refused. *2.* A second writing of anything.

Redress *1.* Satisfaction or payment for harm done. *2.* Access to the courts to get #1.

Reductio ad absurdum (Latin) "Reduce to the absurd." Disprove an argument by showing that it leads to a ridiculous conclusion.

Reduction Turning something abstract (such as a debt) into something concrete (such as a cash payment).

Re-entry Taking back possession of land by a right you kept when you left the land before.

Refer *1.* Point to; direct attention to. *2.* A judge's action of turning over a case, or part of a case, to a person who has been appointed to sort things out by taking **testimony,** examining documents, and making decisions and recommendations. This person is called a *referee* or *special master.*

Referee in bankruptcy An old word for a federal judge who runs **bankruptcy** hearings.

Reference *1.* An agreement in a **contract** to submit certain disputes to an **arbitrator** for decision. *2.* See **refer.** *3.* Mention of a place to find certain information. See also **citation.** *4.* See **incorporate by reference.**

Referendum Putting an important law to a direct vote of the people.

Reformation A procedure in which a court will rewrite or correct (reform) a written agreement to conform with the original intent of the persons making the deal. The court will usually do this only if there was **fraud** or mutual mistake in writing up the original document.

Reg. *1.* **Regulation.** *2.* **Registered.**

Register A book of public facts, such as births, **deeds,** voters, etc. The book is often called a *registry,* and the record-keeping official a *register, recorder, registrar,* or **clerk.**

Registered Listed on an official record. For example, a *registered stock* can be cashed in only by the person who is officially listed as the owner.

Registrar See **register** and **transfer agent.**

Registration *1.* Recording (see **record**). *2.* See **register.** *3.* A *registration statement* is a financial and ownership **statement** required by the **S.E.C.** of most sellers of **securities.**

Regnal years **Statutes** in England are usually dated by the name of the king or queen on the throne at the time and the year of their reign.

Regressive tax Opposite of **progressive tax.**

Regs. Regulations.

Regular *1.* Steady; uniform; with no unusual variations. *2.* Lawful; legal; in conformity with usual practice.

Regulate Control. A government *regulates* business by passing laws and setting up *regulatory agencies* (**administrative agencies**) to write rules and **regulations,** to administer and enforce the regulations by giving **orders,** holding **hearings,** etc.

Regulation A rule that is put out by a local government or by an **administrative agency** to **regulate** conduct. For example, **IRS** regulations apply the *tax* **code** to specific situations, and local governments put out parking regulations.

Regulatory agency See **regulate.**

Regulatory offense *1.* A **statutory** crime. *2.* A minor offense, defined *not* by **statute** but by **regulation.**

Rehabilitation *1.* The restoring of former rights, abilities, authority, credibility, etc. For example, *rehabilitating a witness* means asking questions to restore the witness's believability after the other side has destroyed it or put it in question. *2.* See **Chapter Thirteen** for a *rehabilitation in bankruptcy.*

Reinstate Place back in a condition that has been ended or lost. For example, to *reinstate a case* is to put it back into court after it has been dismissed (thrown out).

Reinsurance A **contract** by which one insurance company insures itself with another to protect itself against all or part of the **risk** it took on by insuring a customer.

Rejoinder   A *common-law* **pleading.**

Relation   "Relating back" or having retroactive effect.

Relative fact   *1.* **Circumstantial evidence.** *2.* An *evidentiary fact* (see **evidence**).

Relator   A person in whose name a state brings a legal action (the person who "relates" the facts on which the action is based). See **ex rel.** [pronounce: re-<u>late</u>-or]

Release   *1.* Give up or relinquish a claim or right to the person against whom it might have been enforced. The document by which a claim is relinquished is called a *release.* *2.* For *release on own recognizance,* see **recognizance.**

Relevancy   See **relevant.**

Relevant   Having an impact on a question or issue; having to do with a disputed issue in a lawsuit. **Evidence** is *relevant* if it tends to prove or disprove a theory or position (by one side in a lawsuit) that will influence the result of the lawsuit. Evidence must be relevant to be admitted (accepted) by the court.

Reliance   Belief in something, plus acting on that belief. See also **promissory estoppel.**

Relief   The help given by a court to a person who brings a lawsuit. The "relief asked for" might be the return of property taken by another person, the enforcement of a contract, money, etc.

Rem   (Latin) "Thing." See **in rem.**

Remainder   *1.* An interest or **estate** in land or **trust** property that takes effect only when another interest in land or trust property ends. For example, if Mary's **will** says, "I leave my house to Joe for ten years and then to Jane," Jane's interest is a *remainder.* See also **reversion.** *2.* Used in a will, *remainder* means "what's left;" for example, "my house and clothing to Joe and the remainder to Jane."

Remainderman *1.* A person who gets what is "left over" under a **will** or when a **trust** ends. *2.* A person who will (or may) get an interest in land at a future time.

Remand Send back. For example, a higher court may *remand* (send back) a case to a lower court, directing the lower court to take some action.

Remedial statute *1.* A law passed to correct a defect in a prior law. *2.* A law passed to provide (or modify) a **remedy** (for example, to create a new **lien**).

Remedy *1.* The means by which a right is enforced or satisfaction is gained for harm done. The means by which a violation of rights is prevented, redressed, or compensated. For example, Ron's *remedy* against Don if Don refuses to give back Ron's book might be to take it back, to argue with Don until he gives it back, or to go to court to either get it back or make Don pay for it. *2.* "Legal remedies" or "court remedies" include such things as **injunctions** and **damages.**

Remise **Release,** end, give up, or forgive (a debt, an offense, a harm done, etc.). The process is *remission.* See also **condonation.**

Remit *1.* Send; send in or send back. *2.* Give up or pay.

Remittance Money (or a check, etc.,) sent by one person to another, often as payment for a debt.

Remitter Being "sent back" to an earlier, better right. For example, if a person who owns property and **leases** it to another is left the lease rights in the renter's will, the owner gets full original rights to the property by *remitter.*

Remittitur *1.* Either the power of a trial judge to decrease the amount of money awarded by the **jury** to the **plaintiff,** or the power of an **appeals** court to deny a new trial to the **defendant** if the plaintiff agrees to take a certain amount of money less than that given in the trial. *2. Remittitur of record* is the return of a case from appeals court to trial court to carry out the higher court's decision.

Remonstrance   A formal protest against governmental policy or action.

Removal   The movement of a person or thing from one place to another; for example, transfer of a case from state to federal court.

Render   *1.* **Pronounce,** state, or declare. For example, a judge *renders judgment* by formally making a decision in a case in court. *2.* Give up or return. For example, *rendition* is a state's returning a **fugitive from justice** to a state seeking the fugitive's return. *3.* Pay or perform.

Renewal   The act of extending a legally binding arrangement for an additional time period, often by entering into a new agreement on the same or similar terms.

Renounce   Reject, cast off, or give something up openly and in public. The process is called *renunciation* and often refers to **abandonment** of a right.

Renvoi   (French) Return; send back. The principle that the laws in your own state or country should be applied to a case when your laws direct you to abide by another state's or country's laws, but those laws in turn direct the use of your laws. [pronounce; ron-vwa]

Reorganization   *1.* See **Chapter Eleven** for reorganization in **bankruptcy.**   *2.* Any restructuring of an organization.

Rep.   **Reporter, reports,** or **representative.**

Repair Fix a defect. Repairs and **improvements** are treated differently for tax purposes.

Reparable injury A wrong that can be compensated by money.

Reparation Payment for an injury; redress for a wrong done.

Repeal Wipe out an earlier **statute** by passing a later one. This is usually **prospective** only.

Repleader **Motion** for a new trial.

Replevin A legal action to get back *personal* **property** wrongfully held by another person.

Replevy Give back personal **property** to a person who has brought a lawsuit for its return.

Replication An old form of **pleading** similar to the modern **reply.**

Reply In *federal* **pleading,** the **plaintiff's** response to the **defendant's answer** or **counterclaim.** The usual order is: complaint, answer, reply. The reply denies some or all of the facts in the answer. Sometimes it adds new facts, but only to counter facts in the answer.

Repo. *1.* A *repurchase agreement* in which a dealer agrees to buy back a **security** at a set time and price. *2.* **Repossession.**

Reporter *1.* Published volumes of decisions by a court or group of courts. Also called *reports. 2.* A **loose-leaf service.** *3.* A *court reporter* records court proceedings and later makes good copies of some of them.

Repossession Taking back something sold usually because payments have not been made.

Represent *1.* To say or state certain facts. *2.* To act for, do business for, or "stand in" for another person. See also **agent.** *3.* To act as another person's lawyer.

Representation _1_. See **represent.** _2_. In **contract** law, a _representation_ is any statement (or any impression given about a state of facts) made to convince the other person to make a contract. _3_. In **inheritance** law, _taking by representation_ is taking **per stirpes.**

Representative action _1_. **Derivative action.** _2_. **Class action.**

Reprieve Holding off on enforcing a criminal **sentence** for a period of time after the sentence has been handed down.

Republication Reestablishing the validity of a **will** that has been revoked.

Repudiation Rejection or refusal. For example, repudiation of a **contract** is the refusal to go through with it, usually with a legal right to refuse.

Requirements contract A **contract** for the supply of goods in which the exact amount of goods to be bought is not set but is agreed to be all that the buyer reasonably needs while the contract is in force. Compare **output contract.**

Requisition A demand or a request for something to which one has a right.

Res (Latin) _1_. A thing or things; an object; a status; for example, the subject matter or contents of a **will** or **trust.** [pronounce: race] _2_. For _res adjudicata_, see _res judicata_. _3. Res gestae_ are "things done," or "an entire occurrence." Everything said and done that is part of a single event, such as threats that are part of an **assault.** Words spoken by others can usually be testified about even if **hearsay** if the words are part of the _res gestae_. [pronounce: race guest-eye] _4. Res immobiles_ are **real** property. _5. Res integra_ means an undecided point of law, one without **precedent** and probably without any discussion in prior cases. _6. Res ipsa loquitur_ ("the thing speaks for itself") is a

rebuttable presumption (a conclusion that can be changed if contrary evidence is introduced) that a person is **negligent** if the thing causing an accident was in his or her control only, and if that type of accident does not usually occur without negligence. It is often abbreviated "res ipsa" or RIL. [pronounce: race ip-sa low-kwe-tur] *7. Res judicata* means "a thing decided" or "a matter decided by **judgment.**" If a court decides a case, the subject of that case is firmly and finally decided between the persons involved in the case, so no new lawsuit on the same subject may be brought by the persons involved. See also **collateral estoppel** and **double jeopardy.** [pronounce: race ju-di-ca-ta]

Rescind   To take back or **annul.** To cancel a **contract** and wipe it out "from the beginning" as if it had never been. [pronounce: re-sind]

Rescission   *1.* The **annulment** of a **contract.** See **rescind.** *2.* The president's request to Congress that certain money already appropriated not be spent. [pronounce: re-sizh-un]

Reserve   *1.* Hold back a thing or a right. For example, to *reserve title* is to keep an ownership right as **security** that a thing bought will be fully paid for; and a judge may *reserve decision* of a legal question by putting it off until the end of the trial. *2. With reserve* in an auction means that the thing will not be sold unless the highest bid exceeds a certain amount (the *reserve price*). *3.* A fund of money set aside to meet future needs, losses, or claims.

Residence   A place where a person lives all or part of the time. Sometimes, this is the same as **domicile.**

Residuary   The part left over. For example, a *residuary clause* in a will disposes of all items not specifically given away.

Residuum (Latin) Leftovers.

Resolution A formal expression of a decision made by an organized group, such as a club or a **legislature.**

Resolve *1.* A **resolution.** *2.* A firm decision to do something; a strong will to achieve a goal.

Resort A *court of last resort* is a court whose decision cannot be appealed within the same court system.

Respondeat superior (Latin) "Let the master answer." The principle that an employer is responsible for most harm caused by an employee acting within the **scope of employment.** In such cases, the employer is said to have **vicarious liability.**

Respondent The person against whom an **appeal** is taken or against whom a **motion** is filed.

Responsive Answering. For example, a *responsive pleading* is a court paper that directly answers the points raised by the other side's **pleading.**

Rest To *rest a case* is to formally end your side's presentation of evidence for a major phase of a case in court.

Restatement of Law Books put out by the **American Law Institute** that tell what the law in a general area is, how it is changing, and what direction the authors think this change should take; for example, *Restatement of the Law of Contracts.*

Restitution Giving something back; making good for something.

Restrain *1.* Prohibit from action; hold back. *2.* Hinder or obstruct. *3.* For *restraining order,* see **temporary restraining order.** *4. Restraint of trade* is an illegal agreement or **combination** that eliminates competition, sets up a **monopoly,** or artificially raises prices. See **antitrust acts.**

Restrictive covenant A **clause** in a **deed** that forbids the new owner (and all later owners of the deeded land) from doing certain things with the land; for example, a clause that prohibits use of the land for commercial purposes.

Restrictive indorsement Signing a **negotiable instrument** in a way that ends its negotiability; for example, "Pay to Ann Jones only."

Resulting trust A **trust** created by law (rather than by agreement) for reasons of fairness when one person holds property for another. For example, if Peter buys a house for himself but puts the **title** in Paul's name, a court may decide that the house is held in a *purchase money resulting trust* for Peter's benefit.

Retained earnings A company's yearly **net** profit minus **dividends.**

Retainer *1.* Employment of a lawyer by a client; the agreement to do so; or the first payment in that agreement. *2.* Holding something back because you have a right to.

Retaliatory eviction A landlord's attempt (prohibited in most states) to throw out a tenant for complaining to the health department, forming a tenants' union, etc.

Retirement Making the final payment owed on a **security** and ending its existence and all obligations under it.

Retrospective (or retroactive) law A law that changes the legal status of things already done or that applies to past actions. See also **ex post facto** laws.

Return *1.* The act of a sheriff or other peace officer in delivering back to a court a brief account of whether or not (and how) he or she **served** (delivered) a court paper to a person. *2.* **Yield** or profit. *3.* See **tax return.** *4.* A *return day* (*or date*) is either the day by which a sheriff must serve a court paper for it to be valid (see #1), or the day by which a **defendant** must **file** a **pleading** after receiving a **summons** to come to court.

Rev. *1.* Review. *2.* Revised.

Revenue *1.* Income. *2.* Profit on an investment. *3.* Describes things that raise money for the government.

Reverse Set aside. For example, when a higher court *reverses* a lower court on **appeal,** it sets aside the **judgment** of the lower court and either substitutes its own judgment for it or sends the case back to the lower court with instructions on what to do.

Reversion (or reverter) Any **future interest** kept by a person who transfers away property. For example, if John rents out his land for ten years, his ownership rights during those years, his right to take back the property after ten years, and his **heirs'** right to take back the property after ten years if he dies are *reversionary interests*. Compare **remainder.**

Revised statutes *1.* A **code.** *2.* A book of **statutes** in the order in which they were originally passed, with temporary and repealed statutes removed.

Revive Restore to original force or legal effect.

Revocation *1.* The taking back of some power or authority; for example, taking back an **offer** before it is accepted and ending the other person's right to accept. *2.* The ending or making **void** of a thing. *Revocation* of a **will** takes place when, for example, a person makes another will.

Revoke Wipe out a thing's legal effect by taking it back, canceling it, rescinding it, etc. See **revocation.** If something can be revoked but has not been, it is *revocable*.

Revolving charge Credit, often provided through credit cards or department stores, by which purchases may be charged and partially paid off month by month. New purchases may be made, charged, and paid off during the same period.

Richard Roe A common name used for a **fictitious party** or a name used along with **John Doe** to illustrate a legal situation.

Rider An additional piece of paper attached to a larger document. A *rider to a bill* is an addition made late in the **legislative** process and often unrelated to the **bill** but "tacked on" anyway.

Right *1*. Morally, ethically, or legally just. *2*. One person's *legal* ability to control certain actions of another person or of all other persons. Most rights have a corresponding **duty.** *3*. For *right from wrong test,* see **M'Naghten rule.** *4*. A *right of action* is a claim that can be enforced in court. *5*. *Right-to-work laws* are state laws that forbid **labor contracts** requiring union membership, preferential hiring, or similar provisions.

Riparian Having to do with the bank of a river or stream.

Ripe *1*. A case is *ripe* for selection and decision by a court or agency that has the power to turn down cases if it involves a real **controversy** and if the legal issues involved are clear enough and well enough evolved and presented so that a clear decision can come out of the case. *2*. A case is *ripe* for decision by a **trial** court if everything but the decision is completed and in order.

Rising of court Any starting or stopping of court activity.

Risk A **hazard** (fire), the danger of hazard or loss (one chance in 10,000 per year), the specific possible hazard or loss mentioned in an **insurance** policy (John's house burning down), or the item insured itself (the house).

Robbery The illegal taking of property from the person of another by using force or threat of force.

Robinson-Patman Act A federal law that prohibits price discrimination and other anticompetitive business practices.

Rogatory letters A request from one judge to another asking that the second judge supervise the examination of a **witness** (usually in another state, and usually by written **interrogatories**).

Roll *1.* A record of official proceedings. *2.* A list of persons or property subject to a tax. *3.* To *roll over* a debt is to refinance it.

Roomer A person who rents rooms in a house, as opposed to a **tenant,** who may have more legal rights.

Royalty A payment made to the creator of a work or the owner of a natural material for the use of that work or material.

Rubric *1.* Overall purpose. *2.* Title. *3.* Category. *4.* Rule.

Rule *1.* To settle a legal issue or decide a **motion, objection,** etc., raised by one side in a legal dispute. The *ruling* is made by the person in charge (judge, hearing officer, chairperson, etc.). *2.* An established standard, principle, or guide. *3.* A **regulation,** often to govern an **administrative agency's** internal workings. *4.* For the *rule against perpetuities,* see **perpetuity.** *5. Rule of law* has many definitions; for example, "a general statement that is intended to guide conduct, applied by government officials, and supported by an authoritative source." Also, *"the" rule of law* is the principle that the highest authority is the law, not the government or its leaders.

Rules (federal) See **federal** *rules.*

Ruling A judge's decision on a legal question raised during a trial.

Run   *1*. Have legal validity. For example, state law *runs* throughout the state. *2*. To continue to count. For example, "the **statute of limitations** is running" means that days are being counted against the maximum allowable number of days before the statute prohibits a lawsuit; and "the statute of limitations has run" means that the statute's time limit has expired. *3*. Be attached to a thing. For example, a **covenant** may *run with* (be attached to) the land and stay with the land even if the land changes ownership.

S   *1*. Section. *2*. **Statute.** *3*. Senate.

SA   Abbreviation for *incorporated* in French and Spanish. See **corporation.**

SB   Senate **bill.**

SBA   Small Business Administration.

SC   *1*. **Supreme Court.** *2*. Same case.

S Corporation   A small (defined by number of owners) business **corporation** that has chosen a tax status that allows it to be taxed as a **partnership** to avoid the **corporate** income tax.

SD   Southern **district.**

SE   South Eastern Reporter (see **National Reporter System**).

SEC   Securities and Exchange Commission. See **security.**

SEP   Simplified Employee Pension; employer payment to an **IRA.**

SM   Service mark.

SS   Sworn statement. A symbol found on many **affidavits.**

SSA   Social Security Administration.

SUB   Supplemental unemployment benefits; a private plan.

SW   South Western Reporter (see **National Reporter System**).

Safe harbor   An approved way of complying with a **statute** when the statute is phrased in general terms.

Said   "The one mentioned before." A word to be avoided in legal writing, as in *"said table."*

Sale   *1.* An exchange of property for money (or the contract that expresses the exchange). *2. "Sales"* is a field of law, now covered primarily by the **Uniform Commercial Code**, which governs the sale of goods.

Salvage   *1.* Property recovered after an accident or other damage or destruction. *2.* In tax law, an assumed value that business property will have at the end of its useful life.

Sanction   *1.* Agree to or confirm another person's actions. *2.* A penalty or punishment attached to a law so that it is obeyed.

Sanity   See **insanity.**

Satisfaction   Taking care of a debt or **obligation** by paying it.

Satisfactory   A general word for "enough" or "good enough."

Save   *1.* Hold until later; reserve; preserve. *2.* For *save harmless,* see **hold harmless.** *3.* A *saving clause* is a provision in a law or contract that makes its parts **severable** (see that word). Also see **grandfather clause.**

Schedule   A list; in particular, a list of specifics or details attached to a more general document.

Scienter   (Latin) Knowingly; with guilty knowledge. [pronounce: si-<u>en</u>-ter]

Scintilla   A very little bit, usually used in the sense "a *mere scintilla* is (or is not) enough **evidence**. [pronounce: sin-<u>till</u>-a]

Scire facias   (Latin) A judge's command to a public official to come to court and explain why a record in that person's possession should not be destroyed, disclosed, etc. [pronounce: <u>sigh</u>-ree <u>fay</u>-sheeus]

Scope of employment   The range of actions within which an employee is considered to be doing work for the employer. See **respondeat superior.**

Seal   An identification mark pressed in wax. Originally, for a document to be valid, it had to have a wax seal on it to show that it was done seriously, correctly, and formally. Later, the use of the letters **LS** took the place of wax. Now, there is little use for a seal except to formalize certain **corporate** documents and documents witnessed by a **notary public**. See also **contract under seal.**

Search warrant   Written permission from a judge or **magistrate** for a law enforcement officer to search a particular place for **evidence**, stolen property, etc. The police must give a good reason for needing these items, a likely reason why they might be there, and some indication that their information is reliable.

Seasonable   In a reasonable amount of time.

Sec.   Section.

Second   *1.* Lower ranking; coming later or farther away; less important. *2.* For *Second Amendment,* see **Bill of Rights.** *3.* A *second-look statute* is a **wait-and-see statute.**

Secondary *1*. See **second**. *2*. *Secondary authority* is either **persuasive authority** or a comment about the law, such as an **annotation**. *3*. A *secondary* **boycott, picketing,** or **strike** is indirect pressure on a business that does business with the one with which a union is actually having a dispute.

Secretary of state In the U.S. government, the **cabinet** member in charge of foreign relations; in most state governments, the official who takes care of many types of formal state business, such as the licensing of corporations.

Secure, secured, and securities See **security**.

Security *1*. Property that has been given as a **pledge**, that has a **mortgage**, that has a **lien,** etc., to *secure* (as financial backing for) a loan or other obligation. A *security interest* is any right in property that is held to make sure that money is paid or something is done. Most property *secured* this way may be sold by the *secured* **creditor** if the debt it backs is not paid. *2*. **Stocks, bonds, notes,** or other documents that show an ownership share in, or a debt owed by, a company. The *Securities and Exchange Commission* **regulates** their sale.

Sedition Stirring up persons to armed resistance against the government.

Segregation *1*. The **unconstitutional** practice of separating persons in housing, schooling, and so on, based on race, nationality, etc. *2*. *Segregation of assets* involves identifying and setting aside one person's property from a common fund or pot.

Seisin Full and complete present ownership and possession of land. [pronounce: seez-in]

Seizure *1*. The act by a public official (usually a law enforcement or court officer) of taking property because of a violation of the law or because of a **writ** or

judgment in a lawsuit. *2.* The act of a law enforcement officer taking a person into **custody** and detaining the person in a way that interferes with freedom of movement.

Selectman A member of some local **legislatures**. Some small towns have the *first selectman* serve as mayor.

Self-dealing A **trustee** (or other person with a **fiduciary** duty) acting to enrich or help himself or herself rather than the person who should be helped.

Self-defense Physical force used against a person who is committing a **felony**, threatening the use of physical force, or using physical force. This is a right if the person's own family, property, or body is in danger, but sometimes only if the danger was not provoked.

Self-executing Describes laws or court decisions that require no further official action to be carried out.

Self-help Taking an action without obtaining official authorization when that action may need authorization. For example, a *self-help eviction* may be a landlord's removing the tenant's property from an apartment and locking the door against the tenant. In many states, some forms of self-help are illegal.

Self-incrimination Anything said or done by a person that implicates that person in a crime. It is normally **unconstitutional** to force or require a person to do this.

Self-liquidation Paying off a loan by the short-term resale of the items bought with the loan money.

Self-serving declaration An out-of-court statement by a **party** to a lawsuit that, if admitted as **evidence** in the lawsuit, would tend to be helpful to the party. These statements are usually inadmissible **hearsay**.

Selling short   See **short sale.**

Senate   The upper **house** of a state or of the U.S. **legislature.** The members are senators.

Senior interest   An **interest** or right that takes effect or collects ahead of others.

Sentence   The punishment, such as time in jail, given to a person convicted of a criminal offense.

Separability clause   A *severability clause.* See **severable.**

Separate   *1. Separate but equal* was the rule, now **unconstitutional**, that when races are given substantially equal facilities, they may be segregated. *2. Separate estate* is property owned by a person as an individual rather than as part of a business or marriage. *3. Separate maintenance* is money paid by one married person to another for support if they are no longer living as husband and wife. In some states, this term means only *temporary* **alimony** or *temporary* **support.**

Separation   *1.* A husband and wife living apart by agreement, either *before* a **divorce** or *instead* of a full divorce. If it is by court **order**, it is a *judicial* or *legal separation. 2. Separation of powers* is the division of a government into **legislative** (lawmaking), **judicial** (law-interpreting), and **executive** (law-carrying-out) branches, each acting to prevent the others from becoming too powerful.

Sequester   To isolate or hold aside. For example, to *sequester* a **jury** is to keep it from having contact with the outside world during a trial, and to *sequester property* is to have it put aside and held by an independent person during a lawsuit.

Seriatim   (Latin) One at a time; in proper order.

Series   A set of law books in numerical order. A new (second, third, etc.,) *series* follows, rather than replaces, an older one.

Servant A person employed by another person (a **master**) and subject to that person's control as to *what* work is done and *how* it is done.

Service *1*. The delivery (or its legal equivalent, such as publication in a newspaper in some cases) of a legal paper, such as a **writ,** by an authorized person in a way that meets formal requirements. It is the way to notify a person of a lawsuit. *2*. Regular payments on a debt. *3*. A *service mark* is a mark used in the sale or advertising of services, usually to identify and protect the service by a distinctive design, title, etc.; for example, Lazy Transport's "*Slotruk Service®*."

Servient Describes land subject to a **servitude** or **charge.**

Servitude *1*. A **charge** or burden on land in favor of another. For example, the owner of a piece of land may be required by the **deed** to allow the owner of adjoining land to walk across part of the land. This type of **servitude** is called an **easement**. The land so restricted is the *servient estate*, and the land benefiting from the restriction is the **dominant** *estate*. *2*. The condition of being a slave or servant.

Session A day or period of days in which a court, a **legislature**, etc., carries on its business. *Session laws* are **statutes** printed in the order that they were passed in each session of a legislature. See also **statutes at large.**

Set aside Cancel, **annul**, or **revoke** a court's **judgment.**

Set down Put a case on the list (or court **docket**) for a **hearing.**

Setback A distance from a street, property line, building, etc., within which building is prohibited by **zoning** or other laws.

Setoff A **defendant's** **counterclaim** that has nothing to do with the plaintiff's lawsuit against the defendant.

Settle *1.* Come to an agreement about a debt, payment of a debt, or disposition of a lawsuit. *2.* Finish; take care of completely. *3.* Transfer property in a way that specifies a succession of owners. *4.* Set up a **trust**.

Settlement *1.* See **settle**. *2.* The meeting in which the ownership of **real property** actually transfers from seller to buyer. All payments and debts are usually taken care of at this time or immediately thereafter.

Settlor A person who sets up a **trust** by providing the money or property for it.

Seventh Amendment See **Bill of Rights.**

Sever a trial Try a person's case separately and at another time from others who might otherwise be in the same trial. Also called *severance.*

Severable Capable of carrying on an independent existence. For example, a *severable* **statute** is one that can still be valid even if one part is struck down as **invalid** by a court. A *severable (or separable)* **contract** is one that can be divided into separate contracts, each valid even if the other is not. Most statutes and some contracts have a *severability, separability,* or *saving* clause.

Several *1.* More than one. *2.* Separate; individual; independent. See also **joint and several.**

Severally Distinctly; separately; each on its own.

Severalty ownership Sole ownership; ownership by one person.

Severance tax A tax on the volume or value of a natural resource, such as coal, taken from the land.

Sewer service Slang for telling the court that you have properly served (officially delivered) a court paper when it has actually been thrown away.

Sexual harassment In a narrow sense, using a position of power over a person's job, salary, and so on, to gain sexual favors or to punish the refusal of such favors. More broadly, *sexual harassment* includes such things as unwarranted sexual innuendoes and maintaining a workplace where employees feel sexually threatened.

Shall Almost always *must*, but sometimes *may* if clearly meant that way.

Sham False or fake.

Share *1.* A portion. *2.* One unit of **stock** in a **corporation.**

Shelley's Case The *Rule in Shelley's Case* is that when a life **estate** is given to a person, followed by a **remainder** given to that person's **heirs**, the heirs take nothing, but the holder of the life estate gets an interest in **fee**. (Under the rule, if John gives land to Sue to use for life and, in the same document, gives it to someone else after that and then to Sue's children, Sue gets it all to do with as she pleases.) This rule is no longer followed; life estates and remainders *are* permitted.

Shelter *1.* The principle that a buyer has as good a **title** to property as the seller had. *2.* A way of investing money to gain tax advantage.

Shepardizing Using a Shepard's **citator** to trace the history of a case *after* it is decided to see if it is **followed**, **overruled**, **distinguished**, etc.

Sheriff *1.* The chief law officer of a county, who, with the help of deputies, is in charge of serving **process,** calling **jurors**, executing **judgments**, keeping the peace, operating a county **jail**, etc. *2.* A *sheriff's deed* is a document giving ownership rights to property sold at a *sheriff's sale* (a sale held by a sheriff to pay a court **judgment** against the property's owner).

Sherman Act The first **antitrust** (antimonopoly) law passed by the federal government to break up "combinations in restraint of trade."

Shield law A state law that protects (shields) a writer's or an informer's information sources, or one that protects anonymity.

Shifting Changing; varying; passing from one person to another.

Shop steward A union official elected to represent workers in one department of a business.

Short cause (or calendar) A lawsuit, or part of one, that must be heard by a judge but is usually scheduled early because it can be disposed of quickly.

Short sale A **contract** for the sale of something, such as stock, that the seller does not own. It is a method of profiting from the expected fall in price of a stock, but large losses are risked if the price goes up.

Show cause order A court **order** to a person to show up in court and explain why the court should not take a proposed action. If the person fails to show up or to give sufficient reasons why the court should take no action, the court will take the action.

Shyster Slang for a dishonest lawyer.

Si (Latin) If.

Sic (Latin) Thus; so; in such a way.

Sight *At sight* means **payable** when shown and requested. A **bill** or **draft** payable when shown is a *sight bill* or *sight draft.*

Silent partner See **partner.**

Simple *1.* Pure, unmixed, or uncomplicated. *2.* Not **aggravated.**

Sine die (Latin) "Without day." A final ending or **adjournment** of a **session** of a court or a **legislature.** [pronounce: si-ne de-ay]

Single proprietorship An unincorporated business owned by one person.

Single-name paper A **negotiable instrument** that has only one **maker** (original signer) or, if more than one original signer, persons signing for exactly the same purpose (for example, as **partners**).

Sinking fund Money or other **assets** put aside for a special, long-term purpose.

Sit *1*. Hold court as a judge. *2*. Hold any session; to be formally organized and carry on official business.

Situs (Latin) "Site"; fixed location; place. Usually the place where a thing has legal ties.

Sixth Amendment See **Bill of Rights.**

Slander Oral **defamation.** The speaking of false words that injure another person's reputation, business, or property rights.

Slating Booking.

Slip decision (or sheet or opinion) A printed copy of a U.S. Supreme Court **decision** (or certain other court decisions) that is distributed immediately.

Slip law A printed copy of a **bill** passed by Congress that is distributed immediately once signed by the president.

Small business Some **administrative agencies** define a business as "small" based on number of employees, some on sales volume, some on number of stockholders, etc.

Small claims court A state court that handles only cases for which the **damages** sought are under a certain money limit. These courts have a more streamlined procedure than regular courts.

Smart money **Punitive damages.**

Smuggling The crime of secretly bringing into or taking out of a country things that are either prohibited or taxable.

So. Southern Reporter. (See **National Reporter System.**)

Sodomy A general word for an "unnatural" sex act, or the crime committed by such act. Although the definition varies, *sodomy* can include oral sex, anal sex, homosexual sex, or sex with animals.

Soldiers' and Sailors' Civil Relief Act A federal law that suspends or modifies a military person's **civil** liabilities, or requires persons who want to enforce their **claims** against persons in the service to follow certain procedures.

Sole Single, individual, or separate. See **single proprietorship.**

Solicitation *1.* Asking for; enticing; strongly requesting. This may be a crime if the thing being urged is a crime. *2.* A lawyer's drumming up business too aggressively. This is prohibited by the **Code of Professional Responsibility.**

Solicitor *1.* A lawyer in Great Britain who handles all legal matters except trial work (which is done by a **barrister**). *2.* The name for the head lawyer for many towns and other government bodies. *3.* The U.S. *solicitor general* is the second-ranking federal lawyer, in charge of all **civil** suits involving the United States.

Solvency *1.* The ability to pay debts as they come due. *2.* Having more **assets** than **liabilities.**

Sound *1.* Whole; in good condition; healthy. *2.* "Sounds in" means "relates to" or "is primarily." For example, a lawsuit "sounds in damages" if the only **remedy** requested is **damages** (money), as opposed to other remedies such as *specific* **performance.**

Sovereign immunity The government's freedom from being sued. In many cases, the U.S. government has **waived** immunity by **statute** such as the Federal Tort Claims Act.

Speaking Bringing up matters not found within the legal papers of the case. This is now usually permitted by court rules.

Special *1.* Limited. For example, a court of *special jurisdiction* can handle only limited matters, such as **probate** cases. *2.* Unusual; not regular. For example, a *special session* is an extra meeting of a court or a legislature. *3.* For *special act or law,* see **private law.** *4.* A *special appearance* is showing up in court for a limited purpose only, especially to argue that the court has no **jurisdiction** over the person appearing. *5.* A *special assessment* is a real estate tax that singles out certain landowners to pay for improvements (such as a sidewalk) that will, at least in theory, benefit those owners but not taxpayers generally. *6.* A *special use permit* is government permission to use property in a way allowed by **zoning** rules, but only with a permit. This is *not* a **variance.** *7.* A *special warranty deed* is a transfer of land that includes the formal, written promise to protect the buyer against all ownership claims based on relationships with or transfers from the seller. *8.* For those *special* words not found here, the reader should look under **general** (the opposite of *special*) or under the other half of the compound word (*special* **master,** *special* **partner,** etc.).

Specialty Another name for a **contract** *under seal.*

Specific performance See **performance.**

Speech Speaking, writing, gesturing, and any other way of communicating ideas.

Speedy trial A trial free from unreasonable delay. A trial conducted according to regular rules about timing, not necessarily a fast trial or a trial as soon as someone wants one.

Spendthrift A person who spends money wildly and whose property the state may allow a **trustee** to look after.

Spin-off A new **corporation** created from an existing corporation, which sets up and funds the new corporation and gives the **shares** of the new corporation to the old one's owners. The process of creating the new corporation is also a *spin-off*.

Split action A lawsuit to recover only part of a single claim; generally, the rest cannot be claimed in a later lawsuit.

Split-off A new **corporation** created from an existing corporation, which sets up and funds the new corporation and gives the **shares** of the new one to the old one's owners in exchange for some of their shares in the old company. The process of creating the new corporation is also a *split-off*.

Split-up The process of a **corporation** dividing into two or more separate new ones, giving its owners the shares of these new ones, and then going out of business.

Spoliation *1.* Destruction by an outsider; for example, alteration of a check by someone who has nothing to do with it. *2.* Destruction of **evidence.** *3.* The failure by one side in a trial to come forward with evidence in its possession, and the inferences that the other side may ask the judge and jury to draw from this failure.

Spontaneous statement rule The rule that makes most statements about an event or condition **admissible** as **evidence** (even though they are **hearsay**) if they were spoken during or immediately after the event or condition.

Spot *1.* Immediate. *2.* *Spot zoning* is changing the **zoning** of a piece of land without regard for the area's zoning plan.

Squatter's right The "right" to own land merely because you have occupied it for a long time. This is *not* **adverse possession** and is not recognized as a right in most places.

Stale check A check that is now uncashable because it has been held too long. The time period is often set by state law.

Stand *1.* The place where a witness sits or stands to **testify.** *2.* Remain; refuse to change. *3.* To *stand mute* is to refuse to **plead** "guilty" or "not guilty" as a criminal **defendant.** The judge will usually enter a "not guilty" **plea** for the defendant.

Standard *1.* Conforming to accepted practice. *2.* A model; something accepted as correct. *3.* A minimum requirement, against which something is judged or measured. The *standard of care* in **negligence** cases is the level of care a reasonable person would use in similar circumstances. A *standard of proof* is a level of certainty to which something must be proved; for example, in a criminal prosecution, a defendant's guilt must be proved **beyond a reasonable doubt.** Compare **burden of proof.** *4.* The *standard deduction* is a specified dollar amount subtracted from taxable income by persons who do not *itemize* **deductions** on their income tax returns.

Standing *1.* A person's right to bring or join a lawsuit because he or she is directly affected by the issues raised. *2.* Reputation. *3.* A *standing committee* is a regular, as opposed to temporary, committee.

Stare decisis (Latin) "Let the decision stand." Refers to the principle that when a court has decided a case by applying a legal principle to a set of facts, that court should stick by that principle and apply it to all later cases with clearly similar facts unless there is a good, strong reason not to, and courts **below** *must* apply the principle in similar cases. This rule helps promote fairness and reliability in judicial decision making. See also **precedent.** [pronounce: star-e de-sigh-sis]

State *1.* Say; set down; declare. *2.* The major U.S. political subdivision. (*State action* is action by a state, such as Ohio.) *3.* A nation. (An *act of state* is action by a country, such as France.) *4.* Condition; situation. For example, the *state of the case* is whether a case is not ready for trial, ready for trial, or awaiting **appeal.** *5.* A *state secret* is a fact that the United States need not reveal to a court or to anyone else because it might hurt national security or an equally important national interest.

Stated Regular; settled; agreed upon.

Statement *1.* Any assertion, whether oral, written, or by conduct, intended to be an assertion of fact, of intent, etc. *2.* A document laying out facts. For example, a *statement of account* lists all the transactions made by a customer for that month. Also, several standard **accounting** *statements* (such as of **income**) accompany a **corporation**'s **balance sheet** in its reports.

State's attorney **District attorney.**

State's evidence A general word for **testimony** for the **prosecution** given by a person involved in a crime against others involved in the same crime.

Status *1.* A basic condition. The basic legal relationship of a person to the rest of the community. A *status crime* is one that depends on what a person *is,* not what he or she has done. *2. Status quo* is the existing state of things.

Statute *1.* A law passed by a **legislature.** *2.* A *statute of frauds* is a state law, modeled after an old English law, that requires many types of **contracts** (such as contracts for the sale of real estate) to be signed and in writing to be enforceable in court. *3.* For *statute of limitations,* see **limitation.** *4.* A *statute of wills* is a state law, modeled after an old English law, that requires a **will** to be in writing, signed, and properly witnessed to be valid. See also **holograph.** *5. Statutes at large* are a collection of all statutes passed by a particular legislature, printed in full and in the order of their passage. [pronounce: <u>stach</u>-oot]

Statutory Having to do with a **statute;** created, defined, or required by a statute. For example, *statutory rape* is the act of a man having sexual intercourse with a woman under an age defined by state statute (regardless of whether the woman consents).

Stay *1.* Stop or hold off. For example, when a judge *stays a judgment,* the judge stops or delays its enforcement. *2.* A stoppage or suspension. For example, the act mentioned in #1 is called a *stay of judgment.*

Steward   Shop steward.

Stipulation *1.* An agreement between lawyers on opposite sides of a lawsuit. It is often in writing and usually concerns either court procedure (such as a time extension to file a **pleading**) or agreed-upon facts that need no proof. *2.* A demand. *3.* One point in a written agreement.

Stirpes   See per stirpes.

Stock *1.* The goods held for sale by a merchant. *2.* Shares of ownership in a **corporation.** Stock is often divided into *preferred stock* (which gets a fixed rate of income before any other stock) and *common stock* (the bulk of the stock). *3.* A *stock association* is a **joint stock company.** *4.* A *stock dividend* is profits of stock ownership paid out in more stock rather than in money.

Stockholder's derivative suit A lawsuit in which a shareholder of a corporation sues in the name of the corporation because a wrong has been done to the company and the company itself will not sue.

Stop and frisk A quick, temporary detention and "pat down" by a police officer of a person whom the officer suspects of being armed.

Stoppage in transit The halting of the delivery of goods even after they have been given to a **carrier**

(railroad, etc.), especially when done as a matter of right when, for example, the buyer is **insolvent.**

Stranger A person who takes no part in a deal in any way; a **third party.**

Straw man *1.* A "front"; a person who is put up in name only to take part in a deal. *2.* A man who stood around outside a court in old England and was hired by lawyers to give false **testimony.** *3.* An argument set up purely to be knocked down.

Strict *1.* Exact; precise; governed by exact rules. *2. Strict construction* of a law means taking it literally, so that the law should be applied to the narrowest possible set of situations; and *strict construction* of a contract means that any ambiguous words should be interpreted in the way least favorable to the side that wrote the words. *3. Strict foreclosure* is a **creditor**'s right, in some circumstances, to take back property and cancel the debt; neither the creditor nor the debtor can sue the other for additional money. *4. Strict liability* in **civil** law is legal responsibility for damage or injury even if you are not at fault or **negligent.** Manufacturers sometimes may be held strictly liable for defective products. *5. Strict liability* in **criminal** law is guilt even without criminal intention **(mens rea).** One can be strictly liable for minor offenses (such as speeding) and special **regulatory** offenses (such as polluting).

Strike *1.* Take out. For example, to *strike* a word is to remove it from a document. *2.* Employees stopping, slowing down, or disrupting work to win demands from an employer. *3. Striking a jury* is choosing individuals from a **panel** to serve on one case.

String citation A series of case names and **citations** that is printed after an assertion or legal conclusion to back it up.

Strong-arm provision A part of the federal **bankruptcy** law that gives a bankruptcy **trustee** powers equal to those of a powerful **secured creditor** (whether or not such a creditor actually exists) to help the trustee gather all the bankrupt person's property.

Style Official name.

Sua sponte (Latin) *1.* Of his or her own will; voluntarily. *2.* On a judge's own **motion,** without a request from a **party.**

Sub (Latin) *1.* Under. *2.* *Sub judice* means under judicial consideration; as yet undecided. [pronounce: sub <u>jood</u>-uh-see] *3.* *Sub nom.* is an abbreviation for *sub nomine,* which means "under the name or title of." *4.* *Sub silentio* means "in silence"; without taking any notice or giving any indication.

Subchapter S See **S corporation.**

Subcontractor A person who contracts to do a piece of a job for another person who has a contract for a larger piece of the job or for the whole job.

Subdelegation **Delegation** of authority.

Subject to Subordinate to; governed by; affected by; limited by; etc.

Sublet A **tenant**'s renting of property to another person.

Submit *1.* Put into another's hands for decision. *2.* Allow; yield to. *3.* Attempt to introduce **evidence.** *4.* Offer for approval.

Subordination A ranking of rights; in particular, signing a document that admits that your **claim** or **interest** (such as a **lien**) is weaker than another one and can collect only after the other.

Subornation The crime of asking or forcing another person to commit **perjury** (to lie under **oath**). [pronounce: sub-or-<u>nay</u>-shun]

Subpoena A court's (or **administrative agency**'s) **order** to a person that he or she appear to **testify** (give **evidence**) in a case. A *subpoena duces tecum* commands a person to come and bring certain documents. [pronounce: suh-<u>pee</u>-na <u>due</u>-kiss <u>tay</u>-kum]

Subrogation The substitution of one person for another in claiming a lawful right or debt. For example, when an insurance company pays its policyholder for damage to a car, the company becomes *subrogated to* (gets the right to sue on and collect) any claim for the same damage that the policyholder has against the person who hit the car.

Subscribe *1.* Sign at the end of a document (as the person who wrote it, as a **witness,** etc.). *2.* Agree to purchase some initial stock in a company.

Subsidiary Under another's control; lesser. A *subsidiary corporation* is controlled by another, the *parent corporation*.

Substance *1.* Reality, as opposed to mere appearance. *2.* The "gist" or real meaning of something. *3.* See **substantive law.**

Substantial *1.* Valuable; real; worthwhile. *2.* Complete enough. *3.* "A lot," when it is hard to pin down just how much "a lot" really is.

Substantiate Establish the existence of something or prove its truth; verify.

Substantive evidence **Evidence** used to prove facts rather than to back up or discredit a **witness**'s believability.

Substantive law The basic law of **rights** and **duties** (**contract** law, **criminal** law, etc.,) as opposed to **procedural law** (**pleading** law, **evidence** law, etc.).

Substituted service **Service** of **process** by any way other than personal delivery to the person named (by mail, newspaper publication, delivery to a family member at home, etc.).

Succession   Transfer or continuation. For example, *intestate succession* is the transfer of a dead person's property by law to **heirs** if the person does not leave a **will.**

Sue   Start a **civil** lawsuit.

Suffer   Allow or permit something to happen.

Suffrage   The right to vote.

Sui generis   (Latin) One of a kind. [pronounce: sue-ee jen-er-is]

Sui juris   (Latin) "Of his or her own right." Possessing full civil and political rights and able to manage your own affairs.

Suit   A lawsuit; a **civil action** in court.

Suitor   A **party** or **litigant** in a lawsuit, usually the **plaintiff.**

Summary   *1.* Short; concise; immediate; without a full trial. *2. Summary judgment* is a final **judgment** (victory) for one side in a lawsuit, without **trial,** when the judge finds that there is no genuine factual issue in the case. *3. Summary process* is an abbreviated type of court hearing available in situations such as **evictions** in which a tenant's failure to pay rent automatically ends a lease.

Summons   A **writ** (a notice delivered by a **sheriff** or other authorized person) informing a person of a lawsuit against him or her. It tells the person to show up in court at a certain time or risk losing the suit without being present.

Sumptuary law   A law controlling the sale or use of socially undesirable, wasteful, or harmful products.

Sunset law   A law that puts an **administrative agency** automatically out of business unless the law is renewed by the **legislature.**

Sunshine law A law requiring open meetings of government agencies or allowing (or assisting) public access to government records.

Superior *1.* Higher. A *superior court,* however, is sometimes a state's *lowest* court, sometimes its highest, and sometimes an intermediate court. *2.* **Dominant.**

Supersede *1.* Set aside; wipe out; make unnecessary. *2.* Replace one law or document by another, later one.

Supersedeas (Latin) A judge's **order** that temporarily holds up another court's proceedings or temporarily **stays** a lower court's **judgment.** A *supersedeas* **bond** may be put up by a person who **appeals** a judgment. The bond delays the person's obligation to pay a judgment until the appeal is lost. [pronounce: sue-per-see-de-as]

Supervening New; newly effective; interposing. For *supervening cause,* see **intervening cause,** and for *supervening negligence,* see **last clear chance doctrine.**

Supplemental pleading A **pleading** that brings up events that happened after the start of the lawsuit.

Supplementary proceedings A **judgment creditor**'s in-court examination of the **debtor** and others to find out if there is any money or property available to pay the debt.

Support *1.* The obligation to provide for your immediate family, or the payments made to meet this obligation. *2.* See **lateral support.**

Suppress evidence Keep **evidence** from being used in a **criminal** trial by showing that it was gathered illegally (this can be done either at the trial or at a pretrial *suppression hearing*), by refusing to give evidence (this may be a crime), or by the prosecution's holding back requested evidence favorable to the defendant (this may be **unconstitutional**).

Sup-pro **Supplementary proceedings.**

Supra (Latin) Above; earlier (in the page, in the book, etc.).

Supremacy clause The U.S. **constitutional** provision that the U.S. Constitution, laws, and **treaties** take precedence over conflicting state constitutions or laws.

Supremacy of law Describes a government in which the highest authority is in law, not in persons.

Supreme Court The highest U.S. court and the highest court of most, but not all, of the states.

Surcharge An extra charge on something already charged; a special payment for a special purpose; an overcharge; etc. See also **surtax.**

Surety A person or company that insures or guaranties that another person's debt will be paid by becoming **liable** (responsible) for the debt when it is made. See **guaranty.**

Surplusage Extra, unnecessary words, or matters not relevant to a case, in a legal document.

Surprise The situation that occurs when one side in a trial, through absolutely no fault of its own, is faced with something totally unexpected that places an unfair burden on its case. When this happens, a **continuance** is often granted and, occasionally, a new trial is granted.

Surrebutter (and surrejoinder) Two forms of **pleading** no longer used. Modern court practice usually stops with two or three pleadings, not the five or more it would take to reach these.

Surrender Give back; give up; hand back; or return.

Surrogate *1.* The name for the judge of a **probate** court in some states. *2.* A person who stands in for another person.

Surtax *1.* An additional tax on what has already been taxed. *2.* A tax on a tax. For example, if you must pay a $100 tax on a $1,000 purchase (10 percent), a 10 percent *surtax* would require an additional $10 payment, not an additional $100 payment.

Survival statute   A state law that allows a lawsuit to be brought by a relative for a person who has died.

Survivorship   The *right of survivorship* is the right of certain property owners, such as **joint** owners of real estate who outlive other joint owners, to own the property. Joint renters may have similar rights.

Suspended sentence   A **sentence** (usually "jail time") that the judge allows the convicted person to avoid serving (usually if the person completes community service, etc.). Compare **probation.**

Suspicion   *1*. More than a guess but less than full knowledge. *2*. "Held on suspicion" is being temporarily held by the police without specific charges against the person being held.

Sustain   *1*. Grant. When a judge *sustains* an **objection,** he or she agrees with it and gives it effect. *2*. Carry on; bear up under. *3*. Support or justify. If the evidence fully supports a **verdict,** it is said to *sustain* the verdict.

Syllabus   A **headnote,** summary, or **abstract** of a case.

Symbolic speech   Gestures and actions meant to communicate a message; for example, holding your nose. Symbolic speech is protected by the **First Amendment.**

Syndicate   *1*. A **joint adventure.** *2*. Any business venture.

T   Term; territory; title; testamentum (Latin for **will**); etc.

TC Tax court.

TM Trademark.

TRO Temporary restraining order.

Table *1.* Suspend consideration of a **legislative bill;** put something aside either temporarily or permanently. *2.* A list of figures. *3.* A *table of cases* is an alphabetical index of cases used in a book, with the page numbers on which they are referenced.

Tacit *1.* Understood without being openly said; done in silence; implied. *2.* Customary.

Tacking Attaching something later, smaller, or weaker to something earlier, larger, or stronger.

Taft-Hartley Act A federal law, passed in 1947, that added several employers' rights to the union rights in the **Wagner Act.** It established several union "unfair labor practices," such as attempting to force an employee to join a union.

Tail See **fee** *tail.*

Taint *1.* **Attainder.** *2.* Loss of reputation. *3.* *Tainted* means gained by illegal means or resulting from something gained by illegal means.

Tariff *1.* An import tax. *2.* A list of articles and the import tax that must be paid on items on that list. *3.* A list of the services, rates, and rules of a public utility.

Tax *1.* A required payment of money to support the government. *2.* *Tax avoidance* is planning finances carefully to take advantage of all legal tax breaks, such as **deductions.** *3.* A *tax deed* is a proof of ownership of land given to the purchaser by the government after the land has been taken from another person by the government and sold for failure to pay taxes. *4.* *Tax evasion* is illegally paying less in taxes than the law allows. *5.* *Tax exempt* may refer to property not subject to property tax, income not subject to income tax, an organization not subject to any tax, etc. *6. Tax fraud* is *tax evasion. 7.* A *tax rate* is the percentage of **taxable income** (or of inherited money, of purchases subject to sales tax, etc.), paid in taxes. *8.* A *tax return* is the form used to report income, deductions, etc., and to accompany tax payments and refund requests.

Taxable income   Under federal tax law, this is either the **gross income** of a business or the **adjusted gross income** of an individual minus **deductions** and **exemptions.** It is the income against which **tax rates** are applied before subtracting **credits.**

Taxing costs   Making one side in a lawsuit pay the other side's costs of the suit.

Taxpayer suit   A lawsuit brought by an individual to challenge the spending of public money for a particular purpose.

Technical   *1.* Having to do with an art or profession. *2.* Minor; merely procedural.

Temporary restraining order   A judge's **order** to a person to not take a certain action during the period prior to a full **hearing** on the rightfulness of the action.

Tenancy   The condition of being a **tenant;** the **interest** a tenant has; the **term** (amount of time) a tenant has.

Tenant   *1.* A person who holds land or a building by renting. A *tenant at will* has a **lease** that can be ended at any time ("at will") by either the tenant or the landlord. A *tenant by sufferance* is a person who wrongly stays in property after the lease has ended. *2.* A person who holds land or a building by any legal right, including ownership. These tenants include *tenants in common* (each hold a share of land that can be passed on to **heirs** or otherwise disposed of); *joint tenants* (like tenants in common, except that they must have *equal* interests in the property and, if one dies, that person's ownership interest passes to the other owners); and *tenants by the entireties* (like joint tenants except that they must be wife and husband and hold the entire land as one individual owner).

Tender   *1.* An **offer,** combined with a readiness to do what is offered. *2.* An offer of money. *3.* "Cash on the line." Actually putting money forward, as opposed to merely offering it. *4.* A *tender offer* is an offer, usually public, to buy a certain amount of a company's stock at a set price.

Tenor   A vague word meaning anything from "the exact words" to "the general meaning" or "train of thought."

Tenth Amendment   See **Bill of Rights.**

Term   *1.* A word, a phrase, or a part of a document or agreement; especially one that has a fixed, technical meaning. *2.* A fixed time period.

Termination   Any ending; an ending before the anticipated end. Under the **Uniform Commercial Code,** the end of a **contract** without its being broken by either side.

Territorial jurisdiction   Either the power of a court to take cases from within a particular geographical area or the power of a country, state, etc., to control its land and, sometimes, surrounding waters.

Territory   Land administered by a country, but not a permanent part of the country or completely integrated into its governmental workings. *Territorial courts* are courts in each U.S. territory, such as the Virgin Islands, that serve as both state and federal courts.

Test case *1.* A lawsuit brought to establish an important legal principle or right; or breaking a law to challenge it in court. *2.* One case selected from many similar ones to be tried first, with all persons involved in the other cases agreeing to be bound by the decision.

Testacy (or testate) Leaving a valid **will.** *Testate succession* is the giving and receiving of property by a will.

Testament A **will.**

Testamentary Having to do with a **will.** For example, *testamentary capacity* is the mental ability to make a valid will.

Testator A person who makes a **will.**

Testify Give **evidence** under **oath.**

Testimonium clause The part of a **deed** or other document that contains information about who signed and when and where the deed was signed.

Testimony **Evidence** given by a **witness** under **oath.**

Theft Stealing of any kind.

Theory of pleading doctrine The **common-law** principle that a person must prove a case *exactly as alleged* in the **pleadings** to win the case. This doctrine is now of limited use because in modern practice pleadings may usually be amended to match the proof.

Thereabout (and other "there" words) A vague, overly formal word meaning "approximately there." Like other "there" words (*thereafter, thereat, thereby, therein, thereof, thereto, theretofore, thereunder, thereupon, therewith, etc.*), it is best left out of a sentence or replaced by the exact thing referred to.

Third degree Illegal methods of interrogation to force a person to confess to a crime.

Third party (or person) A person unconnected with a deal, lawsuit, or occurrence but who may be affected by it. For example, a *third-party beneficiary* is a person who is not a part of a **contract** but for whose direct benefit the contract was made.

Three-judge court A special federal trial court for certain limited types of cases specified by federal **statute.**

Time draft (or bill or loan) A **draft** (or **bill** or loan) payable at a certain time.

Time is of the essence When this phrase is in a **contract,** it means that a failure to do what is required by the time specified is a **breach** (breaking) of the contract.

Time-barred Prohibited by a *statute of limitations* (see **limitation**).

Timely Done within the required or promised time.

Title *1.* The name for a part of a **statute.** For example, "Title VII" of the 1964 Civil Rights Act is known as "Title Seven." *2.* Formal ownership of property or the document that shows this ownership. *3.* A *title search* is a search of land records to see if a title is good or restricted. *4.* A *title state* or *title theory jurisdiction* is a state in which the title to mortgaged property is held by the lender until the debt is paid.

To have and to hold A phrase used in some deeds to make a land transfer valid. The phrase is no longer necessary.

To wit An unnecessary phrase, best replaced by a colon (:).

Toll To *toll a statute of* **limitations** is to do something to delay it from taking effect, to "stop the clock from running."

Tombstone ad A stock (or other **securities**) or land sale notice that clearly states that it is informational only and not in itself an offer to buy or sell. It has a black border that resembles one on a death notice.

Tontine A type of insurance, now illegal, in which many persons pay into a fund and only those living by a certain date split it up.

Torrens title system A system of land ownership **registration,** used in some states, in which the owner gets a **conclusive** "Certificate of Title" to land after a successful hearing. Use of the *Torrens* system is voluntary and supplementary to the recording of a **deed.**

Tort A **civil** (as opposed to **criminal**) **wrong** other than a **breach of contract.** For an act to be a *tort,* there must be a legal **duty** owed by one person to another, a **breach** (breaking) of that duty, and harm done as a direct result of the action. Examples of torts are **negligence, battery,** and **libel.**

Tortfeasor A person who commits a **tort.**

Tortious Having to do with a **tort.** [pronounce: tor-shus]

Total Complete for legal purposes (even if not "total" in the common language sense).

Totten trust A trust created by putting money into a bank account in your name as **trustee** for another person. You can take it out when you want, but if the money is not taken out before you die, it becomes the property of that other person.

Trade name The name of a business. It will usually be legally protected in the area where the company operates and for the types of products in which it deals.

Trademark A distinctive mark, motto, brand name, or symbol used by a company to identify or advertise its products. **Trademarks** (and **service** *marks*) can be federally **registered** and protected against use by others. A registered mark bears the symbol ®.

Traditionary evidence   Evidence of what a dead person said long ago.

Transaction   *1.* A business deal. *2.* An occurrence; something that takes place. A group of facts so interconnected that they can be referred to by one legal name, such as a "crime" or a "contract."

Transcript   A copy; especially the official typed copy of the **record** of a court proceeding.

Transfer   *1.* Change or move from person to person (sell, give, or sign something over, etc.), or from place to place (court to court, etc.). *2.* A *transfer agent* is a person (or an institution such as a bank) who keeps track of who owns a company's stocks and bonds, of dividends and interest, and so on. *3. Transfer tax* is the name for different types of taxes in different places; for example, an **estate** tax, a gift tax, a tax on stock sales, etc.

Transitory action   A **lawsuit** that may be brought in any one of many places.

Trauma   *1.* Bodily injury caused by an external blow. *2.* Sudden psychological damage. *3.* Severe psychological damage caused by a past event.

Traverse   An old form of **pleading** in which facts in the other side's pleading are denied.

Treason   The crime of a U.S. citizen's helping a foreign government to overthrow, make war against, or seriously injure the United States.

Treasurer   The person in charge of an organization's money (taking in, paying out, etc.,) but not usually its financial decisions.

Treasure trove   Hidden money or valuables with no known owner. Depending on the state, it may belong to the finder, the landowner, or the state.

Treasury bill, bond, certificate, or note   A document showing that the U.S. Treasury has borrowed money.

Treasury stock (or shares)   Shares of **stock** that have been rebought by the corporation that issued them.

Treatise   A large, comprehensive book on a legal subject.

Treaty   A formal agreement between countries on a major political subject. The _treaty clause_ of the U.S. **Constitution** requires the approval of two-thirds of the Senate for any treaty made by the president.

Treble damages   **Damages** three times as great as the amount of proven financial harm caused, authorized by **statute** to strongly discourage certain kinds of wrongful actions in certain types of lawsuits.

Trespass   _1._ A wrongful entry onto another person's property. _2._ An old term for many types of civil wrongs or **torts.** For example, the _trespass_ in #1 was called _trespass_ **quare** _clausum fregit;_ modern **contract** lawsuits grew out of _trespass on the case;_ and _trespass vi et armis_ (force and arms) became modern lawsuits for both **negligence** and **battery.**

Trial   The process of deciding a case (giving **evidence,** making **arguments,** deciding by a judge and jury, etc.). It occurs if the dispute is not resolved by **pleadings,** pretrial **motions,** or **settlement.** A trial usually takes place in open court and may be followed by a **judgment,** an **appeal,** etc.

Tribunal   Court.

Trier of fact   The **jury** (or the judge if there is no jury).

Trover   An old type of lawsuit, now rarely used, in which a piece of property was claimed to be lost by someone and then found by the person from whom he or she wanted it back. This got around the problem of proving the thing was wrongfully taken, because all the person had to prove was that it was his or hers and that the other person had it.

True bill An **indictment** approved and made by a *grand* **jury.**

Trust *1.* A group of companies that has a **monopoly.** *2.* An arrangement by which one person holds legal **title** to money or property for the benefit of another. For example, a *trust* is created when a mother signs over stocks to a bank to manage for her daughter with instructions to give the daughter the income each year until she turns thirty and then give it all to her. In this example, the mother is the **settlor** or **grantor** of the *trust,* the bank is the **trustee,** and the daughter is the **beneficiary.** A trust, however, need not be set up explicitly; for example, if a father gives a son some money, saying "half of this is for your brother," this may create a *trust* in favor of the brother. Also, a trust can be set up in a **will;** can be created by formally stating that someone holds money in trust for another person; and can be created in hundreds of other ways, both intentional and unintentional. *3.* A *trust certificate* is a document showing that property is held in trust as **security** for a debt based on money used to buy the property. *4.* A *trust company* is a bank or other organization that manages trusts, acts as **executor** of **wills,** etc. *5.* A *trust deed* is a **deed of trust.** *6.* A *trust fund* is money or property set aside in a trust, set aside for a special purpose, or treated legally *as if* it is held in trust. *7.* A *trust receipt* is a document by which one person lends money to buy something and the borrower promises to hold the thing that was bought in trust for the lender until the debt is paid off. *8.* A *trust state (or trust theory jurisdiction)* is a state in which

title to mortgaged property is transferred to a **trustee** until the debt is paid.

Trustee *1.* A person who holds money or property for the benefit of another person (see **trust**). *2.* A person who has a **fiduciary** relationship toward another person; for example, a lawyer, an **agent,** etc. *3.* A *trustee in bankruptcy* is a person appointed by the court to manage a **bankrupt** person's property and to decide who gets it.

Truth-in-Lending Act   Consumer Credit Protection Act.

Try   Prosecute; litigate; attempt. To *try* a case is to argue it in court as a lawyer, to decide it as a judge, or to participate in it in any of several other ways.

Turning state's evidence   See **state's evidence.**

Turpitude   Dishonesty or immorality.

Tying in   Linking the sale of one product or service to the sale of another product or service. If a seller has a **monopoly** on a product, *tying in* the sale of another product may be a violation of **antitrust** laws.

UCC   Uniform Commercial Code.

UCCC   Uniform Consumer Credit Code. (Also called UC3 and U3C.) A **uniform act** adopted by some states to **regulate** the way merchants and lending institutions give credit to consumers.

UCMJ   See **Code** *of Military Justice.*

ULA **Uniform Laws** *Annotated.*

ULPA Uniform Limited Partnership Act.

UPA Uniform Partnership Act.

USC United States Code. The official law books containing federal laws by subject. They are recompiled every six years, and supplements are published when needed.

USCA *1.* United States Code Annotated. The law books, based on the **U.S.C.,** containing all of the federal laws by subject and partially explained. References to cases from state and federal courts referring to each federal law are part of the *annotations. 2.* **United States Court of Appeals.**

USCCAN United States Code Congressional and Administrative News. A series of books with the texts of and cross-references to all federal laws and some congressional committee reports and administrative regulations.

USCS A set of law books similar to **USCA.**

USDC United States District Court.

UTI Undistributed taxable income.

Ultimate facts Facts essential to a **plaintiff**'s or **defendant**'s case. Often, facts that must be proved by *other* facts and evidence.

Ultra (Latin) Beyond; outside of; in excess of. For example, *ultra vires* actions are things a **corporation** does that are outside the scope of powers or activities permitted by its **charter** or **articles of incorporation.**

Umpire A person chosen to decide a **labor dispute** when the original **arbitrators** disagree.

Unauthorized practice of law Nonlawyers doing things that only lawyers are permitted to do. Who and what fits into this definition is constantly changing and the subject of dispute. If, however, a clear case comes up (for example, pretending to be a lawyer and setting up a law office), the practice may be prohibited and the person punished under the state's criminal laws.

Unclean hands See **clean hands.**

Unconscionability Sales practices that are so greatly unfair that a court will not permit them. For example, a sales contract between a large company and a poorly educated person that contains unfair terms in small print and technical language, and that involves an unfairly high sales price, is _unconscionable._

Unconstitutional Describes laws or actions that conflict with the U.S. **Constitution.**

Undersigned The person (or persons) whose name is signed at the end of the document.

Understanding A vague word meaning anything from "silent agreement" to "valid **contract.**"

Undertaking _1._ A promise, especially one made in the course of a lawsuit to the judge or to the other side. _2._ A venture of any kind, especially the process of putting out financial **securities.**

Underwrite _1._ Insure. _2._ Guaranty the purchase of any stocks or bonds that remain unsold after a public sale; or sell an **issue** of stocks or bonds.

Undue _1._ Improper; illegal. For example, _undue influence_ is pressure that takes away a person's free will to make decisions. It involves misusing a position of trust or taking advantage of a person's weakness. _2._ More than necessary.

Unethical conduct Actions that violate professional standards such as the lawyers' **Code of Professional Responsibility.**

Unfair competition Dishonest trade practices, such as too closely imitating the name, product, or advertising of another company to take away its business.

Unfair labor practice An action by a union or an employer that is prohibited by law; for example, an employer's attempt to force an employee to give up union-organizing activities.

Unified transfer tax A combined federal tax on transfers by **gift** or death. It replaced the separate federal gift and **estate** taxes.

Uniform Regular; even. Applying generally, equally, and evenhandedly.

Uniform acts (or laws) Laws in various subject areas, proposed by the commissioners on uniform state laws, adopted in whole or in part by many states.

Uniform Code of Military Justice Code of Military Justice.

Uniform Commercial Code A comprehensive set of laws on every major type of business law. It has been adopted by almost every state, in whole or in major part.

Unilateral One-sided. For *unilateral contract,* see **contract.** A *unilateral mistake* about a contract's terms usually will not get a person out of the contract unless the other side knew about the mistake when the contract was made.

Union Any joining together of persons, organizations, or things for a particular purpose. A *labor union* is an organization of workers, formed to negotiate with employers about wages, working conditions, etc. A *union shop* is a business in which all workers must join a particular union once employed.

United States attorney A federal **district attorney.**

United States Court of Appeals Any of the thirteen federal courts (one to each **circuit**) that hear **appeals** from the U.S. district courts.

United States courts   The U.S. **Supreme Court, courts of appeals, district courts, court of claims,** etc. These are U.S., as opposed to state, courts.

United States Reports   The official volumes in which **decisions** of the U.S. **Supreme Court** are collected.

United States Statutes at Large   Statutes at large.

Unitrust   A **trust** in which a fixed percentage of the trust property is paid out each year to **beneficiaries.**

Unity   _1_. An identical interest in property held jointly. There are the _unities of time_ (the property was acquired by all **joint** owners at the same time), _title_ (the property was acquired by all through the same **deed** or event), _interest_ (each person got the same ownership rights), and _possession_ (each has the same right to possess the whole property). _2. Unity of person_ refers to the way in which property is held by **tenants** _by the entireties_ because they are married. _3. Unity of possession_ also refers to the **merger** of rights in land.

Unjust enrichment   Obtaining money, property, or services unfairly and at another's expense. This does not include merely driving a hard bargain or being lucky in a deal.

Unlawful   Contrary to law; unauthorized by law. Not necessarily a crime, but at least either a **tort** or disapproved of by the law. _Unlawful detainer_ is holding onto land or buildings beyond the time you have a right to them.

Unnatural act   _1_. **Sodomy.** _2_. Describes making a **will** that gives away most of a person's property, without apparent reason, to other than immediate relatives.

Unwritten law   _1_. A "law" of decent behavior that most people follow because it is considered right, just, or usual to do so. _2_. Any one of several commonly held assumptions about the law that are *not* laws and will not be enforced by a court; for example, the "law" that a husband will not be punished if he kills his wife's lover. *3.* **Common law** or judge-made law as opposed to **statutes, regulations,** etc.

Urban easement The right of most street-side property to get light, air, and free entrance from the street side.

Usage A general, uniform, well-known course of conduct followed in a particular area or business.

Use An old method of holding land, similar to a **trust,** in which one person got legal ownership, but another person got the use of the land.

Use tax A tax on some property brought into a state without paying the state's sales tax.

Usufruct An old word for the right to use something as long as it is not changed or used up.

Usury Charging an illegally high interest rate.

Utter *1.* Put into circulation. **Issue** or put out a check. *2.* Say. *3.* Enough to be considered complete, total, or **absolute.**

Uxor (Latin) Wife. Abbreviated *ux.*

V *1.* An abbreviation for *versus* or "against" in the name of a case. For example, *Smith v. Jones* means that Smith is suing Jones. *2.* Volume.

VAT **Value-added tax.**

VRM   Variable rate mortgage.

Vacate   *1*. Annul; set aside; take back. For example, when a judge *vacates a judgment,* it is wiped out completely. *2*. Move out or empty.

Vagrancy   A vague, general word for "hanging around" in public with no purpose and no honest means of support.

Vagueness doctrine   The rule that a **criminal** law may be **unconstitutional** if it does not clearly say what is required or prohibited.

Valid   *1*. Binding; legal; complying with all needed formalities. *2*. Worthwhile; sufficient.

Value   *1*. Worth. This may be cost, cost to replace, what it could sell for, etc. See also **market value.** *2. For value, value received,* or *for valuable consideration* mean for **consideration.** *3*. A *value-added tax* is a tax based on the sale price of goods and services minus the cost of raw materials and goods purchased to produce the goods and services.

Variable rate mortgage   A **mortgage** with payments that change (monthly, yearly, every five years, etc.), based on a standard index.

Variance   *1*. A difference between what is alleged (said will be proved) in **pleading** and what is actually proved in a trial. *2*. Official permission to use land or buildings in a way that would otherwise violate the **zoning** regulations for the neighborhood.

Vel non   (Latin) Or not.

Vendee   Buyer.

Vendor   Seller.

Venire facias   (Latin) Describes a command to the **sheriff** to assemble a **jury.** A *venireman* is a juror.

Venue   The local area where a case may be tried. A court system may have **jurisdiction** (power) to take a case in a wide geographical area, but the proper *venue* for the case may be one place within that area for the convenience of the **parties,** etc. Jurisdiction is the subject of fixed rules, but venue is often left to the discretion of the judge.

Verbal Spoken; partly spoken and partly written; written but unsigned; or lacking some other formality.

Verdict *1.* The **jury**'s decision. *2.* The usual verdict in a **civil** case, one in which the jury decides which side wins (and how much), is called a *general verdict.* When the jury is asked to answer specific questions of **fact,** it is called a *special verdict.* *3.* The jury's decision in a **criminal** case: usually, "guilty" or "not guilty" of each **charge.**

Vertical In a chain, such as from manufacturer to wholesaler to retailer, as opposed to among various manufacturers.

Vest Give an immediate, fixed, and full right or take immediate effect.

Vested **Absolute, accrued,** complete, not subject to any **condition** that could take it away; not **contingent** on anything. For example, a pension is *vested* if someone gets it at retirement age even if that person left the company before retirement age.

Veto A refusal by the president or a governor to sign into law a **bill** that has been passed by a **legislature.** In the case of a presidential veto, the bill can still become a law if two-thirds of each **house** of Congress votes to *override* the veto.

Vexatious litigation Lawsuits brought without any just cause or good reason.

Vi et armis (Latin) "Force and arms." See **trespass.**

Vicarious liability Legal responsibility for the acts of another person because of some relationship with that person; for example, the **liability** of an employer for certain acts of an employee.

Vice *1.* Illegal (and considered immoral) activities. *2.* An imperfection or defect. *3.* Second in command or substitute.

Vide (Latin) "See." For example, *vide ante* means "look at the words or sections that come before this one."

Vinculo matrimonii See **a vinculo matrimonii.**

Violent presumption Complete, even though indirect, proof.

Vir (Latin) A man; a husband.

Virtue *1.* Worthwhile or good in a practical, not moral, sense. *2.* "By *virtue* of" means "by the power of" or "because."

Vis (Latin) Force or violence. *Vis major* is an irresistible force or natural disaster.

Visa Formal permission to travel in a country.

Vitiate Cause to fail. Destroy (totally or partially) a thing's legal effect or binding force. **Fraud** *vitiates* a **contract.** [pronounce: vish-ee-ate]

Viva voce (Latin) "Living voice." Orally rather than in writing. A *vive voce* vote is sometimes taken on minor questions: the leader decides who wins by voice volume, not head count.

Viz An awkward term, meaning "that is to say" or "these are." Usually a colon (:) alone will do.

Void Without legal effect; of no binding force; wiped out. For example, a *void contract* is an agreement by which no one is (or ever was) bound because something legally necessary is missing.

Voidable Can be made **void.** Describes something that is in force but can be legally avoided. For example, a *voidable contract* is an agreement that one or both sides can legally get out of, but it is effective and binding if no one chooses to get out.

Voir dire (French) "To see, to say," to state the truth. The preliminary in-court questioning of a prospective witness (or juror) to determine the witness' competency to testify (or the juror's suitability to decide a case). [pronounce: vwahr deer]

Volenti non fit injuria (Latin) "A willing person cannot be injured legally." See **assumption of risk.**

Volstead Act A defunct federal law that prohibited the manufacture and sale of alcoholic beverages.

Voluntary *1.* With complete free will; intentional. In this sense, a *voluntary trust* is one set up intentionally rather than imposed by law. *2.* Free; without **consideration.** In this sense, a *voluntary trust* is set up as a gift rather than as a way of protecting, for example, a mortgage holder.

Voting trust An arrangement by which stockholders in a company pool their shares of stock to vote as a block at stockholders' meetings.

Vs. Versus. See V.

W West or western.

WD Western **district.**

Wage assignment An arrangement in which a person allows his or her wages to be paid directly to a **creditor.** It is illegal in most situations in many states. See also **garnishment.**

Wage earner's plan See **Chapter Thirteen.**

Wager of law A practice in old England by which a person accused of something, such as owing money, could swear that the money was not owed and could bring eleven neighbors (called *compurgators*) to swear to the person's general truthfulness.

Wagner Act A federal law, passed in 1935, that established most basic union rights. It prohibited several employer actions (such as attempting to force employees to stay out of a union) and labeled these actions "unfair labor practices." It also set up the National Labor Relations Board to help enforce labor laws.

Wait-and-see statute A state law that avoids some of the problems caused by the *rule against perpetuities* (see **perpetuity**) by allowing time to pass to find out if a **will** or **trust** violates the rule.

Waive Give up, renounce, or disclaim a privilege, right, or benefit with full knowledge of what you are doing.

Waiver The voluntary giving up of a right. (See **waive.**) For example, *waiver of immunity* is the act of a **witness** who gives up the **constitutional** right to refuse to give evidence against himself or herself and who proceeds to **testify.**

Want *1.* Desire. *2.* Lack.

Wanton *1.* **Reckless,** heedless, or **malicious.** *2.* Weighing about 2,000 pounds. *3.* Floating in broth. *4.* In need.

Ward *1.* A division of a city for election and other purposes. *2.* A person, especially a child, placed by the court under the care of a **guardian.**

Warehouse receipt A piece of paper proving that you own something stored in a warehouse. A *warehouse receipt* may be a **negotiable instrument.**

Warrant *1*. Promise or guaranty, especially in a **contract** or **deed.** (See **warranty.**) *2*. Written permission given by a judge (or **magistrate,** etc.,) to a police officer (or **sheriff,** etc.,) to arrest a person, to conduct a search, etc. *3*. An **option** to buy **stock.** *4*. Promise that certain facts are true.

Warranty *1*. Any promise (or a presumed promise, called an *implied warranty*) that certain facts are true. *2*. In land law, a warranty is a promise in a **deed** that the **title** of land being sold is good and complete. *3*. In the law of buildings, a *construction* or **home owners warranty** is the promise that the building was built right; and a *warranty of habitability* is the implied promise to buyers or renters that the building is fit to live in. *4*. In **consumer** law, a warranty is the same as in the previous definitions, plus any obligations imposed by law on a seller that benefit a buyer; for example, the *warranty* that goods are **merchantable** and the warranty that goods sold as fit for a particular purpose are fit for the purpose.

Wash sale *1*. Selling something and buying something else that is basically the same thing. *2*. **Rescission.** *3*. A sale with no profit or loss.

Waste Abuse or destruction of property in one's rightful possession but belonging to someone else, or property in which someone else has certain rights.

Wasting Being used up; depleting; depletable.

Waybill A document made out by a **carrier** with the "who, what, where, how, and when" of goods shipped.

Weight of evidence The more *convincing* **evidence** in a legal dispute, not necessarily the larger quantity.

WESTLAW A computerized legal research source.

Whereas A vague word, often used to mean "because" when placed at the beginning of a legislative **bill** (in the explanation for why the bill should become a law).

Whereby (and other "where" words) A vague word meaning "by means of," "how?" or several other things. This word, like other vague, formal "where" words (_whereas, wherefore, whereof, whereon, whereunder, whereupon,_ etc.,), is best left out of a sentence or replaced by a specific thing, place, or idea.

Wherefore A vague word, often used in a **complaint** to begin the section in which the **plaintiff** spells out exactly what he or she wants from the **defendant** or wants the court to do.

White Acre See **Black Acre.**

Widow's (or widower's) allowance That part of a dead spouse's property that a person may take free of all claims under some state laws.

Widow's (or widower's) election That part of a dead spouse's property that a person may choose to take under some state laws, rather than accepting what was given in the spouse's **will.**

Wildcat strike A strike without the consent of the union.

Will _1._ Desire; choice. See **tenant** _at will. 2._ A document in which a person tells how his or her property is to be handed out after death. For **holographic, nuncupative, reciprocal,** and other types of wills, see those words.

Willful _1._ Intentional; deliberate; on purpose. _2._ Obstinate; headstrong; without excuse. _3._ With evil purpose.

Wind up Finish current business, settle accounts, and turn property into cash to end a **corporation** or **partnership** and divide the **assets.**

Wish Anything from "mildly desire" to "strongly command."

Withholding tax Money held by an employer from an employee's pay, by a bank from certain interest payments, etc., and turned over to the government as prepayment of income tax.

Within the statute   *1.* Defined by the **statute.** *2.* Prohibited by the statute. *3.* Allowed by the statute.

Without day   See **sine die.**

Without recourse   A phrase used by an indorser (signer other than the original **maker**) of a **negotiable instrument** (check, etc.,) to mean that if payment is refused, he or she will not be responsible.

Witness   *1.* A person who observes an occurrence (such as an accident), an event, or the signing of a document. *2.* A person who makes a sworn (under **oath**) statement that can be used as **evidence** (in a court, legislature, hearing, etc.).

Words   *1. Words and Phrases* is a large set of law books that provide definitions of legal (and many nonlegal) words by giving actual quotes from cases. *2. Words of art* are technical terms that are used in a special way by a profession. *3. Words of limitation* are the words in a **deed** or **will** that tell what type of **estate** or rights the person being given the land receives. *4. Words of purchase* are the words in a deed or will that tell who gets the property.

Workers' compensation laws   Laws passed in most states to pay money to workers injured on the job, regardless of **negligence.** Businesses pay into a fund to support these payments.

Work-product rule   The principle that a lawyer need not show the other side in a case any facts or things gathered for the case unless the other side can convince the judge that it would be unjust for the things to remain hidden and that there is a special need for them.

Work-to-rule   A work slowdown in which formal work rules are followed so closely that production slows down.

World Court   International Court of Justice.

Wraparound   Either a **second** mortgage on a property that includes payments on a low-interest-rate first **mortgage** or a new mortgage that makes payments on the old mortgages of several properties at once.

Wrap-up clause   **Zipper clause.**

Writ   A judge's **order** requiring that something be done outside the courtroom or authorizing that it be done. The most common _writ_ is a **summons.** If the writ cannot be served (delivered properly), a second one (called an _alias writ_) may be used. For **prerogative** _writs_, **habeas corpus, attachment,** and other types of _writs_, see those words. These include papers that are no longer strictly _writs_ but have become part of the court's ordinary processes as **judgments** and **orders.**

Write-off   An uncollectible debt, or a business or investment loss, that can usually be claimed as a tax loss.

Written law   **Statutes.**

Wrong   A violation of a person's legal rights, especially a **tort.**

Wrongful death action   A lawsuit brought by the **dependents** of a dead person against the person who caused the death. **Damages** (money) will be given to the dependents if the killing was **negligent** or **willful.**

Year books   Reports (see **reporter**) of old English cases.

Yeas and nays   Oral voting in a **legislature,** usually by calling each name one by one.

Yellow dog contract An illegal employment contract in which an employer requires an employee to promise that he or she will not join a union.

Yield Profit as measured by a percentage of the money invested. For example, a $10 profit on a $100 investment is a 10 percent *yield*.

York-Antwerp rules Agreed commercial rules on international shipping.

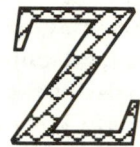

Z *1. Regulation Z* is the set of rules put out by the Federal Reserve Board under the *Consumer Credit Protection Act*. It describes exactly what a lender must tell a borrower and how it must be told. *2.* "*Z*" is a mark used to fill in unused blank spaces on a legal document to keep them from being filled in later.

Zero-rate mortgage A **mortgage** in which a large down payment is made and the rest of the purchase price is paid in equal **installments** with no interest.

Zipper clause A statement in a **contract** that it is an **integrated** *agreement*.

Zone of employment The physical area within which an employee is eligible for **workers' compensation** when injured, whether or not on the job at the time.

Zoning The division of a city or county into mapped areas, with restrictions on land and building use, lot size, architectural design, etc., in each area.

APPENDIX A
Where to Go for More Information

If you cannot find the word you want in this dictionary, if the definition given here does not fit the context in which you found the word, or if you need a more elaborate definition, there are several places to look. They are listed here with the most convenient first and the most comprehensive last.

1. Standard English Dictionaries

A regular dictionary can be useful. Often, legal documents will use an ordinary English word in its ordinary way, but because of its use in an unfamiliar place, the word looks "legal." A regular dictionary may reassure you that the word's ordinary meaning fits perfectly. *American Heritage, Merriam-Webster,* and *Random House* are helpful dictionaries. The *Oxford English Dictionary* is a good source for older words.

2. Large Law Dictionaries

Large law dictionaries are helpful for long Latin phrases, old words and definitions, and situations in which you need several examples of how to use a word properly. The two best known are *Black's* and *Ballentine's*.

3. Hornbooks

If you know the field of law from which the word comes, a good starting place is a students' summary of the law in that field. This is called a "hornbook." For example, if the word comes from the field of torts, try the index in the back of Prosser's *Law of Torts*.

4. Legislation and Cases

If the word comes from a statute (or ordinance or regulation), the statute may contain a specialized definition of the word, often in a definition section (or several definition sections scattered through it). This is always true of the uniform laws and is usually true of major federal and state legislation. For example, important definitions for commercial terms are found in the definition section of the *Uniform Commercial Code*.

5. Words and Phrases

If you want every conceivable use of a term, or if the word has not turned up in any of the preceding sources, you might go to a law library and use *Words and Phrases*. This is a multivolume set of books with quotes from multiple judicial decisions for each word. The supplement inside each volume's back cover provides the most recent uses.

6. Descriptive Word Index

If the word is not a legal word, but you need to know if it ever became entangled with the law, try the *Descriptive Word Index* to West's *Digest System*. For example, if you need to know about tires that blow out during a skid, you might look up "tires," "blowouts," "skids," or related synonyms.

7. Legal Encyclopedias

If you want to get into the general legal subject from which the word came, and if hornbooks are no help, try a legal encyclopedia. The two major ones are *Corpus Juris Secundum* and *American Jurisprudence.*

APPENDIX B
Lawyer Talk

This section is written primarily for paralegals, law students, and others who use legal words in their work. Its message is simple: Legal words are valuable technical tools, but they can complicate, confuse, and prolong any task. Legal jargon smothers clear thinking, clear writing, and clear speaking.

The section is also written for the "person on the street" who uses the dictionary to help with legal questions that come up in everyday life or to learn something about the law. The ability to sort out useful legal language from "legalese" is a big advantage.

Legal words are overused or misused in several different ways:

1. Using TECHNICAL legal words instead of clearly explaining legal concepts to nonlawyers.

2. Using VAGUE legal words when clear English would be more precise.

3. Using TOO MANY legal words.

4. Using certain WORTHLESS legal words.

1. Technical Words

Even when used accurately, legal words may be out of place when speaking or writing to nonlawyers:

Lawyer talk	_English_
An "annulment" voids the marriage ab initio.	An "annulment" wipes the marriage off the books as if it never happened.
Plaintiff alleges defendant is the vendee.	Smith claims he sold it to Jones.
If you don't bequeath it in a codicil, it will go by intestate succession.	If you don't change your will to put it in, some cousin may get it.
I'll move for a continuance, but it may be denied as dilatory.	I'll try to put it off, but the judge will think we are stalling.
You hold the estate in fee, but if you alienate it, you activate the acceleration clause in the deed of trust.	You own the house, but if you sell it or give it away, the whole loan comes due.
You hold legal title on the face of the instrument, but extrinsic evidence shows that Smith has equitable title.	The papers are in your name, but a court would give it to Smith.

2. Vague Words

Some legal words have a "built-in" vagueness. They are used when the writer or speaker does not want to be pinned down. For example, when a law requires that something be done within a "reasonable time" or with "due care," the vagueness about _when_ or _how_ the thing must be done is usually meant to give a court latitude in deciding the time allowed or the amount of care required on a case-by-case basis. Vague words, however, just as often accompany vague thoughts. The following small list of vague words is drawn from many possibilities:

Sounds precise	But is it?
Above cited	Earlier on the page? In the chapter? The book?
Accident	Was it intentional? Negligent? By pure chance?
Adequate	For what? By what standard? Who decides?
Civil death	For all legal purposes? Just some? Permanent?
Community	The "block"? That section of town? The state?
Face	The whole document? The first page?
Facsimile	Exact copy? Close copy? How close?
Fair hearing	Fair in what way?
Final decision	Final before appeal? Final with no appeal?
Fixture	May be removed? May not be removed?
Foreign	Different country? Different state? Different city?
Heirs	Children? All who may inherit? Blood relations?
Infant	Baby? Young child? Under legal age?

Sounds precise	_But is it?_
Reasonable person	By what standards? With hindsight?
Stranger	Not part of the deal? Knew nothing about it?
Substantial	A lot? More than a little? Above a cutoff?
Undue	A lot? Too much? By force? Illegal?

Some legal words have been in dispute in thousands of cases. Judges have decided that many of them "clearly" mean a dozen different, conflicting things. These words can rarely be avoided but should be replaced by specific objects, facts, or concepts whenever possible, even if this requires using extra words. For example, lawyers almost never agree about the following words:

Consideration	Law
Conspiracy	Obscenity
Holding	Preponderance of evidence
Insanity	Proximate cause
Jurisdiction	Willful

3. Too Many Words

Doubling legal words that mean the same thing can be confusing. Good examples of legal word doubling (and tripling) are found on pages 346 to 366 of _The Language of the Law_ by David Mellinkoff (Little, Brown, 1963). Some of these are the following:

Fit and proper	Mind and memory
Force and effect	Name and style
Give, devise, and bequeath	Null and void
Have and hold	Over and above
Known and distinguished as	Rest, residue, and remainder
Last will and testament	Written instrument

If the use of two similar words adds an important shade of meaning, use them with care. Most doublings, however, are just clutter.

4. Worthless Words

Many worthless words are used frequently in legal writing. Some words are worthless because they are almost meaningless. Others mean exactly the same thing as a clear English word. Here are some examples of both types of worthless words:

Aforesaid	To wit
Ambulatory	Viz
And/or	Whereas
Firstly	Here (or There) about
Forthwith	Here (or There) after
Four corners	Here (or There) by
Hitherto	Here (or There) for
Issue (for "children")	Here (or There) from
Party of the first part	Here (or There) in
Re (for "about")	Here (or There) inafter
Said (as in "said table")	Here (or There) to

How can you avoid using legal jargon? Before using a legal word, you should stop and think. Even if it is precise and useful, is it too technical for the situation? Is a vague word being used to smooth over vague thinking? Would fewer words do the job? Is the word on the "worthless" list?

Also, you should learn to recognize jargon when others use it. Legal language is less imposing once the "legalese" is stripped away. Ask for a translation.